# MANNEQUIN

# MANNEQUIN
## MY LIFE AS A MODEL

### BY
### CAROLYN KENMORE

BARTHOLOMEW HOUSE, LTD.

BARTHOLOMEW HOUSE, LTD.
First Printing . . . September 1969

© 1969 by Bartholomew House, Ltd.

Library of Congress Catalog
Card Number: 79–79434

All rights reserved under International and
Pan American conventions. Published by
Bartholomew House, Ltd.,
a subsidiary of Bartell Media Corporation.

Manufactured in the U.S.A.

To Mom
with love

# CHAPTER 1

*There are more red-headed girls around than there used to be, say, six months ago. One sees them glowing like torches, raking their rosy manes with permissive fingers, basking, with a healthily narcissistic delight, in the way people look at them. Most to the point, in the way men look at them.*

—Vogue, April 15, 1969

"Hey, Red. I dig yer bah-dy."

"Don't be stuck-up, baby. What's the matter—didn't you get yours this morning?"

You can't hide it if you're tall. The huge zippered leather portfolio you're schlepping is like a banner unfurled. You have your eyes on at eight o'clock in the morning. There's nothing you can do about it. A working model walking the streets of Manhattan is as visible as a fire engine, as vulnerable as a fly.

"Can I help you, lady? I wanna be your slave."

"Hey, Red, bounce those boobs again just for me."

"Knock 'em dead, Red!"

Whistles went out when sideburns came in. What you get now are jungle noises—cloacal sounds.

"If you was my old lady, I'd never leave home."

You could be blindfolded. But you could still tell from your own sound track what part of town you're in.

"Wow! What a piece of tush!"

When you hear that, you can bet you're on Second Avenue somewhere in the Fifties. You make your turn, you check the street number, you hope for an elevator, and you settle for the stairs. The pounding hard rock sound on the stereo tells you you've arrived. Your watch tells you you're on time for your go-see. You check your face, you shake your hair, and in you go.

1

"You've never done any nudes?"

The bored, bearded, beady-eyed photographer's rep looks at you as though you might possibly be deformed.

"I've done a couple of bubble baths," you hurriedly explain. "And last week I did a booking for Gil Ross wearing nothing but semiprecious stones."

"How many carats?" he wags. "But you don't have a nude in your book," says the rep, flipping through your portfolio like a nearsighted dentist looking at X-rays.

"The ad's not out yet," you explain. "I did a whole layout done up as a nun. That's not in my book, either. I didn't tell anybody about that but my mother." He smiles. You stand there in the lush East Side studio of one of the most famous photographers in the business. Behind you looms a gigantic set that must have cost a few thou to install: a huge sunken marble bathtub mounted on a grassy carpeted altar; acres of mirrors, miles of jumpy orange draperies, golden fixtures and faucets. People flit about, adjusting lights, ironing carpet seams, polishing marble.

"This set cost the client over seven thousand dollars to install," the man explains. "We're spending so much bread I'm looking for just the right girl to put in it. We're pretty sure the client will go for a nude." The rep is doing preliminary casting. For nude shots you get $250 an hour with a bonus plus for a national ad. You stand there wondering if you'll get the chance to wet your feet in that seven-thousand-dollar pond. The ad won't appear until sometime in 1970. By that time *Ladies' Home* will look like *Playboy*. The Pillsbury Bake-off will probably be topless by then, with see-through refrigerators, ovens, and aprons. Every time the agency calls these days, they begin by saying, "Well, Carolyn, it's not exactly a *nude*." Translation: You may get to wear a daisy between your toes. If you're not ready to work nude, you might as well trip down to the unemployment insurance office in your sequined bra and file. By mid-1969 already, if you hadn't had your navel in *Vogue* and your nipples in *Harper's Bazaar*, you began to feel like Whistler's Mother.

"A very impressive book you have, Karen," the rep says.

"I'm Carolyn," you say.

"Sorry, Carolyn," he says. You know he has to ask you if you have any scars, adhesions, children, moles, warts, or scruples. And at $250 an hour on a seven-thou set he can't take your word for a thing.

"Would you mind testing first?" he finally asks. Before you can answer, he says, "Here's a beautiful head shot. Wait a minute—I want to show these to John."

Aha, you hope. You must have made some kind of impact if he wants to show you to the Maestro. He waltzes across the set and shows your portfolio to the famous photographer supervising the whole show.

"These are beautiful," the Maestro says. "Really great stuff." The rep introduces you swiftly, and you smile, and then he says, "Here's a rough pencil layout of the shot as John sees it."

He shows you this huge drawing of a nude lady standing on the edge of the grassy carpeted ledge. Her right arm is bent oh-so-delicately so you can see the bottom of her bosoms as well as the bosoms of her bottom. Up-front cleavage went out with panel shows. Now it's the cleavage you have aft they're after. When I was a tot, Marilyn Monroe was almost ruined when it got out that she had posed for a calendar shot in the altogether. How many centuries ago was *that*?

"We'd like to see how you look from this particular angle," the rep says casually as the photographer retires to his suite.

"You want me to take my clothes off?" you inquire, trying not to sound as modest as you feel.

"Just to get an impression," he says.

"I have no birthmarks or dog bites."

"Let's go to the dressing room if you don't mind." Today the dressing room—tomorrow the world. There's no getting away from it. You'd give your eyeteeth to work with John. Some of the famous ads on display in the dressing room are luscious. If you're taking the plunge, things couldn't be lusher than this. The dressing room is spotless. You can always tell how a photographer feels about models by the looks of his dressing room.

"You want me to take my blouse off and my bra?"

"Yeah, if you wouldn't mind," he says, very offhand, standing there. Very cool, very haughty, you undo the blouse. Then you unfasten your bra. Just as it drops, you lift your arm like the lady in the penciled layout. You don't want him to think he guessed right in suspecting you are shy.

3

"Is this what you wanted to see?"

"Yeah," says he. "That's what I was afraid of. You might be just a tiny bit too big."

"I'm a 34 B. Are you looking for an A?" Your measurements are all a matter of record. The agency sent over the composite days before the rep asked to see you.

Aha. You discover you don't have to look at him to watch him. The full-length mirror in the dressing room catches you from about six angles. But he can't look at you and the mirror too. It's a three-way bank shot, and you wait to catch his eye. Enough is enough.

"I'm not small-breasted—you can see that," you say as you whip your bra on and snap it in the back. He is standing unnecessarily close. In order to make him feel like a gentleman, you act helpless and say, "Would you mind terribly buttoning up the back of this blouse?" He buttons. "Sorry, Mack, but that's the way I'm built."

"Well," says he, "I don't want to draw too fine a line here. There are intangibles John will be more concerned with than I am. Would you be available for a test Saturday morning?"

Saturday *morning?* Nobody works Saturday in this town. Damn few work Friday or Monday. For anyone who has a secretary to cover for him and a country hideout, the three-day week has already arrived.

"If I'm not right for this job, what do you have in mind to test me for?"

"Well," says the rep, "we don't get a set like this in the studio that often. John is giving up his weekend to run as many tests as we can."

"I don't test nude," you say. I didn't say I wouldn't. I didn't say I would. I'm not crazy mad to do it, but on the other hand the nude is it for 1970 and I am curious (auburn).

"Oh, no," says the rep. "You could work maybe in a body stocking. We'll be trying several top girls. Some of them will be wearing clothes."

"Something new and different," you say. "That could be exciting. Why don't you call the agency?"

Don't commit yourself. They might get a gang of girls in that sunken Roman pool—eleven might be wearing fun furs from Jacques Kaplan and only one would be nude. She'd be the star of their 1971 calendar. Another studio pulled something like that last year.

You pick up your portfolio and out you go.

You're waving frantically for a taxi. What screeches to a halt is a truck. "Can I take you somewheres, Red? Come on, smile. Things aren't that bad. There! That's better. I'd like to book you for one night in Jersey—how about it?"

*Even plain redheads get looked at quite a lot. A really good-looking one comes through every door like a thunderclap.*
—VOGUE, op. cit.

I was only trying to do the designer a favor. His new nude jumpsuit allover undergarment was a very big hit—a beautiful fit—and after he had seen me in it he wanted everybody important to its future to see me in it, so when it was going to be shown as part of a huge show at one of the biggest buying offices in Manhattan—one that decides things for thousands of stores—he begged me to wear it for him. "It will only take a half hour of your time, Carolyn," he promised. So I wilted and agreed.

There were twenty top models there set to parade through a huge conference room of VIBs—very important buyers. The fashion coordinator got us all in line in the proper order while someone inside was pitching jewelry and scarves. All twenty of us were showing lingerie and the new, new underthings. Just before we started to move, this elderly lady showed up, reeking with authority—the caked eyeliner and the blue-gray hair and the tan and the puffy lids spilling over her false eyelashes.

"Let me look at your girls before they go in," said she to the fashion coordinator. I was third in line but the first one she landed on.

"I'm sorry," said the lady. "That red-headed girl can't go in there in that nude jumpsuit. There are a lot of men in there."

"But what's wrong?" said the FC. "This is Peter Pan's finest garment. It's the hottest thing in their new line. It's part of my format."

"Well, you'll just have to show it on a hanger. Say there's no model for it," said the other lady.

"Please, girls," I wanted to say. "I've had so much take-it-off trouble today from the DOMs in this business. I can't cope with any DOLLs. This is nothing I'd wear to St. Patrick's Cathedral, but, after all, the designer dragged me over here specially, and I have a bikini under it, and it has a built-in bra, and I brought these strap-back white summer shoes with the nice fashionable clunky heel, and I decked myself out with these hairpieces, these spiral curls. I made them myself. . . ."

"Oh, I didn't mean to criticize you, dear," said the DOLL, sensing what I must be thinking. "Don't get me wrong—you have a beautiful figure and you look marvelous, but I can't have you going in there like this in front of all those *men*."

The FC and the DOLL argued right down to the wire, but the DOLL won and I walked—did not run—to the nearest exit.

Then I called my designer friend, and he said things on the telephone that no girl from Vermont is ever supposed to hear in her entire *vie.*

Indeed, things are in a fearful state of flux and confusion when, in a chic restaurant that imagines itself holding the line, a headwaiter says to a lady, "Sorry, madam, we are unable to serve ladies wearing pants." The lady takes the pants off and walks in in whatever's left.

"Watch out for Bonita Roja, you creep. You gonna ruin her pretty toes, Pablo, you creep."

You're trapped between two garment carts in a side street just off Seventh Avenue. Nobody says another word. It's those gestures.

There are two of us working in tandem. While the blonde is shooting, I'm changing my face and hair so I look like a different lady in every shot. I'm making quicker changes than any stripper, and everything is running smoothly when suddenly they throw me a silly nightie. No pants to match and only a sheer, sheer gown with an Empire waist and ribbons under the bosom. For lingerie you get double rate, so I'm not thinking of filing a grievance.

"Lingerie is double, OK, Marty?" I shout from the dressing room so this can be counted on my voucher. In addition to your other duties, you have to be your own secretary and traveling accountant. Then I slip into the garment, and this innocent, shimmery, divine wedding-night thing makes me look like a cheap cartoon. I might as well be naked. And *that* is with ordinary dressing room light. Under the hot lights on the seamless it will be worse. I was booked to shoot five or six dresses for a winter catalog, and somebody switched the signals. Catalogs are not looking for sneaky nudies. They have one eye out for the graveyard market. They have to go through the mails. What to do, what to DO?

6

Photographers are usually and ultimately men. They can't be depended on for anything—even so much as a can opener or a safety pin. They can have a stylist and a secretary and an assistant and an assistant's assistant—they can have a whole crew to assist them. But a model is absolutely alone—on her own. That's why we've got to be *semper paratus.* Always prepared. That's why we carry thirty pounds of excess luggage around every day in our tote bags. Because you never, never know what in creation you're going to need to pull yourself together for that crucial instant when you're out there alone under the hot lights on that white seamless and the meter is running at something like ten dollars a second. It could be anything from a false nail for your big toe to a pair of old dirty nude stockings to tuck in a bra that's too big for you. If you don't have it the instant you need it, you can feel very dead even though your heart is pumping and you're breathing like a long-distance runner.

With this catalog bit, if I'd wanted to be helpless and dramatic, I could have played *September Morn* and they could have sent the picture to the retoucher. For a hundred-dollar fee he would airspray out the offending contours. Instead I played Miss Resourceful. I cursed myself for not having a nude strapless bra—all I had was a white one. I took a regular nude bra and tucked the straps in. I slipped into a pair of long-line full panty hose in a nude shade. Just to make sure the retoucher wouldn't have any work to do, I took a nude handkerchief and wore it like a spare fig leaf. When the light hit me on that white seamless, I whipped my red hair around until I looked like I just got out of bed.

Who knows or cares how much work and sweat and split-second *semper paratus* thinking it takes to look like the laziest tart in town?

"Hey, Red, how's business today?"

"What kinda fur coat is that, baby—tiger?"

"Can't we run off together, baby? I'll carry your bag."

"Why you hiding behind those glasses, Red? You can scrape me with those eyelashes—I don't mind."

You never look left. You never look right. You never break that stride until a red light halts you. At the curb it's quiet. Too quiet. You feel somebody standing beside you, breathing in your ear, blowing smoke in your ear. You move. He moves. You step aside. He's right beside you, whispering, "I'd like to squeeze a grape into you, *bella rosa*." You move on the green, faster than ever, because you know you've wandered onto Mafia turf.

> *Red is the color of heat, of wine, of fever, of blood. Red is the signal of danger. It is both a welcome and a warning, and even the most civilized man feels a curiously atavistic quickening of the senses at the sight of a red-haired woman. Never mind that she may be a notorious mouse. He knows that, deep inside, she is a quivering mass of passion and fireworks—a thrower of paperweights when displeased. . . .*
>
> —VOGUE, op. cit.

"Call Al Karp," the agency said when I checked in. "He wants to use you." Al is a crack photographer, and I had worked with him several times, so I called him. He asked me to stop in at his studio sometime during the day. "I wanna use you for a lingerie job, a two-hour booking at double rate," he said. So from my list of Wednesday MUST DOs I scratched my shopping and my trip to the bank and told him I'd come by at eleven.

"It's not a great big job," Al told me. "The client is a lingerie outfit that makes a whole line of color-coordinated underthings—bras, matching slips, panty hose, and girdles. They want some big color slides for a presentation, and if we get a hot one, they'll use it for a national ad. But the ad thing isn't firm yet—spec only. The presentation is surefire."

"You could have told me that on the phone," I kidded him. "What's the matter—you're lonesome?"

"No," Al said. "I knew you were right for it. You're looking better than ever, but today you gotta be sure. I haven't seen you in six weeks, and in that time I've seen kids go to hell. Now I want you to go see the client."

I was ready for that. This is one of the reasons you get paid double rate for lingerie. Everybody has to see every one of your pores before they're ready to go. You might have a crease around your middle or a hickey on your shoulder. A whole committee of fat, bloated, ugly, deformed, hairy freaks has to inspect you to make sure *you* are flawless.

Al called the client while I was there to make an appointment. The client was out. Call him back in an hour. Here goes the first hour wasted. Macy's was just a stone's throw from his studio, so it shouldn't be a total loss. I headed in there to do the shopping I had just scratched off my MUST DO list.

When I called the client at noon, he was in and his secretary said come right up. His office was in the midst of the buttons and bows district on Seventh Avenue. His receptionist turned me over to his secretary who took my book into his office. I had beefed up the portfolio with some recent lingerie shots, so in a moment the great man asked for me to be sent in. He sat there at his desk, poring over the lingerie shots in my book in his puffy, hairy hands.

"You do lingerie a lot?" he asked.

"Quite a bit," I said.

It was a ridiculous question. The line between lingerie and dresses has gone with the wind. It's a relic of the dark ages before the see-through cut-out-up-to-here-and-down-to-there fashions busted loose on the scene. Today a girl will go out dancing in below-navel pants and a man's necktie strapped around her bosoms, but if she is completely covered in a slip that would hang six inches below her longest mini-skirt, she gets double rate because in 1902 girls felt different about it.

Once upon a time models who did lingerie ads wore the mark of Cain. They got paid double rate for appearing in bras and girdles—like combat pay in the Army. But today those lines are all down. Everybody does it and nobody thinks anything about it. You have to have a damn good figure to show off a girdle. You have to have the kind of body that doesn't need a girdle in order to get to pose in one. Once upon a time for a catalog shot you wore a blouse and the photographer cropped you off at the midsection. Today you wear nothing but a smile as you cross your arms across your bosom. Once the magazines would accept only fuzzy near nudes for ads featuring beauty products or reducing aids. Now the nude descends the staircase to sell everything from andirons to egg beaters.

"OK," said the client. "I'd like you to try this on." He gave me a bra and a slip and a pair of panty hose to wear. They were inexpensive but cleverly done in a very modern flowered print. His secretary showed me a little room I could change in. When I put on the bra, I knew he was a pirate. The bra was a direct steal from an exclusive new design I

9

had modeled for a big manufacturer only a few weeks before.

Now I was back in his office and he was looking me over.

"That's great," he said. "Very nice. I told him I wanted a girl with a very *now* look because this is an entirely new line. How do the panty hose fit?"

"They're a little big in the rear," I told him. "For me at least."

"Yeah, maybe so," he mumbled. "That's just a sample. Maybe we can take up some slack." He was repulsive-looking, but he had a nice manner as he warmed up, and he was pleased to see the way his precious little garments fitted.

Next he gave me a tiny matching bikini he wanted me to try on. It was a good fit, well-designed, in good enough taste to wear on any beach. "Yeah," he said, even more pleased than before. "You look pretty good in that. That's the look I want in the slides and in the ad. It's very now, isn't it?" he said. "It's up-to-the-minute—the way you gotta be today."

Things were moving so fast that if I played my cards right I might get out of there in time to get to the bank before my one o'clock booking.

"All right," said the client. "Take off the bra now—lemme see what you look like."

"I beg your pardon," I said.

"Didn't the photographer tell you?" he said. "There's a bare top shot in this job."

"Yes," I said. "I understand you want a shot of the girdle alone. For that we hold our arms crossed like this when we're photographed." I showed him how we did it.

"Oh, hell, no," he said. "This is strictly a bare shot. Bare top."

"Well, then I'm not doing it," I said as diplomatically as I could. "If I'm not doing it for the photographer, I'm not doing it for you."

"I think you've been misinformed about the job."

"Perhaps I have."

"No *perhaps* about it. I know what I want."

"Fine, then get yourself a girl who specializes in that sort of thing."

"I want two girls."

"Fine, then let the other girl do it."

"She can't—she's only five feet two." What that had to do with it I couldn't guess. "I got salesmen coming in here from all over the country for this presentation. I want the whole thing on slides so they can see the detailing. Then I want girls at the same time showing things live in the showroom. At the end of the presentation we dreamed up the idea of having this one shot—a sort of Loew's State finish—just one shot of one girl bare top. Just as a fooler. A waker-upper. A nice little yuk for some hard-working guys."

That did it. If Al Karp hadn't been a good friend of mine, I would have let the client have it then and there. I walked into the dressing room to change, and I could hear him on the telephone calling Al.

"Looka here," he was screaming. "You sent a redhead over here, but you didn't give her a rundown on the job. Quit wasting my time this way, will ya? . . . Yeah, the kid is great, but what good is she if she don't understand the job?"

It was the wrong day for any of that guff. I had had it up to there with DOMs carrying on like first-year med school students. I took the bra he had pirated and I walked into his office. He was still on the phone when I threw it at him.

"If you really want a nice little yuk for those hard-working guys, why don't you wear it?" I started to slam the door, but I was so wound up that I heard myself screaming like a regular yenta. " 'Put this on, take that off. I've seen better legs. Yeah, her hips are a little narrow. Lemme see what you look like.' . . . how would you like it if for once in your life a girl told you what *you* look like? You look like you can't wait to have a heart attack. No girdle ever made could pull you together, and you've got bigger bosoms than I have. You're a man who's got everything . . . fourteen chins, and I'll bet you've got diabetes, too, and ulcers and a hernia and varicose veins . . ."

He was so shattered that it took him a few seconds to get up out of his chair and buzz his secretary. When she came in, he hollered: "Get this crazy redhead outa here!"

She tried to take me by the arm, and I grabbed my portfolio off his desk and started swinging. That thing weighs a ton, and if it lands, it lands with a real karate chop-chop.

"Lemme see your legs!" I shouted at him. "I want to see your legs!" The secretary ran for the receptionist. The receptionist was screaming and said she'd call 911, the Police Emergency Number.

"You're too chicken to show me your legs!" I was yelling. "I'll bet you've got short silk socks on, and every time you cross your legs we see two inches of bare leg. What you need is some of your own panty hose. The next time you want a bare top job, do it yourself. I know plenty of girls who'll pay to see it. A nice little yuk for some hard-working models . . ."

When I walked through the outer office, I tried to lower my voice and said, "Good afternoon, ladies." When I got to the elevator, I was furious that I hadn't stuck around to see if the cops would really turn up.

When I got to the lobby, I ran to the telephone booth to call Al. One phone was out of order. The second one had the receiver torn off the hook. Whenever you desperately need a phone in midtown New York, some vandal has beaten you to it. Perhaps it's just as well. By the time I found a booth that was functioning, I had cooled down to the point of worrying if my explosion had cost Al a client.

"I'm sorry, Al," I began, and then he cut me off.

"Don't *you* apologize. *I'm* the one who has to apologize. When this guy barked at me over the phone, that did it. I don't take that from anybody. I told him he could take his job and shove it."

"You did?" I said. "Well, that makes two of us."

"Good girl," he said. "I'll make it up to you."

# CHAPTER 2

Who says you can't go home again? When I get nauseous from New York, I manage many a weekend—spring, summer, autumn, and winter—especially winter. My little yellow Thunderbird is my one luxury. I keep it at the foot of 23rd Street and the East River for twelve bucks a month, and every Friday as early as possible I get out of town. I have a ski rack on the hardtop, and I drive myself to the mountains where I grew up. I peel off my eyelashes and I scrub off my makeup and I pack skis, poles, boots, parka, gloves, goggles, wax, hat, and I slip into my Bogner stretch pants, duofold longies, turtleneck, and Meggi sweater, and I take off. Sometimes when I'm lucky and have no bookings on Friday, I escape on Thursday night, straight up the Thruway to Albany. Sometimes I stay overnight there with my sister Elinor and her husband Bill. Sometimes I drive straight through.

The state line between New York and Vermont doesn't mean a thing anymore, but when I was in high school, crossing it was a big thing. When you're in high school, crossing ANY line is a big thing. You could drink in New York when you were eighteen, and you couldn't drink in Vermont until you were twenty-one, so the thing to do was drive over to New York and have a beer.

If fate is with me, the city limits of dear old Middlebury are only five hours and thirty minutes from Park Avenue. And then I breeze past the Hadleys', the ancestral home of my brother-in-law Bert. Then comes the golf course and the Middlebury College Field House with the ice-skating rink. The cemetery where Great-grandmother and Great-grandfather Novak are buried. The college fraternity houses and then the old high school building that burned when I was a senior. The top floors are all gone, but the first floor has been turned into a neat row of offices. Then comes the gymnasium where I played basketball and danced myself silly at all the proms. And then I turn into Main Street where my bachelor Uncle Ted presides over one of the sportiest Mobil stations in New England. I honk my horn and give my signal: Carolyn's back in town. The yellow T-bird is coming in for a landing. On the right is the Campus Theater.

Frankie was a hippie when I was thirteen and sold popcorn at the Campus Theater. He lived there in the theater behind the screen, and when Cinemascope came in his quarters got the bends. He wore Western silk shirts and blue jeans and played the guitar and sang through his nose when The Beatles were still picking theirs. When the program changed and the letters had to be put up on the marquee, Frankie did it. If Frankie didn't like the title of the movie, he changed it, and if he didn't like a certain actor, the guy didn't get billing, and that was that. Even the actors Frankie adored caused him trouble when it came to spelling their names, and the manager would come out and say, "No, Frankie, that's not right," and he would call out the names letter by letter.

"Hi, Frankie."

"Hi, Carolyn. See you on TV all the time. You tell 'em any time they need me down there in television land, Frankie Labshere is ready."

"You bet, Frankie. I won't forget."

My sister Jean and I were taking in a double feature at the Campus Theater in Middlebury. It was winter, and I had a snow suit on with suspenders. I couldn't have been more than six. We were sitting where we always sat—in the middle of the middle section. We walked to the theater alone, and after the show we walked through Bakery Lane to Grandma Novak's. She always had a treat ready for us, and then Grandpa Elmer would drive us home.

In the theater this man sat next to me, but I didn't notice him until he leaned over me to offer Jean some candy. She took some and said thank you, and then he gave me some, and pretty soon he was out of candy. He said he would get some more between pictures. When Betty Grable faded out and the lights came up, he asked me if I wouldn't like to go out to the lobby with him and pick out the candy I liked best. When we got to the lobby, the candy counter was closed. "Oh, well," he said, "we'll walk to Calvi's." That was the Italian ice cream parlor where they also sold comic books, candy, and cigarettes.

He took me by the hand as we crossed the street. Then he started down Frog Alley. "Wait a minute," I said. "This isn't the way to the candy store. I don't want to miss the movie. I want to go back with my sister." He grabbed my arm and yanked me into Frog Alley where the lumber yard was. He started leading me between all the piles of lumber. When I screamed, he hollered, "Shut up!" I was terrified. I knew this man was nuts, and he was dragging me, but I refused to shut up. I screamed bloody murder when he grabbed me and tried to pull my snow suit off. I was kicking him and screaming and crying, and he was trying to tear my snow suit off, but the suspenders had metal teeth. Unless you knew what you were doing, you couldn't snap them apart. It was only late afternoon, but it can be very dark in the winter at that time in Vermont, especially in a lonely old lumber yard. I screamed as loud as I could, and I kicked as hard as I could.

Then I fell across a pile of lumber, and I knew he had given up and let me go. He disappeared in the darkness. I ran through Frog Alley as if all the monsters of the deep were after me, and through the lobby of the theater. Jean was already in the manager's office when I came in with my snow suit ripped and my eyes red from crying. I was too innocent to understand what the man was trying to do to me. All I knew was that he'd acted crazy and he wouldn't let me go. I poured out my horror story to the manager, and then after Don Williamson, the Chief of Police, came and took us down to Grandma's, I knew I was all right. I thought the man had been trying to kidnap me. Kidnapping was something I had read all about. That four-letter word beginning with r, like most four-letter words was something I was too young to understand.

But Grandpa was livid. He was ready to go on a manhunt, turning up every corner of Middlebury until this maniac could be found. As it turned out, they caught him within hours. In a small town like Middlebury a stranger has about as much chance to hide as a six-foot nun in a crowd of midgets. A man from away from here—as he was described—was spotted and picked up and turned over to the police pronto. It turned out he was a known sex offender who had been released from an institution in Waterbury only days before.

Grandpa took us home, and Mother put us to bed. Nobody talked about what had happened anymore until I started having nightmares. I would wake up screaming, and Mother would come in to comfort me, and she always knew without my having to tell her that I had been dreaming about the man who dragged me into the lumber yard in Frog Alley.

Two stores past the theater is Bakery Lane, where Grandpa and Grandma Novak live—just across from Frog Alley, near Ruby's. I never go past Ruby's candy store without thinking of Patsy. She had long blond ringlets, and she used to come to the house a lot, and Mom used to dress her in some of our things. They were poor, and when her mother died, they were just kids and Patsy was adopted by an elderly couple in town. When her adoptive father died, she lived with her adoptive mother and aunt who ran the candy store. They dressed her in very old-fashioned clothes and kept her in ringlets until she was in her teens—huge, thick ringlets, the kind that are on the cover of *Vogue* today, but then we thought them stupid and real Baby Jane, and she was always embarrassed because she knew other kids were laughing at her and the way she dressed when she helped out in the candy store. Patsy went to college, but she didn't finish, and then she just left town and went to Boston to work. One day just before Christmas I went into the post office and Mr. Baldwin who had worked there ever since I can remember whispered to me: "Hear about Patsy?"

"Patsy who?"

"Patsy Bissette. Murdered last night in Boston."

"Murdered?"

"Yes. The Boston Strangler."

The Grey Shop and Farrell's men's shop and the Ski Haus are still there, and upstairs is the place where we took dancing lessons from the college students. The bridge used to seem like such a giant thing, but now it looks like a little marble mini. Across Otter Creek is the Rexall drugstore. Somebody else is jerking sodas in the spot I used to command. Up Merchants Row to the Park where they still have the church bazaars, past the Park Diner to the Town Hall. It used to be a movie theater, but now it's the Knights of Columbus Hall. The college kids used to come to movies there, and they thought it was just too campy for words when the picture started jumping and then there would be a crash of beer bottles in the projection booth and everybody would holler, "Hey, Jake, wake up in there."

The minister of the Congregational Church had one of the biggest lawns in town, and the Reverend used to let me play football and wrestle there with the boys. We called it the Point. "We'll meet at the Point," we used to say.

At the end of summer the ladies of the Episcopal Church took over the big park in the center of town where the Soldiers' and Sailors' Monument stood and turned it into a fantasy land for their annual church bazaar. They had gaily decorated booths set up where they sold handmade aprons and pot holders and tea cozies and crazy patchwork quilts. The women sewed all winter in order to deck the booths with color and whimsy. Each booth was a little boutique of its own. Some sold maple syrup, others handmade jewelry, homemade cookies, jam. Mom looked forward to the bazaar because she was a bingo fan.

Church bazaars didn't interest me at all. You had to have money to have fun buying things. Any pot holder the Protestant ladies could make I could make better. Besides, by the time the lights went up and the park really started jumping with music and laughter, I was too worn out from wrestling and playing football with the fellows to wash my ears or look for a clean pair of dungarees.

But this certain summer a girl came up to Middlebury from New York. She spent the entire summer in town staying with her grandparents. Her name was Virginia, and she was a year older than I was, but we became buddies. She used to tell me about the kind of concoctions you could get at Schrafft's in Manhattan; she had been to the Planetarium many times and told me they had a model of the entire sky of the world in a single building. She had been to the top of the Empire State Building and Rockefeller Center. She enthralled me with tales of how dizzy you felt when you got up there and the bottoms of the buildings eighty stories below seemed smaller than the tops and it made you sick thinking about it.

Virginia and I used to wrestle with boys together; we rode horseback into wild untracked parts of the woods together; we had picnic lunches of ham salad sandwiches and marshmallow devil dogs. We exchanged favorite back copies of *Screenland*. Soon she would have to go back to school in New York. When she came over and asked me to go to the church bazaar with her, she was all decked out in a new orange dress her mother had sent her from Peck & Peck on Fifth Avenue, and she had a lipstick to match. I hardly knew her.

I was fascinated by the shade of the lipstick, and I asked what color it was. "Tangerine," she said. It looked very natural, and the shade was something you could ask for at the dime store without blushing. I tried it, and it didn't taste bad either. It didn't really taste like a tangerine, but then it didn't taste like Vicks Vapo-Rub either, like some of them did.

"Try it on," Virginia suggested. "It says in *Screenland* you should really always use a brush on your lower lip and outline it with a darker shade, but just smear it on and it will give you some idea."

I smeared it on. Then we went into the bathroom to peek in the mirror. Virginia showed me how to rub my lips together like Linda Darnell did in this movie. "This way it spreads around and doesn't get so thick it cakes."

I liked the effects, but I wasn't sure. Virginia thought it was smashing, scrumptious. "You wear it to the bazaar and see if anyone notices." I was not one to spurn a challenge like that, so I went to the drawer in my dresser where I kept my money and fished out my thirty-five-cent savings. I was ready to take off when Virginia said, "You can't go like *that*. Either you'll have to change into a dress or I'll have to go home and get into levis too."

I compromised. I hated dresses, but I knew Virginia wanted to show off her new outfit from Peck & Peck, so I got a clean dress out of my closet. It was a yellow one, freshly ironed by my mother. Virginia thought it would be a perfect foil for the Tangerine lipstick.

"How about your hair?" she said thoughtfully.

Well, how about it indeed? Mousy-brown pigtails were mousy-brown pigtails. Turbans looked OK on some people in *Screenland,* but I didn't think I was ready.

"Let it hang loose and I'll brush it for you and we'll see how it looks," Virginia said. I knew then she intended wheedling me into getting completely done up. I was humoring her when I let her put a black velvet band on my head. She didn't like that, so we looked all through the kitchen and the broom closet for some other colored ribbon. We finally got a hunk of brown velvet off a candy box. It was almost the same shade as my hair. Terribly monochromatic. Terribly subtle. Too subtle, maybe, for a Middlebury bazaar. Virginia didn't think so.

Each time I got doctored up in one department, another department came on very strong as an eyesore. Now it was the shoes. The shoes were scuffed and absolutely wrong. We tried putting paint on them, and then Virginia got a spot of paint on her dress and got disgusted.

"For Heaven's sake, Carolyn," she said, "if your face is on right, nobody but your mother is going to look at your shoes."

After posing and primping for another hour, we finally got ourselves together and started downstreet. When I saw the lights in the park and heard the music and the laughter, I got weak in the knees and felt like wiping off the lipstick on anything handy. It felt stupid and I felt stupid. But in the rush I had forgotten to bring a handkerchief, and Virginia absolutely refused to waste hers on my fickle whim. We didn't have a piece of Kleenex between us. If I had to spend a nickle on a box at the drugstore, it would seem like a shocking waste of cash resources.

The first boy we ran into was Charlie Adams. He said, "Hi, Carolyn," in a funny kind of way. Another boy whistled, and Virginia nudged me.

She was carrying on a little too much like a fairy godmother to suit me, and I was ready to head for home then and there.

"I'm dying to know what your mother says when she sees you," Virginia whispered. She was still carrying on a little too much like Little Miss Fix-it for me. But after all, since we'd gone to all this trouble, and she was going back to New York on Saturday, and I might die without ever seeing her again, she was entitled to some vicarious pleasure.

So we headed for the roped-off bingo reservation in the northwest corner of the park, with Virginia leading the way. We debated over whether we should blow our spending money on a card that entitled us to be admitted. Virginia came on like a big spender and was ready to pop for two tickets when we were advised that we were underage. We finally spotted my mother at a table with several other ladies. We went all the way around and stood there by the ropes waiting for her to notice us. Mom had both eyes glued to the three bingo cards in front of her, and she listened to the man calling out numbers as if her life depended on it.

We had to wait until the game was over before she even looked up. Virginia waved at her and shouted. Mom waved back, and then in the longest double take I've ever seen outside of a Marx Brothers' movie she looked at her little daughter. She lit up the way mothers do when they look at newborn babies, and she called my name.

"Hi, Mom," I said, very blasé. "We came by to wish you luck."

I had noticed people noticing me before, and it always made me feel uncomfortable. This time it gave me the shivers the way my own mother looked at me. It was like the day I got up at five in the morning to make her breakfast and ended up falling downstairs. It was the real honest-to-God look of surprise and wonder and joy and happiness. The look of love. I knew I wasn't her little tomboy girl anymore. I just knew it. I knew I could never again play football or wrestle with boys. I felt pretty enough to have my face on the cover of *Screenland*.

Everybody has seen that same scene on the Late Late Show umpteen times. We've seen June Allyson do it, and Doris Day has done it. Surely sometime somewhere Sarah Bernhardt did it, too. We have to laugh and camp about it and call it cornball hokum, and yet . . .

In the years between I must have put on enough lipstick to draw a straight line from Middlebury to Fort Knox. But I rarely snap open a tube of lipstick without wondering what happened to Virginia, the little girl from New York who turned me on with Tangerine.

Seminary Street is where we lived when Jean ran away from home. She packed her clothes and made the announcement that everyone was against her and that she intended to end the relationship. Jean is the oldest of us girls, and she had her own room next to the bathroom. Paula and Elinor and I were roommates, and we used to fight over a huge goosefeather quilt that was a relic of Great-grandmother's thirteen-room house where she died. We were supposed to take turns with it, but the transfer of that quilt from one to another sometimes caused a riot, and Jean said, "I'm getting out of here. You girls drive me nuts." Because she was older and better-behaved, she felt she was being taken for granted. She packed all her clothes and stood there on the stairs saying, "Everybody's against me."

And Mom said, "Where are you going?"

Jean said she was going to Grandma's.

"Well, can I help you with your suitcase?" Mom said. "Are you walking or going by bus?"

Naturally Jean didn't want any help from anybody, but she couldn't manage the suitcase, and there were tears all over the staircase, and we all ended up having popcorn together to celebrate the happy ending.

That fence we girls used to climb over to get into that lady's garden

20

and pick flowers is still there. When she spotted us, we used to hide in the evergreen shrubs.

I was in the seventh grade when I first started stopping traffic. I was taller than most ladies in the PTA, so they issued me a white belt, white gloves, and a hat, and I became a sergeant in the school patrol guard. Morning, noon, and after school I had command of the intersection of Main Street and Merchants Row. I stood there like the boss of the universe, stopping trucks in their tracks and shepherding the little ones across the dangerous crossing. I wasn't the slightest bit feminine. I was a confirmed tomboy, and I loved having a little weight to throw around. I figured out a jazzy way of wearing my hat and my belt, and I thought I cut quite an authoritative figure at the crossing. I got to know half the truck drivers for forty miles around. It was "Hi, Carolyn," three times a day from everybody, and I had a smile for every Tom, Dick, and Harry who drove by. I could have run for sheriff, I was such a community fixture. I was fascinated by cars and transmissions and wheel bases and snow tires—anything mechanical was my meat. I could spot a friend coming half a mile away by the make and color of his car. If someone drove by with a new car, that was an event. I had a thing about license plates. I trained myself to commit six or seven digits to memory instantly. If some wise guy didn't respond to one of my hand signals, I didn't have to reach for my note pad. I would keep traffic moving until my tour of duty was over; then I'd write the license down and turn it over to higher authority. I was always on the lookout for out-of-state licenses. When we saw a license plate from New Hampshire or Massachusetts, we never thought of them as strangers or foreigners. We called them "people from away from here." Middlebury, Vermont, was the center of the universe as far as I was concerned.

One day I stopped a man with Pennsylvania license plates on his Chevy. When the school kids had cleared the crossing safely and I gave him the signal to pass through, I saw he was leaning out of his car with a piece of paper in his hand. Motorists sometimes did that when they were lost and wanted to find their way back onto Route 7. He pulled up to the center of the street. I saluted. He handed me the note but didn't say anything. While I was unfolding it to see what it was all about, he whipped into gear and speeded off like a hot-rod Harry. Quickly I

21

scanned his license number. Then I pulled out my pencil and wrote it down on the note he had given me. Then I stuffed it in my pocket. One couldn't be too alert about cars with out-of-state plates. It might even be a stolen car. For all I knew, it might be someone on the FBI ten-most-wanted-men list at the post office.

When my tour of duty was over, I went home wondering if I should telephone the Chief of the Patrol and report the suspicious incident. When I fished out the note and looked at it, I knew something was fishy. It was a handwritten note on engraved stationery, the kind you have to order from a store and have it initialed specially. The note said: "Somebody is crazy about you." And it was signed Franny. The initials on the paper were F.D., so that meant he hadn't stolen the notepaper. He wasn't a car thief or a stationery thief. He was just a plain nut. A nut from away from here. From Pennsylvania.

When I got home, I showed the note to my mother. She didn't think it was so funny. I could tell by the way she reacted that it wasn't one of the things she wanted mentioned to my father. If the Great Rinaldo had any idea that one of his four daughters had been flirted with in the line of duty by some nut from Pennsylvania, some nut from Pennsylvania was likely to get shot.

Mom and I agreed to forget it. It was just one of those things. She knew I didn't have the slightest interest in boys. And even if Franny had a nutty interest in me, there wasn't much he could do about it at the busy intersection of Main Street and Merchants Row.

A few days later I spotted a young man in a corduroy suit and glasses walking past my post with the grade school children. There was something about him that looked familiar. He was almost old enough to be a teacher, but he was dressed like the boys at Middlebury College. He had no business in that part of town at that hour. Five minutes later when I was in the middle of the street halting traffic, he walked past my post again. While I stood there trying to stop one youngster from pummeling another with his schoolbooks, this young man walked over to me and handed me a package in a brown paper bag. His glasses were so thick I didn't recognize him until he said, "Someone is crazy about you." The nut from Pennsylvania—that's who it was. But he delivered the message in such a strange voice, as if he were a Western Union messenger delivering a singing telegram. Or maybe it was some nutty, humiliating thing some of his fraternity brothers had cooked up for him

22

to do before he could get pledged to Phi Titzi Poo or something.

Anyway, as soon as he'd handed me the package, he was off and running as if he'd just robbed a bank. I couldn't wait to tear open the package to see what was in it. I was ready for something nutty, like a five-pound bag of rock salt or carpet tacks or something. When I saw it was a huge box of chocolates, all done up and sealed with cellophane and ribbons, I knew it had to have cost at least five dollars. The one we girls were considering buying for Grandma on her birthday would have set us back $3.95, and it was about half this size. So Franny was not only a nut, he was a rich nut. Unless maybe he was a shoplifter or his parents owned a candy store in Pennsylvania.

I thought about giving the candy away, but there was nobody I could think of who could accept a present like that without talking about it all over town, so I took it home to my mother.

"What do you think we should do?" I asked her.

Daddy wasn't going to feel as relaxed about this as we were. Mom didn't say much, but I knew what she was thinking. "Well, I suppose," she said, "as long as he didn't try to harm you. . ."

"Harm me?" I laughed. "He's *scared* of me. You should have seen him skedaddling up the street."

The way the candy was sealed and packaged there was no way it could be poisoned or tampered with. Mom decided to put it away and say nothing about it.

They wanted to film *Peyton Place* in Woodstock, Vermont, but the people wouldn't allow it. It wasn't the idea that the book was shocking or sensational or couldn't have happened in a small town like Woodstock or Middlebury. It was the idea that the book was written by a woman from away from here. And read by a lot of people from away from here. She didn't know it, so how could she tell it? She couldn't tell the half of it, now could she? She was only writing down what she heard.

*Peyton Place* wasn't allowed on the shelves of the library in high school because it might be read by someone like Vera who came crying one day to our freshman English teacher. The teacher was shocked because she knew Vera was pregnant and felt she ought to help her. But she got off on the wrong foot when she asked Vera who the baby's father was.

"Papa," Vera said, crying her heart out.

"Yes," said the teacher. "Who is its papa?"

Vera kept saying, "Papa," and crying until the teacher finally tumbled. The Greeks had a word for it. But in Middlebury we just felt sorry for the poor child because it had only one grandfather—Papa and Grandpa are just two names for the same beast.

Nobody gets packed off to the insane asylum in Our Town. Dotty people are just accepted, and everybody watches them and takes care of them because everybody knows the ones who really need watching are the people who are supposed to be all right.

At St. Mary's School I was an angel in the fourth grade Christmas play. I had to wear long beige cotton stockings with little garters and a garter belt. It was so cold that winter, and Mom made me wear long underwear under those stockings. I refused to wear them. I wouldn't get up on-stage in granny stockings.

"You're wearing them," Mom said. I stomped and had a tantrum, but I couldn't get out without them. I tried to sneak in the back door and sneak upstairs to change the stockings. Mom was one step ahead of me. She locked the door. My vanity was at stake, and I was determined, so I put my fist through the glass door and unlocked it. Mom was waiting for me. I had to give up. I was finished. My mother knew me like a book. I was furious and weeping, but I went to school and did my number in the play and forgot all about it.

Daddy was the real disciplinarian. He was the one I was really scared of. Mom usually protected me and covered for me when she could, but she couldn't cover up that hole in the back door. So out came Daddy's big black belt. It scared hell out of us when he whipped that thing around. And I would be upstairs locked in my room and the kids would stand in the snow feeling sorry for me. All that fuss over a pair of cotton stockings I thought were ugly. Now the same granny stockings are just too fashiony for words, and I have to carry them around in my tote bag.

When my sister Paula got a little box camera, it never occurred to me to stand behind the lens, clicking the shutter. I was a poser. I had an entire gamut of attitudes I had picked up from *Screenland* and *Photoplay* magazines. I was a fifth grade tomboy, skinny as a string bean. Anything but shorts and jeans looked ridiculous on me. Instinctively I began using stray dogs for props. I would nuzzle any stray hound dog and try to look as sexy as Marilyn Monroe. I would gape at the dog with my mouth open, as wet and juicy as Marilyn in a clinch with Robert Mitchum.

Paula thought I was insane, but when we picked up the prints at the drugstore, everyone had to admit they were great. We didn't know what the pictures were selling, but they were saying something. From every blooper I learned something. I learned how to use the hair of the stray dog to hide my knees. I learned how to keep my hands in line with my body to avoid looking like a Mammy singer. I learned how to freeze at the best angle. I learned how to make my pigtails pick up light. I was ready for bigger things, and I couldn't wait.

We girls went to the movies every Saturday. I was mad for musicals and never tired of watching Fred Astaire and Donald O'Connor. The girls in those beautiful dresses who danced with them were always a big faceless blur to me. I couldn't see anyone up there dancing but me, Carolyn. How can I be that girl?—that was the question. How could I make an instant trip from an Ansco box camera to sharing the spotlight with Fred Astaire? Sometimes I felt I could skate my way to Hollywood like Sonja Henie and Vera Hruba Ralston. We collected pictures of those ladies and even tried to imitate some of their gyrations on ice. But the box camera never caught anything but a shadowy smear. Posing on skates was tricky and film was too precious and expensive to waste. The thought of all those works of photographic art gathering dust in a family album was more than I could bear. I knew it was a waste of time to write to ladies like Sonja Henie and Vera Hruba Ralston. If I sent them a picture and they had any brains at all, they wouldn't show it to a soul. You couldn't expect Sonja Henie to extend a helping hand to a gorgeous young green-eyed thing from Vermont who was waiting in the wings, with her skates on already, ready, willing, and able to replace her. I needed someone who had a big family of his own. A good upstanding member of the Holy Name Society. So I sent my picture to Bing Crosby with a covering letter:

Dear Mr. Crosby:

I have brown hair and green eyes. I can dance and skate and ride horses. I'm afraid to sing in public. I would like to become a movie star and I know you can help in things like that.

Sincerely
Carolyn

Public school was a mystery to us—we had the nuns at St. Mary's until the fourth grade—and then when we switched, it was almost like moving to another town, even though the two schools were only a five-minute walk apart and you could almost see one school from the other. Just as with a new town, you know everybody there, but you're not a part of it until you've been there awhile.

We walked or rode our bicycles to school, and in winter Mom sometimes drove us in the beat-up old Buick we had as our second car. That car made so much noise as Mom drove it up to school that the kids would hear us coming and run for cover. "There they come with the chipmunks in their car!"

There are never any chipmunks in my yellow T-bird. Uncle Ted sees to that. Auto mechanics in the big cities have learned a few things from the surgeons. Whenever you have any trouble with your engine, they yank something out and give you a bill for a transplant. Uncle Ted goes over the innards of my car with me until I know it like I know the map of my face. If I have trouble getting started in the below-zero snow, he sends his truck over to bail me out.

One more corner and I'm on Washington Street Extension and I'm home. Mom puts the teakettle on and Daddy helps me unload—something for everybody from the big city—something for Grandma and something for Grandpa and Mom and Dad—and as I sit there in my ski togs in the kitchen, Park Avenue seems a million miles away. I'm back in my mother's kitchen.

Mom had to braid four sets of pigtails every morning, two black and two reddish-brown, and after getting Daddy off to work at seven, she had another half hour of "Where's my blue sweater?" and "Which is my lunch bag?" (Mom didn't have time to put our names on them that morning) and "I wanna be first—I gotta be early today—I'm on patrol. Is this ready? Did you do that for me?" And after she got us off, there was the baking to do, and then Mom went off to her job of taking care of kids in nursery school, and she liked to listen to Arthur Godfrey on WFAD, and one morning I'll never forget because it was the first time I ever heard Mom complain about anything. It shook me, and I had terrible guilt feelings all day at school, and I wanted to show her all of us loved her but especially me. "I'll show her I care." I had to think of something stupendous as a surprise, like serving her breakfast in bed—this was something that happened only in the movies where people had servants. Nobody had servants in Middlebury. There was only one Negro in town, and she lived in a little doll's house and worked for some people in town every afternoon as a cleaning woman and sometimes for parties. I wondered if she was old enough to have been a runaway slave, and I thought it must be terribly lonesome for her in Middlebury without a Negro man. I wanted to show Mom I would be her slave. We went to bed before Mom did, so I couldn't prepare anything beforehand. I kept waking up every hour all through the night; I had it on my mind. It was dark out when I got up. I sneaked downstairs in robe and pajamas and no shoes so I wouldn't spoil the surprise. I had no idea how to make coffee. Oatmeal I thought I could make, but it came out unbelievable—I had put so much water in it that it looked like clear soup. I made one thing at a time, and I couldn't get things on the tray—the toast and the jam and the whole pot of coffee and the oatmeal and the sugar bowl off the table. The tray weighed a ton, and I got through the door OK, and I was halfway to the landing when I could feel my toe caught in the leg of my pajamas. I was moving so carefully and slowly, but I felt the tray slipping, and I reached for the banister to keep from falling, and I never made it. It sounded like eleven automobiles crashing head-on, and I was at the bottom of the stairs and the coffee and oatmeal soup were trickling down the steps. Mom was up in a flash, and she came to the top of the stairs and turned the light on, expecting a burglar, and saw this mess with me in the middle of it, bawling and crushed and disgraced and too ashamed to tell her what I had been trying to do.

Mom got the whole beautiful message in a minute. "Why, Carolyn," she said, "what a nice surprise! Let's all sit down in the kitchen and enjoy the lovely breakfast you made." My sisters came down and looked at the mess, and they thought both Mom and I had gone out of our minds. But Mom knew and I knew that if you want to tell someone

27

you love them, falling downstairs says it better than any greeting card ever made.

Saturday morning Dad is up early with the snow blower, clearing the driveway so I can take off for the mountain. We have a new interstate highway now that cuts through the Frost country.

He was an old man who lived in the mountains and wrote things. I used to ride horses with his secretary's daughter, and I saw him all the time. And then we all saw him on TV at the inauguration of President Kennedy, and he read one of his poems, and we realized Robert Frost was Robert Frost! And the people he wrote about and the places he wrote about are famous forever.

With the new highway I can make it from Middlebury to Stowe in an hour and fifteen minutes. I can get there and be on my skis at ten in the morning—and in New York on Madison Ave and Park Avenue at that hour most people are having their first cup of horrible coffee in those horrible styrofoam cups.

I take a run or two on Spruce Peak to warm up. Wouldn't it be wonderful to be able to ski like a maniac like David and never worry about breaking a fingernail or tumbling and getting bruises on your legs, which means you'll have to cancel a bathing suit booking? Now I head for the chair lift, ready for that cold, blustery ride up. You get in place with a partner as soon as the last pair has taken off. The attendant steadies the chair while you climb on, and you can't have two left feet because that lift never stops moving—well, practically never. I usually grab a long heavy wool poncho-type lift coat and stick my head through it. It's a long ride up there, and while you're going up, the temperature is going down, down, down. You're enjoying the ride through space, and suddenly you're dangling there in the breeze. They had to stop the lift because someone with two left feet was having trouble getting off. You dangle there with the ten-below-zero wind biting your face, and you curse some unseen idiot who doesn't know his right foot from his left. How is he going to get down the mountain in one piece? When they come down in the chair, they never look to right or left. A round tripper on the chair is a lost soul—it means he doesn't have the guts to face the National or the Nosedive.

When the chair gets to the departing station, you have to be ready—swing the metal safety bar open, get your skis underneath you with the tips up and your poles in your hand. The attendant holds the chair for a second and then off you go, zooming over to the Octagon—a warm eight-sided ski hut with huge glass windows that look down on the trails, and a long counter where hot drinks and food are served cafeteria-style. I snap out of my skis and brace them against the wooden racks. I snatch a cup of tea and head for an empty table—then unzip my parka, strip off my gloves, and warm my hands around the steaming cup.

The ski bums are out early and in force because conditions are perfect—packed powder on a 70-inch base and no ice. More snow is predicted for later, and the lines at the ski lift are getting longer.

I'm sipping my tea and yakking to someone when David walks in—red-nosed and healthy-looking and gorgeous. He grabs me and throws me into the air and catches me. We always try to meet Saturday morning on the mountain.

# CHAPTER 3

Nobody ever was—or ever again will be—as green as I was the day I landed in New York. That shade has been discontinued.

This sweet old brown-skinned Skycap treated me as if I were Lena Horne—just in from Las Vegas. He piled all my things on his cart and shepherded me through the airport maze to the taxi stand. I gave him a smile and a dollar tip and felt like an heiress. I didn't even have to think about how much the taxi would cost, either.

"Roosevelt Hotel, please," I said grandly. I'd never stayed in a big hotel in my *vie*. I walked through the lobby as if my whole life depended on how I moved. The elegant furniture, the palms, the soft, sweet music gave me the shivers. So many men were looking at me that I marched straight to the desk and announced myself. Before I could ask for Mr. Moore, two men came over and introduced themselves. One was the sales manager of the whole organization, and they were on the lookout for Miss Kenmore. Immediately they began commanding bellboys and clerks. I signed my name and we swept into the elevator—an entourage of five. The room looked as grand as a Presidential Suite to me, and there was this gigantic arrangement of flowers and a basket of fruit huge enough to sink the *Queen Mary*. I ripped open the card.

"Welcome to Our Star." Who would believe this in Middlebury, Vermont? Everyone kept asking me if everything was satisfactory, and I was fresh out of adjectives already. Mr. Bigelow told me I'd have a few minutes to powder my nose, and then I was expected in the Executive Suite at six for the cocktail party. A real-life sophisticated, glamorous New York cocktail party, and I was invited! Mr. Bigelow and Mr. Moore would meet me there. The company had thought of everything except that there was nobody I could ask to tell me what to wear. I had enough dresses for ten cocktail parties, but the first one had to be absolutely dead right. Something simple. Since I was already their star, I didn't have to be flashy. I could save that for later when I had a chance to see what the smart New York ladies were wearing.

I settled on a severe backless black with a very demure cover-up jacket. I had worked on my hair for three days. I was terrified that if I ever took it down I would be too nervous to get myself back together. At the last minute I decided to carry a flower—a white carnation. That would remind me to thank Mr. Moore for the gorgeous flowers. I had seen Gloria Swanson carry a single flower once on TV. She said it kept her from smoking, but I suspected she did it to call attention to her rings. It might be a good way to keep me from carrying a drink in my hand. Girls always look stupid at cocktail parties standing there, glass in hand, if they don't drink.

When I got off the elevator, you couldn't miss the party. It sounded like a thousand people laughing and talking. The door of the Executive Suite was open; Mr. Bigelow was waiting, and behind him—wall-to-wall men. They stared at me as if I were the only girl in New York that afternoon. Then Jim Moore materialized out of nowhere, suave and smiling. He didn't look like a Vermonter, but he was. Now I felt better. Here was someone I knew. Here was the man who'd discovered me on the ski slopes at Stowe and called me long distance out of the blue at the sorority house, Kappa Alpha Theta, and told me his company, the manufacturers of Slalom Skiwear, would be showing at the National Winter Sports Show in New York in April, and would I be interested? Would I be *interested* in a modeling job in New York? They wanted someone new—someone who was actually a good skier, someone who looked healthy and outdoorsy—not one of these typical starved-looking hothouse hard-looking models from New York. I had gone to Stowe with three other sorority girls to model some Slalom things on the snowy slopes for a company brochure. It was just another weekend lark, and we hadn't even seen the brochure yet, but the people at the company had seen the pictures and I was just what they were looking for. But how could I cut classes for five days? It was my senior year, and final exams were just six weeks away, and the spring formal was Friday night, and how could I squeeze it in?

Well, that was my problem. I was just what they were looking for. So I crawled on my hands and knees from one professor to the other, pleading and wheedling and reminding them I could have pretended to be sick but I had too much good sense for that, and this WAS a great opportunity, and I was just what the company was looking for, and I would hate myself and everybody at school if they stood in the way of this chance of a lifetime. The professors melted like the April snows, and I got permission, and each of them individually gave me homework to do while I was in New York.

Flying alone all the way to New York for the first time in my life on a plane, so terrified of looking terrified that I was afraid to breathe, thinking: You're going to die any minute and end up as a headline in the Addison *Independent*. And I'm supposed to be doing psychology assignments. The last pretty girl from Middlebury who went to the big city never got any farther than Boston, and she ended up as the sixth woman to be murdered by the Boston Strangler, and that was a big headline in the Addison *Independent*. Mom was too good a sport to mention it when I called her and told her I was just what they were looking for in New York. I told her all my expenses would be paid and I'd make some money besides—they hadn't told me how much yet, and I was too excited to ask—anyway, who thinks of money at a time like that? And Mom got excited, too, and said, "Remember to lock your suitcase and lock your door." They had already made a reservation in my name at the Roosevelt Hotel on Madison Avenue, and the president of the company had met me at Stowe, and the man who was in charge of his advertising had a niece in my sorority, and it was through her that I got the chance to go to Stowe in the first place to pose for the brochure, and now look what's happened. They were from Vermont, which is practically family, so Mom made sure to tell Daddy that, and now I'm here. Look, Ma, I'm here! I'm a New York model.

"Carolyn," said Mr. Moore, "how are you? How was your trip?"

"I'm here," I said. "Oh, the trip was terribly exciting. I'm so excited to be here!"

"Well, we're excited about having you," he said, and then it really began. Everybody in the room looked frightfully important, but they were all pestering Mr. Moore to meet me. They said all the silly, goofy things that men think girls want to hear, and I soaked it all up and was thrilled to bits by every syllable. I was too excited to drink anything, so I just twirled my flower and rattled the ice in a glass of ginger ale and smiled. I had noticed being noticed most of my life, but it suddenly seemed normal and natural and a part of a game called business. After all, if I was what they were looking for to show their ski togs, it was perfectly natural that they should look at me. And if they twitted Jim Moore and said things like "It must be nice to have something like

THAT around all day," it didn't seem bad taste at all. They were complimenting him on having the wit to bring a real born-on-skis girl down from the country. Most of the manufacturers and retailers talked about Vermont as if it were as foreign to them as Switzerland. It never occurred to me that anyone would attempt to get familiar with me because, after all, I was giving a performance and they were all the audience. Sometimes they were all crowded around me and the smoke got a little thick, but it wasn't like a cocktail party at all. It was theater in the round. I was getting paid to attract attention. That was my job.

Driving through the crazy lights, the noisy caverns, the jumble of funny-talking people of Manhattan on a Saturday night was the most exciting thing that had ever happened to me. Every time our limousine turned a corner some other fantastic sight appeared. The store windows were like page after page of *Vogue* in three dimensions. Lights blazed, and skinny plaster mannequins posed, and yet the doors were closed. Mr. Moore saw I was exploding with curiosity, so he ordered the chauffeur to cruise by all the sights. Dinner could wait a few minutes. I think they were shamed into seeing things they had taken for granted too long. When I saw the Hotel Plaza and that corner of Central Park, it was as familiar as the Leaning Tower of Pisa. I had seen it in perfume ads since I was a tiny tot. Yet there was something about the lighting in a late spring evening that made it loom like a foreign castle. Times Square was familiar from a thousand movies, but the only way to see it is to be in the middle of it, with traffic jammed and jumbled from every direction and taxi drivers shouting at pedestrians and pedestrians shouting back and everybody screaming at the top of his voice as if the whole city were on the edge of some strange holiday and everybody had to get somewhere else that very minute.

I almost fainted when we walked into the Four Seasons. The restaurant takes up the whole floor of this gigantic skyscraper on Park Avenue with illuminated fountains. Two huge rooms with terraces, and trees are growing in the middle of the main dining room—at least two stories high. An army of waiters buzzed around us, and when I reached for a cigarette three men were holding flames in front of me before I got it in my mouth. I was too dizzy to order and terrified of asking for the wrong thing. But everybody had a suggestion, so I just let them take over, and when the wine came in they all drank to me, and then these fabulous things began arriving at the table. The advertising

33

manager asked me what Broadway shows I wanted to see so he could get me tickets. Theater, I said. Gee, thank you very much, but I wouldn't want to be shut up in a theater at night in Manhattan for fear I might miss something. I wasn't getting off-stage to sit in the dark in anybody's theater.

That first night I didn't sleep a wink. I kept thinking of all the people I wanted to send postcards to, but I didn't have any postcards, so I made lists, and I tried to remember and write down what I had had for dinner and how much I had seen already. They had given me a pair of gold stretch pants to wear as my basic show outfit, and then I would change parkas and jackets as the different customers wandered in. At 5 A.M. I was up trying them on and parading around admiring the fit. Jim Moore called me early and invited me to join him for breakfast in the hotel dining room. He promised he would look out for me, and he thought of everything. We took a cab to the Trade Building on Eighth Avenue, and it was like a huge convention. They had a gorgeous showroom and trunks of gorgeous things for me to wear—turtlenecks and parkas with fur hoods and ski jackets and racks of gorgeous stretch pants and imported sweaters.

That first morning the man who owns the ski shop in Middlebury came wandering in, and when he discovered who I was, I felt so important and he was so surprised. All the other customers were just little men who owned ski shops all over the country, but I didn't know that. I didn't know enough to be tired. I couldn't get off that cloud.

Mr. Moore had to go to Macy's to pick out a gift for his little girl, and he asked me to go along. If he'd asked me to dive off the Empire State Building, I would have done it if he told me what to wear. So we walked on Seventh Avenue through the crowded noon hour pedestrian traffic—me in my tight gold stretch pants, a beautiful Norwegian P & M sweater, sealskin après ski boots, and big bold sunglasses. Naturally everyone was looking at me. I'm sure now they thought I was giving away free chewing gum or something, but at the time I was sure they thought I was the belle of New York. Jim didn't bat an eye. He was enjoying the show. After all, he'd produced it. He just let me rev my motor and took it in stride. When we got into the misses' department, the section manager came over and looked at me.

"My," she said, "what a beautiful outfit! Are you modeling for Macy's or someplace nearby?"

34

"How did you guess?" I beamed. I wanted to hug her. My public!

When we got back to the Trade Building, I was just one more model doing the same old thing. "Will she deliver my order?" one of the customers heckled Jim.

I almost plotzed when one of his friends came up to him and said, "Jim, you knew what you were doing when you brought this girl in from outa town. She makes these other zingers look like a bunch of tarts."

"False eyelashes and all that mascara are OK for evening things, but they look like hell on a girl modeling skiwear," Jim announced. "We wanted the natural look and we've got it, haven't we, Carolyn?"

At that point I couldn't have looked any other way if I'd tried. If I had a natural look, it was as unconscious as I was.

Whenever traffic slowed down a little in our exhibit, Jim Moore would walk with me through the rest of the show. All the men stared and made the same witty remarks they make every year—but to me they were all shiny and newly coined. And then the editor of *Skiing* magazine came to visit our parlor and asked if I would pose for their cover with three other girls. I didn't know what to say. Getting to be a cover girl on your first modeling assignment—I couldn't believe it was happening. I stuttered and spluttered and said he ought to talk to Mr. Moore. Of course, Mr. Moore said, we'd love it. His hunch was paying off. Now he would get a cover credit for whatever outfit I wore in the picture.

There was never time to change for lunch, so that gave me an excuse to walk around New York in those gold stretch pants. It was a very warm day, and absolutely everybody looked at me as we waltzed into the cool dark caverns of the Brass Rail. Jim introduced me to everyone who came by, and I was soaking it all in.

That night we had dinner at Mamma Leone's, and then Jim told me about the big fashion show the following afternoon. Everyone would assemble in the auditorium, and there would be lights and music and a runway, and I would get to show Slalom things while other models showed things from White Stag and other manufacturers. I walked on air the next day, waiting to do my first real-life live fashion show. They gave us a brief run-through. This gave me my first chance to see what New York models look like.

Those models just didn't seem to understand how glamorous it all was. They were like a bunch of waitresses or factory workers, watching the clock, bitching about the lights in the dressing room, complaining about the color of the clothes, fuming and fussing with the false eyelashes, and scattering ashes all over. They were noisy and funny and all wore too much makeup—especially around the eyes. They carried around huge tote bags full of junk, and they were forever rushing to the telephone to call somebody, and they never stopped complaining. They couldn't wait for it to be over. I wanted it to go on forever.

It was too late for me to compete with them, so I went my own way. I wore no makeup but a little eye liner and some mascara. I left my hair pulled back under a stretch band. I was a conservative Vermont college girl, and I couldn't be anything else. But every time I went out on that runway I felt it was an important occasion and I was a star. To the rest of them it was just a job. I couldn't understand how they could be so cynical. They didn't seem to appreciate how lucky they were.

After the show they took me up to this huge photographer's studio to pose for the cover shot. There were thousands of lights and an acre of white seamless paper. The photographer talked to me as if I knew what I was doing. He tried many groupings. One of the girls was a little chunky, and she tried to stay in the back. Finally he got his picture. I felt as though I had just swum the English Channel. I wanted to know when the cover would come out, and nobody seemed to know—or care. Finally the editor talked to me and told me it would be out in September. A picture taken in April doesn't appear until September? How does a person endure the suspense?

"You're still in school?" one of the girls asked me.

"Yes," I said. "I graduate from the University of Vermont in June."

"Hey," she said, "you should come to New York and become a model."

A lot of people had said that to me. But here was a New York model saying it.

"Thank you," I heard myself saying. "I think I will."

That night, sitting on the floor of a Japanese restaurant, having our last glamorous New York dinner party together with all the boys, I kept thinking about it. How do you *become* a New York model? For the first time in my life I had met someone who might possibly be able to tell me where to begin, and I'd been too ga-ga to ask her.

36

My last day was Thursday. When we got to the Exhibition Hall, the workmen had already begun pulling the booths apart. The wardrobe lady was packing all the beautiful clothes. I cried when Mr. Moore made me a present of the beautiful parka and a sweater and the gold stretch pants I'd been wearing. He gave me this huge check—twenty-five dollars a day and a liberal allowance for nonexistent expenses. What an enormous amount of money to be paid for having the time of my *vie!*

When I got back to school, everyone was rushing around like mad getting ready for the Spring Formal. I got out my gown, and it looked so tacky I wanted to die. I had this terrible fever and didn't know it until a splitting headache rocked me and my throat was so sore I could barely speak. The whole idea of the Spring Formal seemed small-town and tacky. Bruce—this boy I was pinned to—picked me up and, sick as I was, I tried to tell him I was going to have my picture on the cover of *Skiing* magazine. I tried to tell him about the flowers at the hotel and the Four Seasons and the Japanese restaurant and the fashion show and the excitement of the city and the glamorous cocktail party and the woman at Macy's and what she'd said to me and what the New York model had said to me. And he said, "Look, Carolyn, save it for your mother, will you? I live in New York, remember?"

It wasn't just what he said—it was the way he said it. We had a terrible fight, and I gave him back his pin. Who wants to get married, anyway? Maybe when I sent my picture to Bing Crosby when I was a kid—maybe I wasn't crazy. If someone wanted me on the cover of a magazine and a model thought I should become a model, what was I waiting for?

We left the dance early, and Bruce dropped me at the sorority house. I was the first girl in—that had never happened before. And my eyes were red, and my nose was running, and when Mrs. Eddy, the house mother, saw me, I burst into tears. Of course, she wanted to know what was the matter, and I loved her, anyway—I thought she was so great. She actually listened when I told her how nasty Bruce Gordon was and how he didn't want to listen. I blurted out everything.

She listened and listened, and then she said, "Never mind, Carolyn, someday you'll be all those things. You're intelligent. You've got spunk and drive. So you just pitch in and go after it. You'll make it, and you'll forget how nasty he was, and you'll meet the right boy one day."

She put me to bed with Vicks all over me, and then I realized I'd seen exactly the same scene in a Jeanne Crain movie. Or maybe a Mitzi Gaynor one.

Those last weeks of college were torture. I couldn't wait for it to be over so I could head for New York to start my career as a model. When I heard through my sorority that three girls who lived together in Greenwich Village were losing a roommate and looking for a replacement, I leaped at the opportunity. I was certain this would be perfect for me.

I took the Greyhound bus down early Saturday morning to meet them and make all the arrangements. It was hot when I got there. The sidewalks were teeming. The bus terminal was a madhouse. I couldn't get a cab and I had to take the subway. I got lost and had to try again. After walking for miles, I finally found their street and their number. My heart sank when I walked into the hallway and caught a whiff of the smell. Maybe New Yorkers are used to it, but to me it smelled of garbage and dirt and soot and excrement. When the girls showed me the apartment, I had trouble keeping myself from bursting into tears. The three of them lived all cramped together in two dirty basement rooms—with no room at all for their clothes. How they ever managed to cook in that tiny closet kitchen I couldn't imagine. The bathroom was enough to give you acute constipation watching the ballet of bugs under the old-fashioned bathtub.

That night they made a bed up for me on a dirty old sofa that had such an odor I hated to put my head on the pillow. I was awake half the night wondering how anybody, but anybody, could get used to living like this. Maybe you had to be born in a city and have it deteriorate gradually around you before you could take it for granted. As bad as I wanted to snag a glamour job, I couldn't live like this—not even for one night. There was, I decided, more than one New York. There was more truth than poetry in the old saw about its being a great place to visit but. . .

I went back on the bus Sunday morning. I told the girls I would talk to my mother and let them know. I had to think of a decent excuse that wouldn't embarrass them and me and the girls from the sorority, so I told them my plans had sudenly changed and I was going to California to look for a job instead.

38

Then one weekend I met a boy who was raving about the terrific skiing places there are in the California mountains, just a few hours away from the palm trees. So on pure whim I decided I would go to Los Angeles instead of New York to start off as a model.

California couldn't scare me. Not like New York did. It was still just a dream to me. I'd never been there.

When I spotted two nuns boarding the jet to Los Angeles, I was immensely relieved. Even if we crash, I thought, we probably won't *all* die. I had never been on a jet before, and I was absolutely terror-stricken. I checked two suitcases, but still I had all this extra stuff to drag. When the stewardess showed me my seat and fastened my safety belt for me, I got out my missal and put it in my lap. I never moved. The two little nuns were having the time of their lives, but I prayed all the way.

A jolly middle-aged man from Sherman Oaks sat next to me, took pity on me, and tried to talk with me, but I had acute rigor mortis, expecting the plane to drop. I opened my mouth just long enough to say I was going to stay with my aunt and uncle in Glendale, and he tried to explain where that was in relation to Hollywood and Beverly Hills and Sherman Oaks, but the entire lecture was lost on me. I had no time for geography lessons. I was too busy preparing for death.

When it didn't happen on the Great Plains, I knew we were going to crash in the Rockies. When we got past those, I felt maybe I had a chance to survive if we landed in the ocean. At least I could swim. When we came in over the runway, I went into shock. The nice man from Sherman Oaks had to unbelt me and help me off the plane with all my junk. He tried to tell me how to get to Glendale, but I assured him my Aunt Lucille and Uncle Ralph were meeting me.

"Where?" he said. Well, he had me there. I hadn't realized an airport could be so huge. I'd never met them in my life, but I was hoping they would recognize me. When I saw the palm trees, I could finally believe I had survived. I was wandering around ga-ga, taking in all the sights, when I ran into the man from Sherman Oaks again. By now he treated me like a basket case and was terribly concerned because my relatives could not be found. "Did you call them?" he asked. I couldn't tell him I'd been too busy gazing at palm trees to think of anything as rational as that. Then I realized I didn't even have their phone number. I called

Information with a sinking feeling, and she shocked me by giving me the number right away. I dialed. As soon as I heard this Vermont twang saying hello I felt better.

"Uncle Ralph?" I shouted. "It's Carolyn."

"Carolyn?" he said mystifiedly. "Carolyn—Anna's daughter from Middlebury. Well, I'll be—this is a surprise—where are you, Carolyn?" How could it be a surprise? I had written them everything, asking if I could stay with them until I got located.

"I'm at the airport," I said.

"You are? Well, golly, how nice of you to call us first thing! When are we going to get to see you?"

Horrors! They hadn't gotten my letter. What could have happened? Where did I get the nerve to just land on them like this without any warning? How could I have just assumed they'd gotten my letter? Why hadn't I called from Vermont to make sure? It was so embarrassing. I felt like such a fool. In Vermont everybody is your neighbor and you think nothing of dropping in on anybody at any time. But these were people I'd never even met. I was counting on moving in with them, and they didn't even expect me.

"Gee, Uncle Ralph, you're going to get to see me as soon as you're ready," I said. And then I blurted it all out. They were as gracious as could be, and the whole thing became a joke. They told me to take the limousine to the Hollywood Roosevelt Hotel and they would drive over and meet me halfway. "You won't know us, but we'll know you," they said.

My Hungarian gypsy blood pressure got me to the Hollywood Roosevelt Hotel. When Uncle Ralph and Aunt Lucille found me, I was never so glad to see anyone in my life!

I landed in Los Angeles on a Thursday, and by Monday I was a girl Friday. Southern California has more psychiatrists per square inch than any other place on this planet. There is a comparable density in the profession of psychology. I had my B. A. in psychology from the U. of Vermont, but when I examined the want ads in the newspaper I knew it was my high school Gregg shorthand and typing that would open the most doors for me. The first employment agency I landed in gave me some tests. I passed the typing test, doing fifty words a minute. I got a speedwriting book and began brushing up.

I was hired in the first office the agency sent me to, at eighty dollars a week. What I wasn't shrewd enough to figure out was the internal drama going on in the office. It was the kind of enterprise that could exist only in Southern California. They supplied all the merchandise that smiling masters of ceremonies give as prizes to contestants on radio and TV shows. Mr. Peters was the boss. Miss Vance was the vice president who ran the show. Miss Vance hired me. She was a good-looking blonde in her late thirties. Everything was fine until Mr. Peters arrived and starting giving me the once-over. Every time he looked at me, Miss Vance would punish me by giving me enough letters to break my arm. The girl at the switchboard saw what was happening before I did. She tried to help me out, but it soon became clear that Miss Vance was trying to encourage me to get out of there. Before I could figure out what was going on, Mr. Peters came in one morning early and called me in. He wanted me to take some dictation. He was a great dictator. He was so entranced with the sound of his own voice that his letters all came out making no sense at all. When he got completely tangled up, he would ask me to read back to him what he had said. That discouraged him so much that things went from bad to worse.

This morning he dictated a name and a Las Vegas address which he read off a telegram. As soon as he said, "Dear Fred," there was a long pause, while he moved his chair out from behind his desk. He raised his eyes toward heaven every time I caught him staring at my knees. I sat there with my pencil poised while he examined his fingernails. Then he came on with a big beaming smile and said: "What do you think of Las Vegas?"

I knew the question was directed at me, but I ignored it and wrote it down as if it were the beginning of his stupid letter. I kept my eyes glued to my notebook. There was a long pause while he got up from his chair and paced the office with his hands in his pockets.

"Why don't you put your pencil down for a moment, Miss Kenmore?" he whispered. "I'm talking to you."

"I'm sorry, Mr. Peters," I said. "I thought you had some dictation you wanted to get out." Now he was standing behind me, breathing heavily, blowing a stream of mint-flavored air into my hairdo. The smell of shaving lotion and Tums was overpowering.

"When were you last in Vegas?" he wanted to know.

"I've never been in Las Vegas, Mr. Peters," I said. "If you must know."

"How come?" he said. "The first time I laid eyes on you, I swore I'd seen you in Vegas. But I could be wrong, of course."

"Definitely," I said. I didn't panic. I didn't even get flustered. I was very calm, figuring out what I would do when he made his big move.

"That's a little oversight that can be easily corrected," he smiled as he pranced around the office, still with his hands in his pockets. "I get down to Vegas at least two weekends a month. Eventually we'll have to open an office down there. It's the only place to contact the big media people. California is too spread out. Vegas is where the action is. I'll bet plenty of guys told you that already, didn't they? Plenty of guys took an interest in you and wanted to take you down for a weekend where the action is. . .?"

I gave him the blankest stare I could manage. He couldn't face me, so he started pacing the floor behind me. I made up my mind if he got close enough so I could smell his peppermint breath, I would get up and leave.

"Mr. Peters," I said archly, "is this a proposal?"

"Baby," he replied, "this is a straight out-and-out pitch. I know what the score is, and so do you. So why play cat-and-mouse? We're all after the same thing. You want it and I want it, so let's do it right. I'll make the reservations, and we'll meet right on the plane . . ."

When I tried to stand up, he had his two hands on my shoulders. His whole weight was on me. I couldn't move. I was trying to figure how to slither out of it when he slipped both his hands around my throat. I hadn't pegged him for a maniac, but you never can tell. He was slobbering on the back of my neck. I knew if I held very still he would eventually try one of two things. Either he would try to unzip the zipper at the back of my dress or he would start fishing in my bosom. In either case he would lose his grip, and then I would take a dive out of there.

I kept absolutely still while he slobbered. When he started unpeeling my zipper, I took a dive off the office couch.

"Keep you dirty, rotten hands off me," I said quietly.

"Aw, come on, baby," he moaned. He had taken his jacket off, and he was leaning on the couch with his tongue out like a dog in heat. It was too silly a picture. He looked so ridiculous I couldn't resist it.

42

I walked to the door, but I didn't open it. I just stood there and let out the most horrendous scream I could manage. Then I stood there with the back of my dress open, waiting. I have no idea where that particular bit of feminine inspiration came from. I must have seen it in some movie when I was a tot.

The door banged open and in marched the vice-president, Miss Vance. Behind her was the girl from the switchboard. "Myrtle," I said to the switchboard girl, "will you please zip me up in the back?"

Miss Vance got the entire message. I got the feeling this had happened too many times before. I went back to my typewriter, and I just sat there, burning, trying to cool off. Myrtle was finally dismissed, and the door to Mr. Peters's office was closed, and there was a big summit meeting in the office. When it was over, Miss Vance had the gall to tell me she was giving me a week's notice.

"You can't fire me, Miss Vance," I announced. "I have already told Mr. Peters he can take his dictation and shove it." She had the nerve to insist that I had to stay around and finish up all his stupid letters and break in another girl.

"Let Mr. Peters break in the other girl," I said. I picked up my purse, threw the typewriter cover at her, and waltzed back to the employment agency and asked them to get me another job.

I might have expected this kind of thing if I had landed a glamour job in TV or the movies. I wasn't ready for it in this little outfit that was only on the outer fringes.

The agency immediately lined me up something better—in Beverly Hills. A beautiful air-conditioned office right in the heart of the action territory on North Canon Drive. The job was with a firm that manages the personal affairs of film stars and TV stars and record stars. It collects their pay check, pays them their weekly allowance, pays their bills, pays their servants, their taxes, their insurance, and invests what is left over. The office had a certain glamour of its own—the stars would come trooping in and out from time to time, and the boss had a big Thunderbird which I used to run errands and zip around in. In between I answered the telephone, acted as receptionist, secretary, and all-around girl Friday.

The main rub was transportation. In order to get to Beverly Hills from Glendale I had to get up at five o'clock in the morning to catch the bus. At that hour it was cold enough to wear a fur coat as you sat on a deserted, woebegone little wooden bench waiting for the bus while the air-conditioned limousines zipped by on their way to and from the freeway. It took an hour and a half to get to Beverly Hills on the bus. By that time you were carrying your coat—it was so hot after the sun came up that you needed nothing but a bikini. Then you went into an air-conditioned office, and when you came out at night the chill hit you, and if you rode home on the bus, by the time you got to Glendale it was 8 P.M. and you could use your fur coat again to walk home in. I loved being with my aunt and uncle, but I knew I had to make enough money to get a place of my own—and with my salary under a hundred a week and rents so high, a roommate was inevitable.

I was treading water, waiting to get time and money to get into modeling someway. I wanted to cross over from a secretarial spot into a glamour job, but I didn't know where to begin. I couldn't wait to be discovered. In Middlebury I had been one of the prettiest girls in town. In Hollywood I was just one more pretty face in the crowd. I wanted to be a star at something, but I was ashamed of wanting it, because in Hollywood everybody wanted it, and I didn't want to be part of any mob scene.

Skis must do for me what sequins and satins and sables do for other girls. I had been flying around Hollywood and Beverly Hills for days—sitting in deserted bus stops in Glendale, on a stool at Schwab's drugstore on the Sunset Strip, driving around Beverly Hills in a Thunderbird, and nobody—but nobody—ever seemed to notice me. Finally I took a weekend off and went up to Mammoth Mountain.

Up there on the slopes where the air gets thinner and the snow gets thicker, the girls get fewer and fewer. The competition is mostly in the après ski lounge at the Mountain Inn.

This tall, tan, terrific skier glided up to me and said, "I've been watching you." He had a hint of a foreign accent I couldn't place. "You move very well for a California girl."

"I'm not a California girl. I come from Vermont."

"Oh, that explains it. You grew up on these things like I did."

He was really the first European man I had ever experienced, and I was enjoying the difference. His name was Pollo, which was short for Leopold, and he was a Swiss citizen, except that he was really German, and he had come to this country to work during the Korean War and had joined the American Army. When he got out, he became an

44

American citizen and went back to Europe. He was good enough to be a ski instructor and good-looking enough to be an actor. He might have been terribly famous, for all I knew, and I didn't feel like asking. Finally he said he was a model. He didn't seem to be thrilled about the admission until I stretched the point and said I was a model too.

"I knew," he said. "I can always tell. I've worked with enough of zem to know. Who's your agent?"

I not only didn't have an agent—I didn't know what an agent was. So I told him I had been stretching the point to say I was a professional. Actually, all I'd done was a few little jobs here and there. I told him I had posed for the cover of *Skiing* magazine, but the issue wouldn't be out until September. "But you have to have an agent, schatzi," he insisted. "We'll have to do somesing about zat."

When I told him I was working as a secretary and just waiting and hoping and looking and not knowing quite what to do, he got very efficient. He was a real go-getting Teutonic type. "You could be doing commercials like crazy," he said. "I'll take you to zis agent I know. You won't have to sleep wiz him," he said casually. "I already took care of zat. I'm his favorite Storm Trooper, schatzi."

I wasn't quite sure at first what he was telling me. I knew there were boys who like boys. There were various names for them, like gay, pansies, faggots, homosexuals, and queers. Was Pollo telling me he was one of those? Or was he telling me that a male model went around sleeping with other men in order to get ahead? Or was he convertible, or AC-DC as they called it in Hollywood, or bisexual as they called it in Psychology III? Maybe they have a different way of looking at these things in Europe.

He wanted to know if I had a portfolio of pictures. I told him I had a few but that I really needed some more before I could go out after any jobs. It turned out he knew photographers in Paris and London and New York, but there was nobody good in California he could send me to. He said we could safely leave that to his agent. "Let him work a little for his money," said Pollo.

When he took me down to the Inn's après ski lounge to buy me a drink, all the other girls were swooning over him. He was the best-looking thing on the slopes. But a fine romance that was! He sat me down in a corner and proceeded for a full hour to pour out his troubles to me nonstop. He was deep in love trouble. He was madly in love with

45

a French actor who didn't love him. He had had a breakdown and gone to a psychiatrist in New York. Then, to complicate things, the psychiatrist fell in love with him. When Pollo left this psychiatrist and went to another psychiatrist, the first psychiatrist had a breakdown and was threatening to sue him for professional services at the rate of thirty-five dollars an hour. Pollo had fled New York to avoid process servers, and now he was living with an American actor who loved him but whom he didn't love at all. One of the big studios wanted this American star to go to Germany on location for a picture, but he refused to go unless Pollo could go with him, so the studio offered Pollo five hundred dollars a week to go along and keep their actor happy, and Pollo was outraged at their crudity. "Zay treated me like a piece of trade, schatzi," he complained. "I told zem my rate was fifty dollars an hour, and zay couldn't afford to pay me zat."

I wondered how he ever found time to work with all this drama in his life. I had majored in abnormal psychology at the University of Vermont, but I was in way over my head. I wished I could help him as much as he helped me. He gave me the name of his friend, the agent. He told me he could call him and set up an appointment. He insisted I would not have to tell any lies at all. I could leave that to him. He would say he had worked with me in New York—that I was out here on a skiing vacation where he had run into me.

"Zat's why you didn't bring your pictures," Pollo suddenly explained to me. "So many terrible people in New York are after you to do so many crummy jobs, and you just had to get away from it all. Money isn't your scene. Your family is hideously wealthy. If he needs pictures to send you around for jobs, let him send you to some of his faggot photographer friends."

There was only one trouble with Pollo's elaborate little plot. He forgot to ask me if I was a member of the union. How could I have done all these commercials in New York without ever getting into the union? It was one of the first questions the agent asked me when I went in for the interview. I couldn't think of any answer. He explained to me that I would be allowed to do only one job, and then I would have to agree to join the Screen Actors Guild. At that point I would have joined anything.

When Pollo called me that night to find out how the session had gone, I told him we had tripped ourselves up. How could I explain being such a hot number in New York if I didn't have a union card?

"Screw zat, schatzi," he said. "He's not supposed to be asking you questions. He's supposed to be helping you because you're a friend of mine. I'll tell him any more of zat union jazz and I'll have him blacklisted with the faggots' union."

The agent sent me around to a photographer he recommended to have some test pictures made. I took an afternoon off from work to sit for them. They weren't terribly good, and a few days later the man gave me a bill for forty-seven dollars. When I confessed that to Pollo, he was furious with me for being so stupid, and he was even more angry with the photographer.

"Nobody pays for test pictures," he screamed at me. "You're a big New York model, and zis faggot is lucky you went near him. Where does he get the nerve to charge you for zat? Tell me his name and I'll scratch his eyes out. Don't pay him—let him sue you!"

"He says no money no pictures."

"Zen let him keep his lousy pictures. We'll find some ozzer faggot photographer."

I know Pollo had the best of intentions, but his dramatic love life intervened. One night he called me and said he had to go back to Europe. His lover had been in an auto accident and was in a plaster cast. "I have to go back and play Nurse Edith Cavell," he said. "I told that faggot agent if he didn't get you a commercial in ten days I'd scratch his eyes out."

How he would accomplish that by long distance I never knew. But something happened for some reason, and one day the agent called me and sent me out on an interview for a job with Chevrolet. I always tried to squeeze the interviews in on my lunch hour. But this one wouldn't squeeze. So I talked to my boss, and he said I worked hard enough around the office anyway, and if I needed more time I could make it up by coming in on a Saturday. So off I went to my first real interview.

It was a full hour trek on the bus to the office of Young & Rubicam just off Hollywood Boulevard. The casting director was interviewing dozens of girls, but after he took one look at me, he didn't even bother to look at my photographs. He sent me to see the director.

The director took one look at me and said, "Fine, we'll use you, Miss Kenmore." I didn't know what he meant by that, and I was too scared to ask. He asked me if I could be available next Saturday. They would be shooting a commercial for the new Chevrolet outside the branch office of a big company in the San Fernando Valley. They picked Saturday because the office would be closed and they could shoot all day undisturbed by crowds.

"I'll give you a quick rundown on the story board as it's mocked-up now. Your boyfriend drives up in front of your office in his new Chevrolet. He waves to you, and you wave to him, and you come running out of your office right after work, and he picks you up, and you drive off. We're picking two other couples in order to show three Chevrolet models in the one commercial. OK?"

This was type casting right down to the ground. I had just run out of my office in the exact same simple linen dress I wore to the office in order to get the part of a girl who just runs out of her office. If I had tried to fix myself up into something I imagined they might have wanted, I couldn't have done it. The only thing unnatural about me was that I didn't know anybody with a Chevrolet. I had to take the poky old bus. I asked the director what clothes I should bring, and he said offhandedly to bring half a dozen outfits in different colors—the same general kind of apparel as I had on and the stylist would choose one for color.

I floated back to the office and told the girls I had the part. Nobody seemed as surprised as I was. But Beverly Hills is blasé about everything except fires and floods.

Friday night before my debut I was up until dawn. I laid out my clothes and packed and unpacked and repacked. Six dresses were about my limit. If he'd asked for seven, I'd have had to go buy one. I shampooed my hair. I shaved under my arms. I smoothed my legs. I creamed my elbows and knees. I did my toenails and my fingernails, and after I was in bed and set the alarm I creamed my hands and put my gloves on. Two hours later, at 4:30 A.M., I got up and uncreamed my hands and combed out my hair. Then, with extras of everything I could possibly use in the event of any disaster that could possibly be imagined stuffed into my huge suitcase, I struggled to the bus stop to catch the bus for Hollywood where we were to get the chartered bus to take the cast and crew to the San Fernando Valley. We had to be made up and on the set ready to shoot at 8 A.M. They made arrangements for us to use one of the offices in the building as a dressing room, another for makeup. There were two makeup men for three girls, but it was no big production. They tried to preserve our natural California look.

The cars got more attention than the girls. They had been delivered to the set the night before and washed and shampooed and creamed and manicured and wrapped in Saran wrap, and every time one of us touched the door handle of a Chevrolet during rehearsal, two little propmen walked over afterward to wipe our fingerprints off the chrome. They sat there twinkling in the early morning sunlight like twentieth century shrines.

I didn't know black and white from color or film from tape, so I listened avidly to every snatch of conversation among all the cast and crew. I didn't dare let on to a soul that this was my first SAG job. After the director picked out one of my six outfits—a lime-green linen suit—the assistant director came around with these imposing oversize printed contracts for us to sign. I tried to sign mine casually, as if I had signed hundreds of these in my life, but at the same time I tried to give a quick look-see. All I could really see was that my name was typed in and my category was principal player and my SAG rate was a hundred and five dollars per day plus an extra five dollars for the use of my own wardrobe.

One hundred and ten dollars a day! That was more than I made at the office in a week. I'd thought twenty-five dollars a day was a fortune when I worked that ski show in New York. This was for me! And I was starting as a principal player. The bus was filled with kids who were supposed to mill in and out of the office building and decorate the front of the building while my Prince Charming drove up in his gleaming, manicured, shampooed Chevrolet and waved to me.

The director couldn't have been nicer. I was terrified he might speak in some kind of technical lingo I might not understand, but it was as simple as ABC. We rehearsed the action a couple of times, and then he said, "This is a take." The extras streamed out of the building, the car drove up, and I burst out on the steps, smiling and waving, and then I dashed with this butchy blond handsome model who looked like Tab Hunter across the street and climbed in the car and drove off. I worked harder and harder at every take. I felt some of the extras were coasting and not giving it everything every take. But they knew the camera never strayed very far from that gleaming, glistening Chevrolet and any acting you did when you weren't touching the automobile was a waste of muscle.

Before I even dreamed of getting hungry, this huge vehicle pulled up near the set. It was the size of a transcontinental bus and inside was a complete restaurant, with cooks, waiters, and maître d'. Out came the tables, and we had a gorgeous hot catered lunch served to us as if we were a stable of Hollywood stars.

We went back to work, and we shot that little scene from every possible angle for the rest of the afternoon. Close-ups and long shots and zoom shots and dolly shots and crane shots and traveling shots until there wasn't a nook or a cranny of those gleaming automobiles that hadn't been captured at its peak of moving perfection.

When I rode back to Hollywood in that bus with the rest of the cast and crew, I wasn't a would-be any longer. I had gotten my feet wet. I had my first commercial under my belt. Even though the car was the star, I had been a principal player. Tomorrow I was eligible to join the same union Elizabeth Taylor belonged to.

When I got home, I wrote my mother and told her I was on my way. I was so excited I began spending the check a week before I got it. I alloted some of it to the dentist, part of it would go toward paying off my college loan, and the rest of it went into a kitty I was building for getting my own apartment closer in to Hollywood and Beverly Hills, where the action was. I even let myself dream about getting an old used car to run around in. If I was going to hang onto one job and chase after commercials, I had no more time to wait for the bus.

Within a month my first commercial was out. Aunt Lucille and Uncle Ralph never missed *Bonanza* on Sunday night, anyway, and when I came on they were paralyzed with excitement. They called my folks in Middlebury, but they had missed it. For the next month my entire family and I were glued to television watching for me. They watched every Chevrolet program on every network. I saw myself three times. It was a little disappointing to discover that most of my acting had ended up on the cutting room floor. But the family thought it was a star part. Everybody in Middlebury was talking about it, Mom wrote me.

Soon after that I teamed up with another girl and we rented an apartment. When the apartment doorbell rang twice one evening, I was sure it was my roommate dropping by after work with some guy. That was our signal to clear the aisles, dive into the bathroom, and get out of sight if you weren't ready for company. But I was ready for anyone, so I opened the door.

There stood this gorgeous gentleman caller. He looked like something out of a surfer movie, tall as a poplar, tan as a lifeguard, and with a smile as big as Texas. When he said, "Hello, there, little lady," I didn't know whether to laugh or melt. He sounded as homespun and comfy as Andy Griffith, but he was sending out all kinds of waves on all channels.

"I'm Spike Henry from Abilene, Texas, and I figure I musta done something pretty nice sometime for somebody somewhere along the pike in order to be lucky enough to happen onto someone as goldarned outasite pretty as you are this minute."

I must have been hypnotized, because it never occurred to me he could be what he was until it was too late. "I know you movie actresses are mighty busy people," he apologized, "but I wonder if you have just five little old minutes for a friend to talk to you like a friend about something as important to all God's creatures and critters as our health and well-being."

I was so entranced by the way he talked and the way he moved that he was inside the door before I knew what had happened. When I discovered he had slid a leather suitcase in behind him, it finally dawned on me that he had to be selling something. Well, that would be easy and charming. I couldn't afford to buy a thing. I still had my car to pay for, and I still owed money to my dentist.

"It isn't a question of my time," I said. "I don't want to waste *your* time, because I'm not interested in buying anything. Besides, I'm not an actress—just an ordinary working girl with bills to pay, and anyway, I don't live out here—I'm just here for a while. You see, I'm from the East."

"I could see that," he smiled. "Eastern ladies have that certain reserve that stands out here. What part?"

"Vermont," I told him.

"Maple sugar country," he said. "Well, wouldn't you know. So it won't be long before you head back there to set up housekeeping for yourself. Now you can't tell me I'm not right about that."

I wondered what he was selling. I wasn't the tiniest bit scared. Grandpa Elmer Novak sold vacuum cleaners all over Vermont, and he had more friends than the Governor of the State. There's nothing wrong with door-to-door salesmanship. After all, it's nothing but live commercials. If someone latched onto this gorgeous hunk of man as a TV pitchman, I wouldn't be surprised.

"No," I said, "I'm going to stick it out for a while. I'm not getting married, if that's what you're getting at."

"That's what they all say," he laughed, "But there's nothing in this world like it. And whoever the lucky fellow is, you're not going to want to make the same mistake so many women make by not taking care of him properly. You know, the amount of nourishment that goes down the kitchen drain every day in the year because ladies don't know what they're doing—this has a lot of big people worried. Out here we have all this natural abundance, and what are we doing with it? We're destroying it in our cooking."

He seemed so intense and concerned about what was going on in California kitchens that I wondered what his answer was going to be. It turned out to be this waterless cookware for $14.95 guaranteed to seal in flavor and whatnot. Before I knew what was happening, he had whipped out a length of red velvet, folded it over his suitcase, which turned into a display tier, and on it was all this dreamy kitchenware. My living room floor had suddenly been turned into a store window display. He was on his knees spieling and singing as he lifted lids and stacked the various utensils into myriads of combinations. He wanted to cook something for me to show off this fabulous equipment. The colors were beautiful, and the items stacked so that they took up virtually no room. It was a special introductory offer. If I bought the beginner's set, he would throw in a complete set of stainless steel Swedish cutlery and a full set of china for twelve people. I couldn't believe it. But after all, this was California. On my first job, a whole office full of people made a living out of making tie-in deals to give products away for publicity.

He caught me when he mentioned that after the product had been thoroughly tested in one hundred California homes, they wanted to get testimonials and photographs of certain select women in order to pick one to do an advertising pitch for their big national campaign. Like an idiot, I told him I had been auditioned for a Chevrolet commercial. That was his cue to ask me for my name so he could write that out on his survey form. If I'd refused, I'd have looked like a nut. Besides, I had confidence in him. These things can happen only in California.

Lana Turner was discovered in a drugstore. Someday someone had to be discovered at home. Besides, I'd been working for weeks now and hadn't bought a thing for myself. If I ever got out of debt to the point of thinking about getting my own unfurnished apartment, the first thing I'd need would be something like this. I didn't need it now, that was for sure. But I would need it if I was lucky. So I told him the thing looked beautiful but that I wouldn't be in a position to buy anything for at least four months.

"I'm in debt up to my ears—you know how it is," I smiled.

"Oh, that's no problem at all," he confided. "We'll just make delivery in two months and you'll have sixty days before you have to make the first little old cash payment. We'll split the difference—how's that?"

Well, you couldn't be fairer than that. He assured me that this arrangement wouldn't impair my chances for getting on the list of the first one hundred California ladies to test this new marvel, out of which the manufacturer and the ad agency would pick one or two ladies to star in the national TV campaign. By now I was really interested in the waterless cookware. I was on my knees in the red velvet display and he was showing me the literature when my roommate walked in the door.

She stood there, not saying a word, gasping with shock like an asthmatic lesbian who's just barged in on her girl friend's honeymoon. I hoped she was thinking what I thought she was thinking. I suddenly felt as uncovered as Eve in the Garden. Who would believe I was just playing dollyhouse with an umemployed cowboy on a red velvet carpet in the middle of the living room? It would be just too humiliating if she was to suspect that this beautiful man wasn't after my body and only wanted $14.95 of my money. He wasn't the slightest bit concerned. When he continued with his spiel, I cut him off short.

"Don't say another word and I'll sign the paper," I whispered. "My roommate boils frozen peas and throws away the water. She wouldn't appreciate this at all."

"I get it," he said.

Diana had flounced into the bedroom, so I rushed in to explain. "This is a new product they're going to introduce later on TV," I said. "I have a chance to get to do the commercial."

"I thought I'd heard of all kinds of casting, but door-to-door auditioning is something new—even out here," she said dryly.

There was no time to argue with a frustrated secretary. I had to get that junk off the living room floor and get that gorgeous Texan out of the house someway. When I gave him the signal, he packed up in a flash. When he handed me the yellow paper, I signed it with a flourish. When he was out of the house, I could breathe easier.

Next morning, when Diana opened the door to leave for work, three giant cardboard cartons blocked the threshold. I was too terrified to look at the labels. Somehow I knew they weren't addressed to the people next door. Or the people across the street. They were too heavy to move.

"They're for you, Carolyn," Diana said icily as she climbed over them and out the door. "All for you."

I knew in my bones that beautiful cowboy had conned me. I had signed his paper only to get that junk off the living room floor, and now I had three times as much junk on the living room floor. He had promised to deliver a $14.95 set of cookware in sixty days. Instead I had a kitchen shower the morning after. This was a king-size mistake. But where was the paper I'd signed? I couldn't believe I had signed something without reading it and without even keeping a copy. But I had—of course I had.

I had no time to do anything. I tried shoving the cartons into the closet, but they were too huge. I had to just leave them there like tombstones. Maybe I could call the Better Business Bureau in my lunch hour. But I didn't even know the name of the company to complain about. I looked over the cartons. There seemed to be no name, no address on them except mine—as big as life. I'd change my name and send them back to the post office unclaimed, I decided. But there was no postmark, either. They must have been delivered in the dark of the night. Maybe I could put them back on the lawn and pay somebody to steal them.

The more I tried to think my way out of the mess the more trapped I felt. I was too ashamed of myself even to tell my mother. I wrote Mother every day and told her everything good and bad and indifferent. There had never been anything I couldn't tell her. But this was too much. I fretted all day, but it wasn't until I got home that night that the cold sweats got to me. In the mailbox was this lovely blue copy of the yellow paper I had signed. A beautiful letter congratulating me on my taste in kitchenware and a beautifully bound coupon book for me to tear out and send this fly-by-night company $26.83 a month for the whole year. I thought I was buying a $14.95 waterless cooker and they had me for three hundred dollars PLUS interest PLUS carrying charges PLUS fine print. And the first payment was due next Monday. That first $26.83 would have to come out of this week's check. I was too ashamed to talk to anyone about it except Mr. Buck Henry or Spike Henry or whatever his name was. I called the number and got no answer. I barely slept a wink all night.

The moment I got to the office next morning, I got them on the phone. I began outlining my beef in distraught emotional detail, and this very cool lady interrupted me.

"What was the name of your salesman, miss?" she snapped.

"Mr. Henry. Mr. Spike Henry or Buck Henry. He said he was from Texas."

"Mr. Henry is no longer with us."

Omigod, maybe the law caught up with him! Why did I have to be the last pigeon? Why couldn't they have caught up with him the day before he got to me, not the day after? I wanted to ask what jail he was in, but I restrained myself and merely asked where I could find him.

"I'm sorry, I can't give you any information on that. All I can tell you is he left the firm."

"Then let me talk to someone else. Whom do you suggest?"

"I'll give you our district supervisor, Mr. Marquis."

"Thank you," I said.

I began with Mr. Marquis and told him the whole story. How the salesman had told me I wouldn't receive the waterless cookware for sixty days and would only have to pay $14.95 sixty days after that. He waited for me to go into all the details.

Then he came on like a cheap TV mobster. "Look, honey," he said, "just send us the money like a good little girl. Send us the check every month and nobody will bother you."

Nobody will *bother* me? Until that point I'd been merely embarrassed and ashamed. Now my dander was up. I was angry. I knew the swindlers were counting on my being so embarrassed over my own stupidity that I would keep quiet about it. The longer I kept quiet about it, the more rope this would give that sweet-talking, handsome, unemployed Texas cowboy to whip that red velvet carpet around in living rooms from Glendale to Pasadena.

I had all the stupid papers and the contract with me. When my boss came in at ten-thirty, I looked him straight in the eye and said: "Mr. Webster, I've done something stupid. The most stupid thing I've ever done in my life. I'm going to be no good around the office until I tell you about it. Maybe you can suggest what I ought to do."

I guess he thought I had stolen the company credit card and given an orgy at the Coconut Grove or something because he said, "Sure, Carolyn, come right in." When I told him my tale of woe, he knew I'd need a lawyer to extricate me. I'd never been near a lawyer in my life. Lawyers in Beverly Hills cost three hundred dollars a minute. Mr. Webster looked in his rollidex and wrote down a name and address. "You go down first thing in the morning and see Henry Carne at the Legal Aid Society. Tell him just what you told me and take your papers."

I got up half an hour early in order to get to downtown Los Angeles. I found this dingy unair-conditioned second-floor office in an old building. I felt frivolous in my crisp white-and-yellow sleeveless shirtwaist dress. The waiting room was crowded with Mexicans and Negroes. Their faces seemed so tortured and tormented with agony and injustice that it was almost more than I could bear to look around the rattrap. If Beverly Hills was the front, this was the backside of the city. Suddenly my woes began to seem like very small potatoes. I remember Grandpa telling me about the old Hungarian game in which everyone puts his troubles in an imaginary pile in the center of the room. Then, on signal, everyone gets a chance to lighten his burden by exchanging his troubles for someone else's. Of course, the upshot of the game is that each man goes away happy if he is able to get his own troubles back out of the common pile and not have to carry someone else's burden.

A young legal assistant looked at my papers and heard the beginning of my story. Then he said, "I guess you'd better talk to Henry." I was embarrassed because they seemed to want to put me ahead of some of the other troubled visitors, but I did as I was told.

Mr. Carne could have played a judge in the movies. He had white, white hair, he wore old-fashioned suspenders, and he chomped a long cigar while he talked on the phone. He was direct, tough, crisp, and never wasted a syllable. He was scanning my papers while he finished his phone call. After that for what seemed like five long minutes, he never said a word. My heart was pounding until he smiled.

"Well, Carolyn, maybe we can do something for you. I know this outfit. We've had a little trouble with them before. Got quite a file on them, as a matter of fact. We'll get them good one day. What's it worth to you to get out of this jam?"

Omigod, I thought, what do I have to do now? There was a joke I'd heard around Beverly Hills about this young actress who was unhappy with the studio, and who went around asking everybody, "Who do I have to sleep with to get *out* of this picture?"

"It's worth quite a lot to me," I stammered.

I started rattling off the gory details, but he brushed all that aside. "We know how they operate. It's always the same," he said resignedly. "Can you get fifty bucks together and charge it up to your education?"

I was so relieved I opened my purse. I had two twenties and a ten, which I produced pronto. He drafted a letter to the Credit Bureau. He told me to deliver the three cartons of unopened kitchenware to their office and get a receipt for them.

"That's all I have to do?" I asked. I couldn't believe it.

"All you have to do," said Henry. And it was, too.

"I'll never do it again," I said. "I was caught off-guard, but it'll never happen again."

"You got off easy," said Henry. "I know a little old lady in Pasadena. She was rich, but she broke her bifocal glasses. She signed a paper for a handsome attorney. She thought she was selling her shares of General Motors. She found out she had authorized her nephew in New York to have her committed to the cuckoo farm for spending too much of her own money."

Next day I got a boy I knew with an open car and lots of muscles to cart the cookware to the Credit Bureau. We got a receipt. I was so relieved it was over and I could finally write my mother. I made her a promise that if I ever did anything that stupid again—if I ever signed anything without reading it—I would come back to Middlebury so Daddy could break both my arms.

Every night after work I would drive our community jalopy to Westwood Boulevard and pick up Francine, who had moved into the apartment when Diana had moved out. One night as we pulled into the carport we noticed a tiny, timid little rabbit of a man turning away from

57

our front door. As we crossed the lawn, he spoke to us from the sidewalk.

"Do you girls live here?" he inquired politely.

"Yes," said Francine. "Can we help you?"

"I know you actresses are very busy people," he began, "but I wonder if you have just five minutes for me to talk to you about something as important to all of us as our health and well-being."

Francine looked at me, and I looked at her. The refrain seemed familiar, but I couldn't quite peg it.

"I know it won't be long before one of you young ladies or both of you has to think about setting up housekeeping for herself. You're not going to want to make the same mistake so many women make. You know the amount of nourishment that goes down the drain every day in the year because ladies don't know what they're doing? The Lord gives us this natural abundance, and what are we doing with it?"

"Wait just a minute," I said. "What are you selling?" He seemed too startled to reply. He stood there like an actor who has forgotten his lines.

"What have you got in that suitcase?" I demanded.

I was moving toward him now, swinging my handbag. "Tell me what's in there!"

He was moving away from me slowly. "Why, a beautiful waterless cooker. Why?" he mumbled.

"Waterless cooker! I knew it!" I shrieked. Now I was swinging my heavy handbag wildly in the direction of his dear little head.

"Carolyn, what's the matter? Are you out of your mind?" Francine was screaming as she tried to restrain me. He was running, I was swinging, and Francine was trying to hold me off so the little man could get away.

"Show us your waterless cookers!" I was hollering. "Come on—don't be chicken. I want to see your waterless cookers. Let's spread that red velvet rug out on the lawn. Come on—get out that red velvet rug!" The poor little rabbit of a man was off and running as if he had two police dogs after him.

It was only then that I realized that I had been rooming with Diana when it happened and that Francine was totally in the dark. So she naturally assumed I had gone stark raving berserk. So I had to sit her down and tell her about the beautiful Buck Henry from Texas and his red velvet throw and how it took the Legal Aid Society and fifty bucks to ruin my chances of being the Betty Furness of waterless cookery on Channel 2.

As a native Californian, she was not shocked at all. After all, she said, they still sell cemetery lots in the sky to the old ladies in Glendale. Out here it's not who do you know. It's who do you owe.

Out here everybody gets so far in debt that sometimes the only way to get out is to go out and hustle and get a commission on helping other people get into debt.

"You got a great build, Carolyn," my new roommate was always saying to me. "Why don't you get rid of that mousy brown hair?" She had dyed black locks and was always cha-cha-cha-ing around, and she couldn't wait to get everyone else in the dye pot with her. I thought her hair was horrible, but she never let me alone about mine. I told her every break I'd gotten up to now had come about because I looked natural. I was leaving well enough alone. She used to have a fit because I wore a regular one-piece bathing suit. She was forever urging me to try on one of her many bikinis. She wanted me to look like her and everybody else. She would heckle me and call me Little Miss New England. I thought I had come a long way. I wonder what she would have said about some of the girls back home. In Middlebury I would look pretty jazzy just as I was.

Then one day my agent called me and suggested I show up for a mass interview with NBC. They were doing a big important commercial for some hair product and would be using as many as a dozen girls. He thought I had a chance. The interview was at eleven in the morning so I had to wangle time off from my job. But everybody in the office was rooting for me. My Chevrolet commercial was still running on *Bonanza*, so I was really a model working part-time as a secretary.

The night before the interview I washed my hair and set it with particular care. Suppose the commercial was for one of the hair-coloring products and they were looking for a mousy brown wren to turn into a radiant redhead? What would I do? Could that be the reason the agent had sent me over? I never asked questions in those days. If there was an opportunity I heard about, I only needed to know the time and the address and I was there. It never occurred to me that there were ways of getting inside information on *what* they were looking for.

Even if I knew I wouldn't know how to make myself over into any other type than what I was.

When I got to NBC for the interview, I felt it was hopeless. There were more than a hundred ladies milling around with at least a hundred different shades of hair. Blondes galore, brunettes came in second, redheads third. But there were only about three or four of us mousy browns. Everyone seemed to know they were casting for Lilt, the home permanent product. It was all very casual, and when my turn came I was shown into a room where three men and two women sat at a table. The women were older office types, but the men were young and casual-looking with their open-necked shirts or turtlenecks. One lady asked me if I had ever colored my hair. I said no. "Have you ever had a permanent?"

Oh, boy, I didn't know what to say. Maybe they wanted someone who used their product. I didn't. Then the other woman got up and came over to me and began to feel the texture of my hair. Meanwhile the men just looked at me. They exchanged little looks, and then the woman asked me to lower my head so the entire panel could feel the texture of my hair.

I felt stupid standing there with a jury examining my scalp. One woman had a little magnifying glass, and she was looking at the ends of my hair. Wow, these people are thorough, I thought. They didn't seem to be interested in the color so much as the texture. One man looked at my book, and then they asked me to leave one of my pictures for their files. I wondered if that meant I had a chance or was this something they asked everyone.

"Will you be available next Wednesday and Thursday?"

I'm just a girl who can't say no. I hadn't even learned to hesitate or pretend to be so busy I might have to check with my agent or at least look in my appointment book. "Oh, yes," I said. On my first job I got the answer right away. I didn't know then how rare that was. I had yet to learn that after an interview it might be hours or days before you get an answer. Sometimes not getting an answer at all is your answer.

That night the agent called me at home. "Lilt wants to use you," he said. "They don't know yet exactly what they want you to do, and it's only a one-shot, but you'll get two days' work out of it. This is their big deal commercial for the Academy Awards!"

A one-shot means a commercial that will be used only one time—you get paid and that's it—no residuals. But going from *Bonanza* to the Academy Awards—that was the big thing. Nobody in Middlebury would miss that. I was so elated I couldn't find a pencil to write down the details.

Naturally my raven-haired roommate wanted to know if I'd won the Irish sweepstakes or what. It was my turn to rub it in.

"Miss Mousy Brown New England is doing a hair commercial for the Academy Awards," I announced.

The next day I had to show up at the NBC wardrobe department for a fitting. I got there early without intending to. I discovered that was the smart thing to do. When there are a dozen girls to be fitted, it's first come first served just as in a department store sale. When I saw this rack of fantastic long ball gowns, I began to get really excited. "This will look great on you," the fitter said as he pulled out a soft green strapless deal with lots of shimmery beads on it. I didn't think I was the beady type, but the fitter winked at me and said, "Always grab glitter when you're in a mob scene. It picks up light."

Then we were instructed to show up Wednesday morning with our hair in rollers. Their hairdressers would decide when they combed it out what style they wanted each of us to wear. So I showed up in my rollers, all excited. I couldn't wait to get into my green gown. The mystery and suspense were killing me. I couldn't wait to find out what I was going to do. While we were having our hair done, two members of the staff kept looking at us and making notes. Finally we found out what it was all about. They were picking two girls to have a Lilt home permanent on camera. They didn't pick me, and I was happy about that. I wouldn't have let them do it anyway.

Before the hairdresser went to work on us, we were taken to the makeup department. One man spent a full half hour fixing my face. He really made me feel like a star. The hairdresser fretted and sweated, giving me an elaborate hairdo. He must have worked on me for an hour and a half. I began to feel what I was about to do had to be important if I was worth this much attention. When I was principal in the Chevrolet commercial, it was a lick and a brush and we were on the set. This certainly meant there were some close-ups coming up.

Then I was led into wardrobe and the fitter helped me into my dress. It took most of the morning to get us ready, and then there we were—eight belles of the ball. Blondes in blue and brunettes in beige and others in pink or green. But everyone was in medium tones—nobody stood out. Next we were led onto the biggest sound stage I had ever seen. Giant pillars and steps and hedges and flowers and gates and fountains and what seemed like blocks and blocks of gleaming, glistening floor. Then the director brought in eight handsome lover boys and they began pairing us off. After we were paired off, on came some syrupy Andre Kostelanetz music and they asked us to dance. After that was over, they picked certain couples to dance and other couples to sit. My escort and I were picked to dance. I thought that was just too divine. At first, that is. If I had known we were going to dance all afternoon and the next morning too, I might not have been such an eager beaver. I never knew anything could be as difficult as filming seems to be. We would dance, and then they would holler cut, and then they would fix the lights, and then we would dance some more, and then something else would go wrong, and then we would dance some more, and then something in the background was thought to be interfering, and the set designer and the director would fight about that, and then the producer would have to be called to referee, and then the fountain would be moved, and then it would be moved back because we had already taken some shots that might not match with later ones if the fountain wasn't in the same place. A platoon of hairdressers and makeup men stood around watching us eagle-eyed to see that there wasn't a shine on a single nose or a lock out of place in a single hairdo. Fortunately they had asked us to bring our own shoes, so I didn't have trouble with my feet. There didn't seem to be any podiatrist on the set, but that was about the only profession that wasn't represented. No wonder commercials cost a fortune. An army of technicians stood around. Each man had one little button to push or one little lever to pull. They were falling all over one another in between times. After we did long shots of the ballroom with dancers whirling around, they moved in for close-ups. Finally the director got to my partner and me and began to give us little bits of business to do. Turn my head and talk to someone else, then smile. I thought the camera was on me every minute so I was giving a performance for five continuous hours. When quitting time came, I was limp. We were told to be back the same time in the morning when the shooting would be resumed. Off came the ball gowns, off came the makeup. The hairdos we could take home with us if we wanted. They had to be completely redone the next morning, and every curl had to match what had been done the day before. The hairdressers kept notes and sketches.

That night I was so exhausted I soaked in a hot tub for almost an hour. I'd had enough dancing to last me for a while. No wonder movie stars go to bed early. But the excitement made it worth it. I could forget how tired I was as soon as I remembered I wasn't going to an office tomorrow morning to sit behind a typewriter or run errands. I had to report on Stage 4 at NBC! I had already signed the contract, and I wasn't sure how much money we would be making, but certainly twice what I had gotten for the Chevrolet deal—something more than two hundred dollars at least.

I was feeling so wealthy I decided to splurge on a long-distance telephone call to my mother. I told her I was working at NBC doing a commercial for Lilt that would be shown the night of the Academy Awards. She said she would alert everybody to watch it. Since it was a national hookup, everybody would see me at the same time all over the country in California and Vermont.

The next morning we found out who the real stars of the production were—the girls who had been picked to get Lilt permanents. I should have known. When they brought them in, their dresses were just a little bit flashier, their hairdos were just a bit more stupendous; they got to wear the jewelry and the glitter that picks up light. They moved in and they became the belles of the ball. That was the whole point. If you use the right home permanent, life can be a continuous ball.

When I saw the commercial at Academy Award time, I wanted to crawl under the bed. I got one fleeting close-up that came and went so fast only my mother could spot me. In the dancing scenes that ruined my feet, my lover-boy partner and I looked like a couple of ants. All that work—all those hours in wardrobe, in makeup, and with the hairdresser, and we could have been bald and nobody would have noticed.

On Oscar night I learned my lesson. Even if you're doing twelve commercials a week, keep your mouth shut about it. Don't sell reserved seat tickets to your family and friends. Let your fans discover you.

And don't count your close-ups before you see them on the box.

Christmas in California almost did me in. I am not a city girl—I found that out in Los Angeles. I can't live without the four seasons—especially autumn, which is my favorite. But an air-conditioned Christmas with red and green lights in palm trees and no skiing and no snow—I was so homesick I was miserable.

I knew by now that if I wanted to make it as a model I would have to make it in New York. California was limbo for me. My three sisters were all married and all living on the East Coast. Elinor in Albany, Paula in New Jersey, and Jean in New Haven, Connecticut. Jean had married a man I picked out for her and introduced her to. So I wrote and asked her if I could stay in Connecticut with her and commute to New York until I got started. If I was going to take the big gamble, I needed the security of being close to my family in case I got bruised, blinded, or burned.

One night I got a telephone call from Jean. She was so excited she couldn't wait for me to come to New Haven. She had found the perfect guy for me and time was of the essence—she wanted me on the next plane. She gave me a rundown on him, like a marriage broker. He was tall and handsome, a Dartmouth graduate, a real New Englander, a bachelor, the outdoor type; he loved to ski and sail and was keen on all kinds of sports, and he had a Bonneville convertible.

Meanwhile I could only guess the kind of buildup Jean was giving me at the other end. "Where did you meet him?" I finally asked her.

"At work," she said. "He's an IBM salesman, and he had to get past me before he could get anywhere." Jean worked as a receptionist in a big fabric dyeing plant. "He was too good-looking to let past without a rundown, so I asked him if he was new in New Haven. He's just been transferred from Boston. So I asked him how he and his wife liked New Haven. 'Oh,' says he, 'I'm not married.' He was a Marine in the Pacific, and he's traveled through the Orient, and he's been to Japan."

"All right, Jean, all right," I told her. "You don't have to sell me anymore. When did all this happen?" If I knew Jean, she jumped on him and had him tied up somewhere.

"Just this morning," she said.

Well, I promised her I would give notice on my job and head East. When I notified my boss, he was very sweet. He understood, and then he made me a counter offer. He was just about to take off on a trip through the Orient. He needed a jet set girl Friday to go along for meetings with clients and inspection of investments. Since I was familiar with the office and since I wanted to leave anyway, I was the logical candidate for the job. I thought it over for about five minutes. Jean had just told me the lover she had picked out for me had traveled through the Orient. Maybe it would be more fetching and more glamorous if I returned to little old New Haven via Bangkok, Singapore, Hong Kong, Tokyo, Canberra, and Honolulu. So that's exactly what I did.

Jean and her husband Bert picked me up at the airport. They had arranged a big welcoming party for me so I could stun Prince Charming into submission. Jean had it all choreographed, and then he couldn't come. We had to go through with the party anyway. Two days later Prince Charming arrived in a pair of blue levis and a polo shirt. Jean is a great one at enlarging things, and I knew she had built me up to the point where he was expecting some kind of glamorous Hollywood star, and she had built him up to the point where he seemed too good to be true.

But as a marriage broker, I would have to give her an AAA rating. Within five minutes after meeting him, I turned to melted butter. I would have died if he hadn't finally, after what seemed to me an eternity of days, asked me out for dinner.

# CHAPTER 4

Brave and foolish and giddy and green and innocent as I was, that first morning I headed for Manhattan posing as a professional model began to loom up like the first day of kindergarten. I needed someone to hold my hand. David volunteered to be big brother.

"Why can't I take you to the train?" David said. I was thrilled to bits at his offer, but I never thought it would work. He would have to get up an hour early to drive from his apartment to my sister's house to pick me up, deliver me to the station, and then drive back through the traffic to get to his job at nine.

He insisted. When he saw me struggling to prepare the typewritten resumes I would need for scattering all around the various agencies in New York, David showed up with a huge IBM Executive typewriter. He showed me how to work it and lent it to me for as long as I needed it to get my *curriculum vitae* together.

With all the commercials I had done on the West Coast, I still had nothing in the way of photographs to back up my experience. So a glamorous resume of past triumphs was a *sine qua non.*

But I kept saying to myself, "This is all very well, but why doesn't he ask me out?" Finally two evenings later he called at dinnertime. He had just driven back from Boston. Oh-so-casually he said to me, "Have you eaten yet?" Jean and Bert had already started dinner, but I was not lying when I said no. He said he would come by and pick me up in fifteen minutes. I didn't know whether he would arrive in levis or not, but I took a chance and got into something a little bit dressy. He looked gorgeous to me in anything, but that night he was particularly handsome in a very Ivy sports jacket and slacks. He took me to a fancy restaurant. It must have cost him thirty bucks for dinner—more than he'd ever spent on a meal or a girl in his life.

We got along so well I couldn't believe it. The band played "The Girl from Ipanema," and that became our song. I knew I had met the love of my life, and I could only hope he felt the same way about me.

Falling in love with David was the biggest thing in my life at the moment. Making it as a New York model began to look like some sort of extracurricular lark.

"What ever happened to Barbara Ann?" said the model to the receptionist." I hear she's no longer with us." They were talking about her as though she had committed suicide in a not very chic hotel.

"We just loved her, dear," said the receptionist to the model. "But she was too limited for us. Her legs were really *too* heavy. That doctor in Switzerland tried to help her, but it didn't take. We really felt we were holding her back."

"Isn't that a shame," said the model.

"It really is," said the receptionist. "She had such a fabulous face, and she was really such a sweet thing, but that only made it more grim. Eileen really loved her, but we had to face it. This is not really the place for her."

They caught me looking at my legs. Mine weren't too skinny, either. The model made me feel much too dressed-up. My white dress and my polka-dot scarf made me feel like a nice little girl from the suburbs. I should have been much more casual. The model wore huge ugly tinted sunglasses and had a real don't-give-a-damn look that spelled a cool sixty bucks an hour. I had tried too hard and ended up looking like a would-be. The butterflies in my stomach had been stirred into action by the bitchiness in the outer office. Receptionists in model agencies always seem to be would-be dropout models. They wanted to be models, they're passing as models, but they've really settled for that regular pay check and the tiny bit of power that comes with being on the other side of the cage: They're not selling, they're buying. They can't really help anybody. Or hurt them either. They can just wound them slightly or rub salt in wounds already there. But I didn't know it then.

My gratitude to the Revlon executive who had made the appointment for me began to evaporate by the second. He had been as sweet as he could be. Men usually are, where girls are concerned. But he had been too high up on the slippery executive slopes to know anything about what went on in the advertising department down below. All he knew was that all Revlon models were hired through the top model agencies, so what I needed was a top agency. Why not go see Eileen Ford at the Ford Agency? He knew her personally. He called her and set up the appointment. And here I was, wondering why he bothered and I bothered.

Somebody in the agency was in a rancid mood; you could tell the way models scurried in and out, the way the receptionist snapped on the intercom. Finally I heard a voice say, "Have her come in."

"Miss Ford will see you now," the receptionist announced.

When I walked in, I could barely see her behind this huge desk with pictures piled high. She was talking French a mile a minute on the telephone, so I sat down on the sofa and pretended not to listen. But Grandma was French and Daddy was French so I knew enough to get the general drift. Somebody had done somebody dirt, and it was never to be forgiven. I knew the Ford Agency had a lend-lease arrangement with Suzy Parker's sister, the famous model of the forties who now operated a model agency in Paris. While Miss Ford spouted French, she was flipping the pages of a portfolio on the side of her desk. She flipped the portfolio shut. *"Je t'embrasse, cherie,"* she said sweetly into the phone, and then she hung up.

When she shouted, "Stand UP," it was in another tone of voice completely. Then I knew the rudeness was directed at me. I stood up, scared stiff, and wondered whether I should turn around or not. And then she said, "Darling, you're not pretty enough for us." I wondered if she was strong enough to throw my portfolio across the room at me. I knew I was strong enough to throw it across any room at her. It wasn't what she said, it was the way she said it. She couldn't say I was too short or too thin or too fat. I wondered if anybody had told her recently that she didn't look like the picture on the book she wrote either. I wanted to cry or die or talk to poor Barbara Ann, the girl with the heavy legs, and ask her how long it took her to get over it. So I picked up my tired portfolio and I thanked her and I left. If I had made a mistake in dressing like a nice little girl from the suburbs, I would act like one. Anyway, the suburbs was halfway between the country and the city. And since I was a country girl, maybe I was only halfway there. I could turn and run or I could keep plugging. I had to call the nice man from Revlon and tell him what she said. I had promised, so I might as well get that over with.

"Well," he said cheerily, "how did it go?"

"Not very well," I said. My pride wouldn't let me quote her exactly. "She said I'm not quite right for her."

He made me promise to try the other agencies Revlon used. "Keep building up your portfolio with more pictures. If anyone over here can use you, we'll call you direct."

Her name was Josephine, but most of the models called her Jo. She was a booker at one of the biggest agencies casting for TV commercials and she interviewed all the new people. She talked with a lighted cigarette dangling from her lower lip and dribbled ashes all over my portfolio as she leafed through my twenty-three poses. She was skinny as a rail, homely as a hedge fence, with a horrible hairdo and no makeup—a rough, tough lesbian with a voice like a buzz saw. This was the second agency my friend from Revlon had steered me to. If I wasn't pretty enough for Eileen Ford, maybe I was plain Jane enough for Comet or Ajax or Lux or Duz. Jo looked at my pictures, then she squinted at me. Then she got up from her desk and walked around me as if she were trying to study the roots of my hair.

"Jesus on top of Jesus," she said brusquely. "You look like the 'other woman.'" I was stupidly about to ask *what* other woman I looked like when she said, "Sweetie, you look like a real split-level homewrecker. The women of America won't buy Ex-Lax from you."

"OK," said the photographer. "Move!"

I was a gazelle. I was a giraffe. I could hear the seamless cracking underfoot as I whirled and turned. I leaped and I darted. Then I froze and leaped again.

"What was *that*?" the photographer inquired, coming out from behind the camera. "Modern dance? You look like Isadora Duncan in heat." It's a good thing I didn't know who she was or I would have burst into tears.

I didn't know what to say. I knew it wasn't what he wanted. It wasn't what he expected. For days and days I had trudged from office to office. I had to build up a portfolio. Finally this photographer liked my looks and volunteered to do some test shots with me. My hair was right, my makeup was perfect, I thought. Yet from the look on his face I could tell I'd laid a big fat bomb. He took my arm and led me over to this dirty old desk in the corner.

"Look, Carolyn," he said. "Don't feel too bad. Every newcomer goes through this. I'll tell you what to do. You go home like a good little girl. You take all your copies of *Vogue* and *Harper's Bazaar.* Tear out the pages and spread them all over the floor. Then get down on your hands and knees and look at them closely. Look at the dresses. See the way the girls stand. See what they do with their hands. See how they turn their bodies. Study the position of the feet. Make a note of what kind of gowns you stand in and what kind you lie down in. Then take the ads for lingerie and nightgowns, study what the girls do with them. Look at them as if they were paintings. Study the composition. They'll begin to repeat themselves, so put them in little piles. After you've studied them, take little pieces of Scotch tape and tack them up on the walls. Then start moving. Learn how to stand, how to face the camera three-quarters. Dope out what you have to do to make the gown look good. Take one of your dresses, study what made you buy it, then figure out what you have to do to sell it. Work on the positioning of your body until you can move from one pose to another and still keep it fluid. You do that for ten days until your elbows ache, and then you come back and we'll try it again."

Now I really wanted to cry. He was the first person who had told me how awful I was and then went to the trouble of telling me why. He wasn't running a school. He wasn't sending me back to school. He was telling me how to be my own teacher.

"Wait a minute," he said as I was slinking out the door, on my way home to lick my wounds. "I know a guy who only pays a straight two dollars a shot. It's nothing fancy. He does fur coats and wedding dresses—making glossies for salesmen's portfolios and catalogs. It's basic stuff—pretty easy. He's a good photographer and a good friend of mine. He keeps grinding out a helluva lot of work. You can learn something working for him. I'll give you his name and you go see him."

Men are wonderful, I decided all over again. So I went to see his friend Sy. He hired me on the spot to do half a dozen shots for him. He threw me a mink coat and put me up against a rear projection of a Fifth Avenue mansion. I had no idea what to do with the coat until he showed me a picture of another model he had taken in fur.

"See how she puts her elbows out to show the cut of the sleeve?" Sy suggested. "Angle your body at three-quarters. One hand in the pocket and one hand under the collar. One leg forward with toe pointed and knee bent. It's the coat makes you warm, not the light. Remember that. That's better. Much better."

Then Sy dug out a picture of his favorite model—one he used a lot. "Look at what she does with a silly thing like an umbrella," he said. Each time I did one tiny thing right or improved the slightest bit under his tutelage, he was pleased as Punch. He gave me a sleeveless suede coat to pose in and showed me what to do with my hands. If your hands hang down too long, the blood pools in the veins and looks ugly. So you show the side of your hand instead of the back of it. "How a model uses her arms and hands can make or break her," Sy explained.

We did the six shots in less than an hour, and Sy wrote me out a check for twelve dollars right on the spot. He had faith, hope, and charity all in one. I knew I wasn't loosened up and I had a lot to learn, but I had learned a lot in an hour and Sy was willing to try me again.

When the prints came up, he called me to come over and look at them. I was amazed at how good they were. His lighting was fantastic. He knew exactly what he was doing. No temperament. No artistic pretension. No whimsy. What pleased me most was that photo number six was infinitely better than number one. The lighting was so good on my face and hair that he made enlargements of them and gave them to me to put in my book.

Then he offered to make some test shots with me some evening when we were both free. I was delighted. In California I had had to pay a photographer to do test shots for me, and then they weren't very good. They already looked very amateurish and dated to me. Now Sy was going to test with me. Out of it he hoped to get something for his portfolio, and I might get something for mine.

The unwritten law on testing is that in return for working for free the model gets one black-and-white print of every test picture she likes. On color prints the photographer gives the transparencies to the model; they split them; the model usually pays for the color prints. Later on, if the photographer sells one of the pictures for editorial or commercial use, the model signs a release and she is paid her regular rate—just as if it were a booked job. A model has everything to gain and nothing to lose from testing. Beginners especially. And no matter how experienced a model is, she can always use new test shots for her portfolio. The trailblazing tests of today are the commercial photographs of next season.

The evening I showed up at Sy's studio for the test session, I schlepped two suitcases and three hanging racks full of clothes—practically every presentable outfit I owned. Sy sat there patiently while I tried on one thing after another. But I knew there was something wrong.

"Look, Carolyn," he began explaining patiently, "there's nothing wrong with the clothes. For a commercial job they'd be fine. But a test is not a commercial job. For a test we wanna do something that's never been done on a commercial job. You oughta wear something you always dreamed of wearing but didn't dare. Something really way-out. In a test we're free. We got no product to sell. We got no client to please. We got no account executive to tell us what to do. We want to wing it—we oughta do something real crazy with your hair—wear a wig you wouldn't be caught dead in in the street. Maybe just a bra and a pair of panties and some galoshes."

I saw how right he was. If I had spent five minutes thinking it through instead of spending twenty-four hours collecting my entire wardrobe, I would have been further ahead. I hated myself for not having the wit to bring anything to the test session except a hundred and nineteen pounds of flesh and a hundred pounds of rags. Where's your imagination, lady? Suddenly I was more critical of myself than Sy dared be. That is always my first reaction. My confidence always swung like a pendulum. I could swing in an instant from stupid overconfidence to absolutely no confidence at all. I would completely withdraw until I was out of it, ready to quit, resigned to resigning. That would last for only a moment, and then I would snap back.

I dug into my suitcases and began scrambling things. I took a pair of white ducks and ripped them into the shortest shorts around. Sy trotted out his favorite prop—the parasol that his favorite model could twirl so well. We began kidding around and improvising on the spot. Things began to happen. He got excited when he found a new angle. He began to play with the lights. I loved Sy and I loved being in front of his camera. I loved being able to please him and excite him and surprise him, and finally I astonished myself when I felt a kind of wordless rapport with this strange yet familiar little man.

I had heard about girls falling madly in love with photographers. Now I knew why. The test session is the mad love affair, the click of the shutter is the orgasm, and the photograph that's lifted out of the fluid in a few hours—that's the baby. Not his, not hers. Every photograph has a life of its own.

If I'd told the truth and said I was from Middlebury, Vermont, it might never have happened. But I didn't want everybody to know I was green as clover, so when I went out for TV commercials I began saying I was from the West Coast. That's where my track record was, as they say around the agencies. There was the Chevrolet thing and the Academy Award spot for Lilt. Some New York agents automatically assumed that any girl from the Coast was a real swinger.

Dick was working on casting for one of the biggest TV agencies in New York. He wanted to be a producer like everybody else, but meantime he was making a living sorting out girls. After he sent me out on a few interviews and I got a few little jobs, he suggested I stop by the office at closing time one day and we would have a drink at his apartment. I was naive enough to think that's what he meant. So I called David in Connecticut and suggested he drive in and meet me afterward and we would have dinner in town. I gave him Dick's name and address without a second thought.

When we arrived at Dick's apartment, I found it was a real showplace. The terrace was a dream with a fantastic twenty-eighth-floor view. He had trees and flowers and bushes of all kinds growing up there. The living room had a wall of glass; huge mirrored panels brought the outdoors inside and multiplied all the growing things with reflections. All the furniture was convertible indoor-outdoor stuff— very smooth and very modern. For contrast he had an old-fashioned womb of a library, with bound copies of the classics on three walls, the room furnished with British antiques. He gave me the grand tour, explaining that work was still going on; the gardener and the decorator were a long way from being finished. He had a little bar in the library, but before he offered me a drink, he went over to the shelves, pulled down a leather-bound copy of *The Anatomy of Melancholy,* and handed it to me. I thought he expected me to admire the binding. He opened it up in my lap. It wasn't a book at all. It was a box disguised as a book. When you opened it up, there was a little compartment filled with cigarettes.

"That's darling," I said. "Did you get this in England?"

He looked at me as if he had bet on a wrong horse, and then he took one of the cigarettes out of the box and sniffed it.

"Are all your books falsies like this, or just certain ones?"

He had taken a cigarette and then politely offered me one. Funny, I thought, I had never seen him smoke before. Most casting directors and agency people smoke continuously, but not Dick. Now he was puffing away, making whooshing noises as he inhaled, closing his eyes and making sinuous movements with his shoulders like Veruschka gone wrong.

"Come on," he said. "Take one."

"No, thanks," I said. I was happy as a lark with my Lark.

"You don't know how groovy it is," Dick was moaning. "I can't wait until this time every night when I can come up here with the trees and flowers and groove off on my grass." He wandered out on the terrace. I thought I'd better follow him. The smell of marijuana was so thick in that little library that I'd be inhaling it whether I wanted to or not.

On the terrace he spread himself out on a chaise longue and began talking to me as if I were his psychiatrist making a house call. He started calling a roll of girls. Each time he mentioned a girl's name, he would follow it with a short story setting forth exactly the temperature, the humidity, the time of day, and the particular spot on the terrace where he had balled her. All this data he was dredging up might be a gold mine for a psychiatrist, but it was pretty boring for me.

"Ah, Angela baby," he was chanting," you peeled off your stockings, and the winter wind picked them up like lotus petals and carried them off in a downdraft toward Thirty-ninth Street."

Damn, damn, damn, I kept thinking, I hope David isn't stuck in traffic. I wish I'd told him to pick me up at six-thirty instead of seven. If I have to listen to this for another thirty minutes, I'll start throwing things, and it won't be panty hose.

"We balled together right there. Right," said Dick, staggering up as if the exact spot were of towering importance, "there." He indicated a spot on the flagstone terrace floor between two azalea bushes.

"Do you have radiant heating here off-season?" I asked.

"Oh, you foolish, funny girl," Dick said. He seemed to feel sorry for me and all the fun things I was missing. I didn't know whether his amatory memoirs were designed to arouse me or impress me. He didn't make the slightest attempt to come near me. It was as if his importance at the agency turned him into some kind of pasha and as one of the girls who worked out of the agency—or hoped to work out of the agency—I was supposed automatically to get into the swing of things and start carrying on like one of his harem.

Suddenly I felt I needed a drink. There were two huge bars in the place, but I didn't feel like waiting on myself. After all, I was his guest. "I'd like a vodka and tonic unless you find that too disgusting," I said.

"No, baby," he said. "You help yourself, but if you booze and I groove on grass we're going to be on different planes. Nothing's going to happen." I felt I could survive that catastrophe, for one evening at least, so I poured myself a drink. Dick finished his stick of pot, and then he wandered into the library and took another book off another shelf and lit up again. Plainly, the ritual of hiding different types of grass in different kinds of books was all part of the fun. I'm sure if the Narcotics Squad came around on a raid, the cigarette boxes were the last places they would ever look. First they would start tearing apart the library.

I was no particular prude about marijuana. I had heard all the arguments for and against, tobacco versus marijuana, and liquor versus marijuana, and pills versus marijuana. It was something that was very much around. You were apt to encounter it anywhere. My view was a simple one. I didn't appreciate *any* kind of anesthetic. I even refused Novocain when I went to the dentist. Any time I wanted to withdraw from this world I would get into my Thunderbird and drive back to Middlebury. Meanwhile I didn't want to make a habit of hanging around premises where oh-so-hip people made a practice of flaunting their familiarity with it. If people wanted to use it and take their chances on getting arrested and all that, that was their privilege. But please leave me out of it.

I wanted to get out of there. I thought I would make my excuses and just stand down in front of the building until David arrived. But what if I was standing down there waiting and something happened on the highway and he called to tell me he'd be late or to meet him somewhere else? Well, Dick seemed harmless, so I thought perhaps I'd better stick it out.

We stayed there on different planes together for a bit, getting further estranged by the minute, until the blessed doorbell rang. Dick came out of it in a hurry. He dashed into his library to make sure that all the books were in place. He tossed a roach over the side of his terrace.

Then he began to flail his arms, beating the air as if it were a dirty rug, trying to get the smoke out of there. I hated to interfere with his delusions of high drama, but I felt I must.

"I think it may be my boyfriend coming to pick me up," I said.

"Your BOYFRIEND!" he said indignantly. "You mean to say you made a date with your boyfriend to pick you up here?"

"Yes," I said. "We're having dinner together in town."

Now he was roaring with laughter, as if this were the funniest thing that had ever happened to him. "I gotta hand it to you. Everybody tries to be different, but you *are* a novelty. You're a novelty all right, and this is novelty night."

When he opened the door, David stood there, all spick-and-span, bright-eyed and bushy-tailed.

"Hi, David," I said. "Dick, this is David." David made a gesture of shaking hands, but Dick was laughing as if he were being tickled to death. David's eyes began roaming around the room, taking in the whole setup—the lush terrace, the glass doors, the low-slung mod couches, the trees, the bushes, and the flagstones. And then he began sniffing the clouds of smoke that were wafting around.

I thought of offering him a drink until I saw the look on his face. Then I realized how it might look from his point of view. Men see things differently than women do. David is a gentle soul, but he is very handy with his fists. If Dick said just one weird thing that was totally out of line, I was afraid David would let him have it. All three of us were on different planes.

"Come on in, fellow," Dick began. "Have a drink. We're celebrating novelty night." David looked baffled, but I decided I wouldn't try to explain. I babbled some excuse, and we got out of there, leaving Dick in the clouds on the twenty-eighth floor.

David wasn't exactly angry. He just wanted to know what was going on. I explained how important Dick was in the business and what a coup I had thought it was to discover he liked me enough to invite me for a drink. Then I told him about the marijuana and the books and everything.

"He never made a pass at you?" David wanted to know.

"Not exactly," I said. "I think he was giving me the opportunity to do what he says other girls do...."

"Like what?"

76

"Tear off their clothes and throw them to the winds and then ..."

Suddenly I thought of Grauman's Chinese Theater in Hollywood. Those blocks of cement with all the footprints of the stars. Maybe that's what Dick was up to—putting together a flagstone terrace made of all his memories cemented together. I could see him giving a conducted tour, saying, "That one over there is where I balled Angela.... And then Dee Dee—it happened with Dee Dee over there by the daffodils.... No, Johanna was the fragile type—she danced on the desk, but I couldn't get her to move off the sofa."

"David," I said, "I think some of these big lechers would much rather talk about it than ball anybody."

"Ball" was one of the four-letter words David wouldn't let me use. Everybody in the business used it, and David hated it.

"Do you think girls have to sleep around with these people in order to get anywhere?" David asked.

I honestly didn't know. But if you started that with casting directors, where would it all end? A booker in a model agency—all he could do for you, really, was tell you where the opportunities were. He could send you out on interviews, but from then on your fate was in someone else's hands—the casting director of the ad agency. All *he* could do for you was show you to the art director. If the art director liked you, he passed you along to one of the assistant directors working on the commercial. This would take you just so far, and unless the director himself liked you, that was the end of the line. After the director had finally picked the girl he wanted, it was all up to the client: the Boss Man of the big company whose product you were expected to sell. A girl might have to run the gauntlet with as many as a dozen men to get one job. Even if she slept with only half of them, she wouldn't have any time left to make her rounds. I tried to explain the staggering mathematics of the business to David.

I think agents are no different from other men. They're looking for all the extracurricular activity they can handle. And if a girl is innocent enough or stupid enough to think she's getting ahead that way, they'll let her.

"No man is going to tell a girl she's wasting her time by going to bed with him," I said. "Or is he?"

David didn't answer. After all, men are men. They've all got their mystery to worry about, too.

Every once in a while after that David would ask me if I ever saw Dick again. Of course I did. Dick sent me out on lots of little jobs, and he was always very nice when he called me. He always asked about David, and once or twice he laughed about "novelty night," as he called it, on his terrace. Finally I told him I was just passing as a swinger from California, that I was really a small-town girl from New England. "Good for you, baby," he said. "You swing your own way. That's all you got, so hang onto it."

The big subway poster shouted: I GOT MY JOB THROUGH *THE NEW YORK TIMES.* I had seen those huge billboards in the subway stations the first day I got brave enough to ride the IRT. Underneath somebody's happy picture appeared the title of some intriguing, unusual job someone had bagged through reading the *Times* Classified columns: Fashion designers and airline people and computer experts.

The want ads hardly seemed the route to a glamour job. But neither did the hit-or-miss sidewalk-pounding approach I had been using. Being the methodical type, I thought, why not give it a whirl? It was mid-afternoon when I tried to buy a *Times,* and the East Side newsstands were fresh out of morning papers. So I headed for the office of the *Times.* I had some time to kill, anyway, and the walk would do me good.

The *Times* lobby turned out to be an amazing place. Copies of the newest classified ads were posted on the walls in glass cases, and the place was full of people scanning the fine print the way Connecticut commuters pore over the latest stock quotations. In case there were no openings for models I might even see what was happening in other departments. Jobs had been few and far between. I couldn't go on forever spending five dollars a day on train fares. At this rate I was working for the railroads.

I found the display case where the M's were posted. Medical Secretary. Messenger. Midget. Models Service, 1457 Broadway. Interviews Daily 10-4. It was still only three-thirty, and 1457 Broadway was just a spit away from the *Times.*

I expected to find droves of girls in the waiting room, but I was all alone. The secretary smiled at me and gave me a simple application form to fill out. When I'd completed that, she whipped out a tape measure, filled in my vital statistics and initialed them. She took the application into an inside office, and within seconds she came out and said, "Miss Newman will see you in a moment if you can wait." It was all very casual, very businesslike. No wasted conversation. None of the uppity female bitchery I had encountered in other places. I had my portfolio with me, but nobody asked to see it. I discovered Models Service doesn't handle print work. They don't book you for photographers or for TV. Their forte is real live models who breathe and move in fashion shows, on ramps, and in showrooms in the garment district, in trade shows and boat shows and auto shows and the like.

When I was ushered into Miss Newman's office, there were no silly questions. She simply said, "All right, Miss Kenmore, walk for me." I walked and she watched me like a hawk. It took her all of thirty seconds to make her decision. "All right, Carolyn," she said. "You'll do fine. Now let's see. I've got someone who wants a girl on Wednesday." While she shuffled papers, she talked straight and to the point. "I won't lie to you, darling," she said. "I'm here to make money. I can't make money unless you make money, so we're partners. If you want a permanent job and I get you one, you pay me one week's salary even if you stay there ten years. If you're interested in temporary work, I take ten percent of everything you earn. OK?"

"You are what you think you are"—that was her motto. "A girl has to have a good opinion of herself if she's to get one from the people she works for," Miss Newman said. "The better job you do, the more valuable you become here and the faster your rates go up. I don't put up with any hanky-panky. Plenty of my girls married the men they went to work for, and lots of them are millionaires today. That's something I'm proud of. But any time one of my girls gets a shady reputation, that's it. I don't send her out anymore. Rule One is always be on time. Being on time means being fifteen minutes ahead of time. I don't want a client chewing his nails at five minutes to eleven wondering whether a girl of mine is going to show up or not and calling me on the telephone. I don't have time for that. If you're late and make a habit of it, I just don't bother to send you out anymore. Rule Two is just simple cleanliness. I have to make a point of it because you wouldn't believe some of the girls who come in here. They're not fit to wash anybody's clothes except their own, and yet they think they're model material. My clients are looking for girls who are wholesome and, above all, clean. That means being spotless morning, noon, and night—underwear clean and neatly pressed, your bra spotless. When you walk in on a job, you have to be ready to stand there and have another woman look you over. You'll be stepping into some garment that represents an investment of a lot of time and money. Nobody needs a girl from Models Service who isn't as spotless as the dress she's going to wear on the ramp."

While I sat there, she excused herself to answer her telephone. Despite her no-nonsense manner, you could tell she spent some time playing Mama on the side. The first girl who called had starved herself for four days in order to get down to a Size 8. When she made it, she went out and stuffed herself. Now she was dying. Miss Newman underlined the obvious lesson. If you haven't sense enough to take care of your health, nobody else can. Another girl had money problems. Miss Newman was brisk. She told her to come up before the close of business and her assistant, Virginia Stone, would advance her some money against her next booking.

"Today more than ever before a girl has to have good legs," Miss Newman told me. "If she doesn't, she's limited to wedding gowns and pants, and who has time to bother with a girl who has problems?"

Even Jackie Kennedy Onassis couldn't make it as a professional model. She rode those horses too much as a kid.

I had no idea when I found her that Cecelia Newman and her Models Service would be my ace in the hole for two solid years while I was breaking into print. The first job she sent me out on was with the Ozite Carpet Company. They were introducing their indoor-outdoor carpet at a trade show in the building at 295 Fifth Avenue where the floor-covering business is centered. Rudy Langone was running the show; he was a mature man with a wicked twinkle in his eye, and he hired me on the spot. He had already hired a brunette model named Gayle. He wanted us to wear red leotards and black textured stockings in order to stir up traffic and lure them into the showroom. It would be solid work from nine to five for three days at thirty-five dollars a day.

"You'll like Gayle," he told me. "You'll be great together."

She was fun to work with. She was trying to break into print work, too. We started that first morning in our red leotards and our black mesh stockings, hair falling to our waists. Rudy gave us baskets of carpet samples. We were supposed to wander around the floors, inviting people to pick out pieces of carpet which were cut like a jigsaw puzzle. In the Ozite showroom they had a huge master puzzle on the wall. If you got a lucky piece, you won a dinner in town, a camera, or a TV set. We were getting paid to attract attention, but at first I wasn't ready. On a burlesque runway at least the cash customers have to keep their distance, and sometimes the loud music can drown out the rude remarks. We had to stay pleasant and smiling no matter what the carpet market wits felt like saying to our faces.

"Which type are you, darling—indoor or outdoor?" was almost the most civilized comment. At the end of the day I was groggy from being on my feet for eight solid hours, but on my way to the train I stopped in at Woolworth's and bought myself a ninety-eight-cent wedding band. I had the strange small-town notion that this might discourage some of the buyers from pawing me. The next morning I flashed it as I was giving out sample carpet pieces. It didn't make the slightest difference. Rudy got a big kick out of having everybody at the show talk about his models, but Gayle and I got a little weary of being talked about as if we were pastrami on a plate.

Rudy was generous with us and gave us every break he could. He knew we were trying to squeeze in go-sees and interviews, so after the first day, as long as one of us was on duty, covering for him, he let us sneak off and go about our extracurricular business. With that $105 I made from Rudy, less $10.50 commission for Models Service, in three days I had made enough expense money to commute for three weeks.

As soon as that job was over, another one came up—dressing up the exhibit of the U.S. Gauge Corporation at the New York Coliseum. It wasn't long before my rates went up. I got fifty dollars a day for demonstrating a desk-top computer for the Olivetti Underwood Corporation at the Coliseum computer show. For this one you needed traffic-stopping looks plus enough brains to run this complicated machine. I wasn't sure I could handle it, but after a quick cram course I was out there punching. Any man who dropped by and wanted to know how much of his monthly mortgage payments went into interest and how much went into amortization, after three questions and a couple of twirls of the machine I could give him the breakdown to take home to the little woman. This introduced me to the whole world of the industrial model. Some girls find their way into this field and never leave, graduating into marketing and sales. They find they make much more money than editorial models or commercial models doing print work, and the cost of wardrobe and other items is not so steep. You don't have to be as skinny and flawless as you do for print. It's a way of making between fifty and a hundred dollars a day. It's money in the bank. But this wasn't what I wanted.

Working out of Models Service gave me confidence. I found out how versatile I could be. There was never a job call that came in that I couldn't handle. If you had to be bright enough to run a computer, I could do it. If you had to be pleasant to the public, I could do that, too. If you had to do a little bit of selling, I was not above it. If they wanted a model for glamour togs, I could handle them. Bathing suits as well. I could do lingerie and brassieres, girdles and galoshes. I was tough as an ox—I could stand for eighty-nine hours a week or I could do a quick change job in five seconds. I like the fashion shows best, and Virginia knew it, so she always booked me on the best ones that turned up.

I wore beautiful clothes, but that wasn't what I wanted. I wanted to be photographed in the clothes and have my photographs on the brassiere packages. I was determined to break into print and get a toehold in TV.

Cecelia Newman is an institution in this business. You always know where you stand with her. If you do a job, you get top rates and you always get your money. Many, many models who work with the chic, fancy agencies would starve to death if they couldn't do a little moonlighting at Models Service.

Models are supposed to be dumb. Sometimes it helps to be as numb and dumb as I was at the beginning. If you knew what was really going on, you might be too embarrassed to breathe.

One day the Stewart TV agency called me and asked me to run down to Wylde Films, Inc., and take my bathing suit. All they told me was that I had a chance to get a product extra buy-out part in a commercial for American Telephone & Telegraph. So down I went, all done up and looking like a dream walking. The casting girl asked me to jump into my swimsuit. After she got a look at me, she asked me to hold still while she sent for the producer. He came in and looked at me, fore and aft, and then he said, "Fine. She'll do."

But what will she do? That is always the question. They told me it was a location job scheduled for shooting at Point Pleasant Beach in

New Jersey. "Would you be available next Saturday, Miss Kenmore?"

I knew that automatically meant double pay, which was tempting enough. But Saturdays and Sundays were my days with David. We were so madly badly-off wacky-crazy about each other that if we didn't get to spend Saturdays and Sundays together it was like the end of Western Civilization, and what was it all about anyway?

"Yes," I said finally without any enthusiasm. They told me to report at the studio at 7:30 A.M. for the trek to the beach. This would mean catching a 5 A.M. train from New Haven. When I told David about it, of course he volunteered to drive me. It was late September, and the beach would be sad and deserted, but what did it matter as long as we could be together—and get double time for our trouble.

We were up at dawn and at the studio promptly at seven-thirty. The director and the crew were waiting, and with them was a gorgeous hunk of male model with a fabulous build—you could see that even through his tweeds.

They had two station wagons full of equipment ready, and when we came out of the studio and the director saw David waiting there, smiling and gorgeous in his big convertible, he said, "Who is *that*?"

"Oh," I said blithely, "that's my boyfriend. He drove me in from Connecticut. I don't live in the city, and I thought if he drove me out we could go directly back to Connecticut and you wouldn't have to worry about getting me home."

"Oh," said the director. I could feel the frost beginning to form. I knew I had done something wrong, but I was not completely aware of the enormity of my indiscretion. It was Saturday morning, too late to drop me and get another girl. What could they say?

We proceeded to New Jersey on our little safari, and when we got to the beach the sky had completely clouded over. It would be a long wait for the sun. The cast and crew assembled in the nearest diner and ordered a huge breakfast. The seating was arranged so David was in the Jim Crow section of the table with the grips and assistants. He couldn't get lost even if they wanted him to. The beach was deserted, and this was the only water hole open for miles. Gee, I thought when the check came up, I hope David thinks of paying, because he's an extra man, really, and not part of the crew entitled to charge bacon and eggs to A T & T. But David has his own way of establishing his existence. Pretty soon we were all one big happy family drawn together by the vagaries of the weather. The elusive sun—not my boyfriend—was the fly in the ointment.

The cameraman worked out his setup, and the male model and I got into our swimsuits. We did a couple of run-throughs. The male model and I ran away from the camera toward the water, with him leading the way and me tagging behind. We did it about a hundred and eleven times, and then we practiced a reverse shot running out of the water into the camera, with him leading the way. The ocean water was like ice, and I was grateful that we weren't being asked to do anything more than get our feet wet for good old A T & T.

With the first glimmer of sun we started rolling. We did it again and again, as the cameraman tried desperately to time our cavorting so that he caught the waves breaking just right. David slouched on the beach, drinking beer and patiently waiting while I romped with this gym teacher with the fabulous build. I began to suspect that the male model was always in the foreground, for some strange reason, and I was always bringing up the rear—when we were facing the camera. When we had our backs to the camera, I was always in the foreground. I began to wonder what kind of commercial this was supposed to be. So I asked my gorgeous partner.

"Oh, didn't they tell you?" he said. "We shot the commercial two weeks ago. All we're doing today is reshooting a couple of shots that didn't work out." In other words, somebody else had the star part and I was hired to be her double?

"Well, I guess so," said the male model. "Kimmie and I play this couple at a resort on vacation. But Kimmie went to the West Coast right after we did it, and she's not coming back."

"Oh," I said. "Then why did they pick me?"

"Well, you're her height and coloring, and you look like her in the buns," he said.

Well, I could feel my sphincter muscles contracting. Here I had tripped down to the casting session looking gorgeous. I'd worked on my makeup for hours to be sure it was exactly right. No wonder nobody paid the slightest attention. All they were looking at was my derriere. I got the job because I looked like Kimmie from the rear.

For the rest of the afternoon's shooting I was completely turned off. The waves broke. We ran toward the camera, and as soon as I got anywhere near the lens, the director called cut. When we ran toward the ocean, I did all my acting with my hindquarters. My only consolation was signing the contract which entitled me to $270 for the day.

Finally we finished and they broke the set, collected the gear. I got out of my chilly bathing suit. It was all over but the amenities. I thanked the director and the cameraman and all the crew for being so nice. I said good-bye to Mr. Gorgeous Gym Teacher.

"Thanks very much, fellas. I really enjoyed it," I lied.

"OK, Carolyn," said the director. "Only next time don't bring your boyfriend."

If they wanted me in Manhattan, it took one forty-cent toll call and I hopped the train. If nobody wanted me on Madison Avenue, that could be lovely, too. When I didn't have to go to the city, David would come over and I would whip up a very seductive *Cosmopolitan* magazine mantrap lunch. I could be disappointed but never really crushed. One day I was just about to spring this jazzy lobster aspic onto a bed of spectacular green romaine when my agency called from New York. "How soon can you get into town?" I slept, ate, cooked, and washed my hair with a train schedule in my hand. I looked at it. Damn, damn, damn. There were dead spots in the afternoon. It would take me two and a half hours by train. David's beautiful convertible was parked in front of the house. But I couldn't ask him to drive me to New York. He had his own career to further. He'd never get to the top at IBM by chauffeuring me around.

I hedged and mumbled until they told me what the deal was. Ford Motor Company's ad agency was casting for a boy and girl to model. They would be on the road for two whole months driving around visiting suburban shopping plazas, parking and looking windblown and sensational, and doing this little skit to show off the car. They were going to try it out in the East Coast cities first. The job would pay a flat rate of two hundred a week for each one, plus all expenses, so that it would amount to two hundred a week free and clear.

Well, this was something I *had* to try for. There was a little script, and I'd have to read for it, but they didn't want an actress—they wanted someone very natural. It would take me away from David for two whole months, and that would be gruesome but not fatal. And it would mean almost two thousand dollars free and clear with all expenses paid. I could pay off everything I owed and end up with a nest egg big enough to take an apartment in New York. It was this commuting that was holding me back—I knew it. I had to get to the center of things where I could be available anywhere in Manhattan on twenty minutes' notice.

David heard the excitement in my voice, and I didn't even have to ask him. He was always there like the Marines, *semper fidelis,* when I needed him. "I'll drive you," he hollered, diving for the rolls and sampling the lobster aspic hungrily, spooning it right out of the mold. How long, oh, Lord, how long? Finally I told them we might make it in an hour and a half, but that would be pushing it, so to be safe, I told them I would be there in two hours.

David hated makeup and false eyelashes with real western Massachusetts passion, so I never wore even a spot of gook when he was around. "Put it on in the car," he said majestically as he called his office and made enough excuses so he could steal the afternoon off. I hated myself for not having cooked something less fancy and more picnicky so we could eat it on the way. But David was already addicted to the lobster aspic, so I put it in a basket and off we flew. "Bring a spoon—you can feed it to me while I'm driving, in case it melts." I threw in the rolls, grabbed some fruit, and off we flew to the Turnpike.

When I told David more about the job interview, he was as excited as I was. The only catch was that if it worked, the Ford Motor Company would come between us for two whole months. How could we stand it?

"Look at it this way, Carolyn," David said between mouthfuls of aspic. "They're looking for a very natural couple, right? Well, what could be more natural than you and me together?"

"But, David, the way you hate makeup and all the nonsense of this business, I never thought for a moment you'd consider—"

"Maybe it's the only way we can be together. For that I'd take a flier at anything." Why hadn't I thought of it? David was better-looking than half the male models they paired me off with. He was a whiz of a driver, he knew everything there was to know about cars, he just didn't happen to have a Ford in his life at the moment.

"Between us we could be pulling down four hundred a week, and they pay all expenses. In two months we could both get out of debt. I'd even turn this in on a Ford if they asked me."

I was trying to attach my false eyelashes and get some fresh gook on my mouth when I heard the sirens. I looked at the speedometer, and when I saw how fast we were going, I knew a cop was after us. David was a great one with explanations. He made my appointment sound like a matter of life and death, but the arresting officer remained unmoved by it all.

"Half the people on this highway are trying to get to some theater or TV show in Manhattan at this hour. If we let them kill themselves, they'll do it," he said very politely and sanely. He wrote out a ticket. Now we were fifteen more dollars further in debt than when we started out.

David found a spot to park within spitting distance of the agency office when we reached New York. This was a miracle, and we took it as a good luck sign. I checked my makeup in the rear-view mirror. David automatically started carrying my tote bag and my portfolio for me. Then it hit me. What is he *thinking* of? He has no *pictures.* If you don't have a portfolio, you're just not a model. He might be a star of the Metropolitan Opera, the Green Bay Packers, or the Mets, but without pictures what could he do? Well, the best thing was to tell them he was an actor and was just moonlighting as a model. If they liked his looks, we'd be like Scarlett O'Hara and think about that tomorrow.

We waltzed into the agency, smiled at the receptionist, and after she asked us to sign in, she handed each of us a copy of the script. We were ten minutes early, so we had ten minutes to give it a quick study. They took my portfolio and sent it into the inner sanctum. When they asked David for his, he said it had been stolen out of the car. "He's really an actor, and he worked this summer in stock with the Stowe players in Vermont, so I think they'll understand." I volunteered all this while David smiled his angelic smile.

When I looked at the script, my heart sank. At least I had a little experience at winging it with these crazy scripts. But all I had to do in this was smile and say, "Yes, sir," and "OK," and be very cute. The boy's part had enough dialogue to strangle Sir John Gielgud. He was supposed to pretend he was a magician because it would take a magician to understand all the magic that Ford had packed into this smoothly silent universal joint and this crypto electronic supersonic catatonic transmission and the lifetime-sealed magic of the hydraulic brakes and ... it went on for pages. Bluff is bluff, but I knew we were in trouble. David does have a marvelous voice, but this stuff looked as though it had been written by a German engineer and translated from the Portuguese. Every sentence was a king-sized mouthful with dangling participles that could trip up even as glib a word juggler as Danny Kaye.

I knew I could do it, but I wondered if David knew what he was getting into. "What do you think?" I asked the poor boy.

His mouth was too dry to answer me. "Do they expect me to memorize this junk?" he pleaded.

"Eventually you'll have to, David dear," I said, "but now all you have to do is read it convincingly. Take it slow and easy and land hard on every other word. Maybe it will help if you underline," I said, handing him a pencil.

Before he could make a scrawl, the receptionist smiled and showed us into the inner sanctum. Three men sat there with the inevitable secretary and the clipboard. "OK, kids," the man said. "Stand back there and give it a whirl." We stepped back a few paces. David had the first line. I smiled until I thought my makeup would crack. But I didn't hear a sound. I stole a look out of the corner of my eye. The poor boy just stood there rigid. The worst case of rigor mortis I'd ever seen.

"You kids had a chance to give it a run-through, didn't you?" the man asked helpfully.

"Yes, sir," David replied, as if he were pleading guilty to the most horrendous sex crime.

I was so embarrassed I didn't know how long I could keep smiling. Finally David began. I don't know how I sounded to him, but to me he sounded more like a mortician than a magician. It was positively pitiful. When it came time for me to react to his excitement over these magical innards in the new, new Fords, all I had to say was "Yes, sir." I sounded so phony I could have spit.

We got through it someway. I expected to be thrown right smack out of there on my ear. I was hoping for it, I think. The absolutely last thing I wanted in the entire world was to be asked to do it over again.

"OK, kids," the number two man suggested, "let's give it another whirl. And try to really pitch it this time. Remember, we're selling the car. You'll be real uptight close. Sell it like you were pitching to your friends and neighbors."

We did it again, but it was still pitiful. I'll have to admit the others must have been horrible, too, because instead of giving us a quick "Thank you," they started looking through my portfolio. "We'll have to have a picture of you, young fellow," they said to David. "Miss Tannenbaum told us you had your portfolio stolen, but we like to send the pictures to the Ford people in pairs. When do you think you can bring yours in?"

"Will a couple of days be soon enough?" David mumbled.

They had a huddled conference about that. Finally they admitted they would be auditioning and screening couples for the rest of the week, so if David brought them some pictures by Friday we would get in under the wire.

Well, you never know. When you think you're great, you can be horrible and not know it. When you think you're horrible, maybe that's what they want. Maybe they're staging a real amateur night and looking for a couple of comedians. Certainly they wouldn't make all this fuss about the picture for no reason. Maybe we had a chance, after all. We left the inner sanctum, threaded our way through the outer office and managed to get to the corridor before we collapsed with relief and laughter. "Now I gotta get some pictures," David was saying. "What do I do?"

"David, don't you realize how perfectly terrible we were?"

"I don't think they know what they're doing either. Especially the guy who wrote that spiel. Anyway, I promised. If you won't take me to one of your photographer friends, I'll get my picture taken in New Haven."

We had to surrender our parking place anyway, so we drove back to New Haven in order to get there before the photographer closed. David called him and told him he had to have the pictures the next day. The poor man said the best he could give him would be some proofs. So David rushed to the studio to pose, rushed over the next day to pick up the proofs, rushed over to me so I could help him write all the lies on the back about his phenomenal career in summer stock in Vermont plus the truth about his collar size, glove size, hat size, shirt size, waist, inseam, height, and the color of his eyes—as if any of it mattered. Just to make it look a tiny bit professional, I typed in the comment: "Excellent hands," the way they do it at the agency. Then David called and they asked him to bring the photo in in the morning. He rushed in there like a marathon runner so they could put it in a pile on the desk.

After all this hurry-up rush-rush-rush, you wait. And wait.

I was used to all this hurry-up-and-wait business by now, but David's only experience had been in the facts-and-figures world of International Business Machines, where two plus two makes four. On Madison Avenue two plus two means enlarging the committee and delaying the decision. Days went by and we heard nothing. Days turned into weeks. Our vision of a dreamy two months' sprinting around the East Coast shopping plazas, smiling from the luxurious interior of a Ford convertible, began to evaporate like one more summer romance.

"Don't they ever tell you anything, Carolyn?" David wanted to know. "How can you work this way? You're always in the dark. Couldn't they at least send you a postcard saying, 'Better luck next time'? You girls invest all that time and money, and they won't even invest five cents in a postcard to tell you you struck out. By the time they made up their minds they wanted you, you could be off somewhere on another job." He began to sound like a union organizer. "If you want to start a union, David," I told him, "I'll be your first member."

Long after I wrote the Ford job off as a lost cause, David still asked me about it. When youth wants to know, youth wants to know. So finally one day I happened to have a go-see in the same office building, so I dropped in. The art director knew he knew me from somewhere, and he happened to be in the outer office. The atmosphere was suddenly so chummy that I didn't mind asking him at all.

"By the way, what ever happened to that Ford thing you tested me for?"

"Which Ford thing was that?"

"You know," I said. "You wanted a boy and a girl to tour the East Coast shopping plazas for two months doing this little skit about the magic of the supersonic universal joints and blah-blah-blah."

He looked as though an ulcer had suddenly grabbed him. "Oh, that," he said painfully. "Why did you have to remind me? Nobody could do that magician routine to suit the client, so we hired a real magician. Then we had to give him more money. Then he looked like such a sharpie we had to cast a real sharp chick to go with him. The one we picked happened to have an illegitimate kid she didn't tell us about. She brought the six-year-old on the honeymoon. They tried to hide her in the trunk of the car or the motel somewhere while they did their number. The motel complained to the law about the kid being left alone, and the magician's wife got into the act. We had to replace the girl, and then finally it was so much trouble that the agency fired the guy who cooked up the whole stupid megillah in the first place. What's new with you? You're looking great. You're lucky you didn't get in on the act, believe me. We'll use you in something else."

I still have that rush-rush photo David had taken specially for the job. Every time I look at it I have to laugh. He got a nice education in what the glamorous world of modeling is all about. And he's never held still long enough to have his photo taken since.

For weeks that summer and fall David drove me to the train every morning and picked me up every night. In all that time we got our signals crossed only once. I waited and waited and David didn't arrive. Oh, Lordy, I thought, our luck has finally run out. He's had an accident. His home phone didn't answer, so I knew he had to be somewhere between his place and mine. When he finally telephoned, his calm, tranquil "Hi, honey," almost drove me up the wall.

"David," I yelped, "where *are* you? I have to catch the eight-o-three or I'm doomed. I have this crucial appointment at Rockefeller Center at nine-thirty. I have to make that train."

"I thought you told me you weren't going in this morning."

"Everything's changed. I have to make that train, David. I have to." I could hear him swallowing hard. Then he finally said OK. I was so intent on my own crisis that it never occurred to me to ask him what had gone wrong for him. I stood in front of the house as usual, waiting. Time was running out when he finally appeared. I jumped into the car while it was moving, and he gave it the gun. Our all-time speed record for making the station was fifteen minutes. That morning he made it in nine. He seemed not quite his usual cheery self. Something was bothering him. So I asked.

It turned out IBM had a special early breakfast meeting for all its salesmen. They had gathered from all over the Eastern territory. I guess he'd told me about it, but I just hadn't been listening.

"Well, what did you do, just walk out?" I said sheepishly.

"No, I went to the boss and told him I was sorry but there was something I had to do."

"You didn't tell him what."

"I couldn't tell him I had to drive my girl to the train."

"Oh, David," I moaned, "you should have told me. You could lose your job for doing something like that, couldn't you?"

"I suppose so," he smiled as we wheeled into the station.

I felt like the most dense, the most self-centered prima ballerina assaloutissima of all time. At the same time I was so touched I could hardly talk. Sir Walter Raleigh had only risked dirtying his coat by spreading it over a muddy puddle. And they called him a cavalier. I wanted to hug David like crazy, but all that would accomplish would be to ruin my makeup and smear the gook he hated all over him. So I squeezed his hand and dashed for the train.

All the way into New York it bothered me. He was so reckless and so impulsive and so beautiful! What would I ever do without him? I'd do anything to avoid hurting him, and yet look what I'd just done.

The very day I needed all the time I could get to navigate the rush hour between Grand Central and Radio City, the train was eight minutes late. I had to invest in a cab. I lunged for the crowded elevator and I got to the office with about thirty seconds to spare. I checked my hair and makeup in the corridor, and then I made my entrance.

The receptionist was working on *her* makeup when I walked in. The cartons of coffee had just arrived and were being distributed through the office. I gave her my name and told her Mr. Ridgefield was expecting me.

"Do you have an appointment?" she said.

My heart sank. "Yes. Of course I have an appointment. It was made by my agency, Rice-McHugh." I was about to say I'd come in specially from New Haven, but then I remembered I always had to keep it a secret that I was a commuter.

"I'll check with his secretary. Won't you have a seat?"

*They* can be late, I told myself. But we can't.

The receptionist was whispering into the phone. I couldn't hear what she was saying. There was a little pause, and then Mr. Ridgefield's secretary appeared—very stiff, very gray, and too polite to be bringing anything but bad news.

"I'm *so* sorry, Miss Kenmore," she said. "Mr. Ridgefield just telephoned. He has a virus, and his doctor wants him to stay in bed for a few days. I'll have to reschedule all his appointments."

A virus! They can be sick; we can't. David risked losing his job to get me to the train. It cost me $4.57 in train fares and more in cab fare to get here on time to find out Mr. Ridgefield has a virus.

"I'm *so* sorry," she kept saying.

The big leather chair was soft and comfortable. I found it difficult to get up and pick up my heavy tote bag and portfolio. Mr. Ridgefield was supposed to send me to his photographer for some test shots. After that I was supposed to have lunch with him and the art director. The agency had asked me not to make any other appointments until three. Now it was nine-thirty-five, and I had five hours to kill. I didn't know if I could face it. I had spent so much time lounging in the lobbies of the Roosevelt and Biltmore Hotels that I was afraid the house detectives had me on their lists as a hooker. I couldn't stand the public library anymore. I was afraid to go into St. Patrick's Cathedral. A girl I know dozed off in there once and a pickpocket snatched her portfolio, her purse, and her tote bag and was gone before she could scream Dies Irae. There was no place in midtown where you could have a cup of coffee in peace. If you tried to kill five minutes on one of their stools, they expected to sell you a five-course meal. There isn't a movie open at that hour except the 42nd Street grind houses, and a girl doesn't dare walk into one of them without a baseball bat or a police escort.

This was cruel and unusual punishment for being so thoughtless with David. I felt like canceling my three-o'clock appointment, taking the train back to New Haven, and grabbing a nonglamour job.

I finally summoned the strength to yank myself out of that comfortable chair. I took the elevator down and walked aimlessly through Rockefeller Plaza. For once I had time—plenty of time—to look at the flowers.

"You're a model, aren't you?" The voice sounded like my sister Elinor. It came from a pretty little girl of about twelve. She was with her mother. Mom smiled indulgently.

"You don't possibly have a picture to spare that you could autograph for me, do you?" said little Miss Twinkle Eyes.

"Baby doll," I felt like saying, "this morning I'd give you my whole portfolio. I'm tired of schlepping it around."

"Sharon has seen you on television. She doesn't know your name, but we recognize your face," her mama said, smiling.

I know, I know, I thought. Sharon wants to be a glamorous model when she grows up.

"I hope we're not holding you up," Mama said.

"Not at all," I said with great conviction. Maybe I could kill five hours just standing here near the pretty flowers and giving out autographs to the tourists. I found an extra glossy in my portfolio, took it out and wrote on it: "For Sharon. Best of luck always." Then I signed my name.

Sharon and her mama walked off, as pleased as if I'd given them the keys to Fun City.

You'll need them, honey. You'll need them.

Media bigwigs can commute from their country homes to Madison Avenue every day and nobody thinks anything of it. But if a model tries to do it, she'd better keep quiet about it. I had to keep it a secret that I slept every night in New Haven, Connecticut. I had to encourage the illusion that I was always just around the corner, ready, willing, and able in full makeup, with eyes on, within twenty minutes of the spot where someone wanted me. For this ruse I needed a special kind of answering service. Someone at the Stewart agency understood the problem and gave me some good advice. He told me to use the Ju 6-6300 answering service—it was used by oodles of models. Miss Galaro there worked out a system of covering for me without making the telephone company rich with toll calls to Connecticut. She would call me from New York person to person. If I was there, I would refuse to take the call. I would hang up the phone and call the agency station direct and get my message, saving two dimes every time.

Then David and I began using the same sneaky trick to save more money. When I was through for the day in New York, I would call his house in New Haven and make the call person-to-person for his brother Peter—the man who was never there. David would answer and say he was sorry, Peter wasn't there. Then quick, before the operator could disconnect us, I would say: "Operator, will you please tell the party that I will try to reach him again at six-fifteen?" This was our code. It was my way of telling David that I would be on the six-fifteen train. He would drive to the New Haven station and pick me up.

Sometimes when lines were busy or operators were slow, I would do the whole spy bit and get the message through and end up missing the train. Then I'd have to start all over again.

Every day it got more and more difficult to find an empty telephone booth at Grand Central Station. Sometimes I suspected half the commuters were using the same secret system.

Sometimes when I had good news—like a job or a promise of a job—I'd be bursting to tell someone and I couldn't wait until I got back to New Haven. I'd splurge—go to the newsstand, buy a paper, get a handful of nickels and dimes and quarters, and call David direct.

One night at Grand Central I found a booth, propped my huge portfolio up against my feet. David was delighted at the good news I had and when I finished talking to him, I was floating. I rushed to catch my train, and I was going through the gates when I realized I didn't have my book. MY BOOK. MY PORTFOLIO. I didn't have it in my hand. I dashed through the rush-hour crowds at Grand Central to find the phone booth. There it was, but the portfolio wasn't there. No more than a minute and a half had passed, yet it was gone. My stomach felt as though someone had just kicked me. I couldn't breathe. I ran across the corridor to the newsstand and began asking the dealer if he had seen anyone with a black leather portfolio. As soon as I heard myself asking the question, I realized how ridiculous it was. I might just as well have asked him if he'd seen someone walk by with a black umbrella with an initial on the handle. I found a policeman and poured out my tale of woe to him. There was nothing in the portfolio but my precious pictures—all the accumulated tools of my trade. I had my name and address in it, and the contents would be of no conceivable use to anybody. The policeman suggested I try the Lost and Found. By that time I knew I'd never see the portfolio again. Somebody would throw away the pictures and sell the portfolio in a minute for five bucks. Maybe, just maybe, somebody would realize what it meant to me and turn it in to the Lost and Found. I went through the motions of making a report, but I knew it was gone. Somehow, someway, I'd have to start over again, collecting pictures, begging new photographers to test with me.

I climbed on the train wondering what I had been so ecstatic about fifteen minutes before. Now I was right back where I had started three months ago. Tomorrow I would come in with a few extra copies I had in a manila envelope. I felt out of balance when I walked. That huge leather thing was like an extension of my arm, and I felt like a cripple without it.

A model without portfolio is like a fiddler without a bow. I bought myself a brand-new portfolio, but the duplicate pictures I had left were pretty slim pickings. They wouldn't fill half the yawning spaces in that huge book. I had to get busy and get some new test shots. The Rice-McHugh Agency was after me to get some outdoor boy-girl shots in my book. But that amounted to quite a production. It meant finding a photographer who wanted to go on location for a day, and it meant locating a male model who was right for my vis-à-vis. So for a few days I was making rounds of photographers' studios on my knees. I had to get some new outdoor pictures before the snow began to fly.

Joey must have sensed my desperation. He was a photographer's rep, and like a lot of them he was a frustrated photographer himself. He hadn't been able to make it with his pictures, so he was working for somebody else.

"If you want some great outdoor shots, you ought to go see Sherman Fairchild. He might invite you out to his mansion for a weekend. There'll be lots of photographers there, and you could get everything you need."

I didn't know whom he was talking about, but I was scared to admit it to him.

"I'll call him and make an appointment for you. If he likes you, I'll take you one weekend," Joey promised. I knew there was a catch to this somewhere, but I had to give it a try.

Next day Joey called me and told me I had an appointment with Mr. Fairchild at two. You'd have to have millions to have a town house like the one he had on East 65th Street. It looked a hundred years old on the outside. Inside it had been done in completely modern style. You felt you were in a museum of avant garde furniture and paintings as you walked up the starkly modern spiral staircase. A very sedate and distinguished-looking housekeeper or secretary escorted me to a drawing room on the top floor and asked me to wait. The salon had a giant grand piano, a sofa, and the walls were covered with huge photos. Against the avant garde furnishings the blowups looked curiously out-of-date—like a gallery of also-rans in the Miss Rheingold competition of 1955: red, red lipsticks, curly fussy hairdos, and Rita Hayworth poses.

After a few minutes Mr. Fairchild came in to meet me. He was a charming man in his seventies, dapper and distinguished-looking. He wanted to see my portfolio, and when he looked at it he smiled. I needed new pictures as badly as his walls did. Then he asked if I would like to see some things he had done. He brought out a huge portfolio of lushly and expensively printed and mounted photographs in color and black-and-white. The best thing about them was the settings: antique furniture, iron gates, formal gardens—the kind of settings that would take a fortune to assemble in a photographer's studio. They made all the girls look very sleek and very professional, very expensive, very *Harper's Bazaar.* Mr. Fairchild explained that he took all the pictures at his home and gardens in Huntington, Long Island. I was thrilled when he invited me out there and told me he would call me in a week or two to discuss a date.

But the next week it wasn't Mr. Fairchild I heard from—it was Joey. He said Mr. Fairchild liked me and would therefore take me out to his country house for the weekend. Joey seemed to think it was all set. I wasn't so sure. Huntington, Long Island, wasn't so far away that one couldn't commute. Why did it have to be a safari for the entire weekend?

I started taking a poll among other models I met on the job. Some of them thought it was the break of a lifetime and were longing to get asked. When I asked one girl who had been there about it, she looked me over carefully, then took me aside.

"Well," she said, "it depends."

"What does that mean?"

"It depends on what weekend you go out there and who brings you. I've heard it can be very straight and nice, but the weekend I went out there it was real *la dolce vita.*"

"Who did you go out there with?"

"A rep who wants to make it as a photographer. The place was full of the same kind of guys. I looked 'em over, and then I said to myself, 'Whose pleasure am I?' I had to fight off guys all weekend, and I never got anything out of it I could put in my book."

All the girls agreed that the house was fabulous and the food was fabulous and the service was fantastic and Mr. Fairchild's equipment topped anything in town. I hadn't made my mind up. Joey kept pressing me, and finally he insisted on taking me out to dinner. He asked me to meet him at the studio around seven. When I walked in, he was all alone in the joint, and he embraced me like a husband just back from Vietnam.

"What's the matter?" he said. "Are you frigid?"

I told him I wasn't used to guys who were so hungry they wanted to devour my whole mouth and ears before dinner. "You're the softest woman I ever met," he said, "but why are you so cold, so tense?"

I wanted to tell him he was not my idea of heavenly bliss, but I had to be diplomatic. Reps get around, they talk to everybody and see everybody in the business, and if I got on his blacklist, it might cost me a lot of work.

"You need a weekend in the country to loosen you up. In this racket, baby, you got to be free and easy. You gotta swing. You're uptight, you're so tense—a real rigid frigid." I had really begun to wonder if this was something I was asking for or whether all models went through this. You've only seen me when you're here, I wanted to tell him.

We had a standoff at dinner, and for the next ten days I made myself very scarce. I didn't want to offend Joey, but I decided I would wait for the safari to Huntington, Long Island, until I found another sponsor.

Fate works in funny ways. Just when I thought I had blown my chance of getting some new outdoor test pictures, a good photographer, Alan Kleban, called me and asked me if I could join him and a male model for an all-day test session at Montauk Point—at the very end of Long Island. He had arranged the day and the girl he wanted had to back out. "Her friend arrived this weekend ahead of schedule," he said. "You know," he said, "the curse is really the curse in this business. It's always raising hob with things."

I finally understood what he was talking about. That had happened to me only once—and I thought I would die when my period—or my "friend," as he called it—arrived the very day I had an important booking. If you're important and in demand, you can cancel. I was just a beginner, so I tried to psych myself into carrying on. It worked for a while, and then I got so woozy I had to leave the showroom floor, terrified I was going to be sick all over the dress, the buyers, and the ramp.

But one girl's curse is another girl's opportunity, and this weekend the opportunity was mine. The photographer told me to bring all my clothes. According to custom, the model packs the lunch and the boys buy the beer. We left at four o'clock Saturday morning. I was still sleepy at seven-thirty when we pulled into a roadside spot for breakfast. By nine o'clock I had my makeup on and the male model and I were romping on the beach. We shot bathing suits and slacks and sportswear and summer dresses, and then in the grass along the dunes Alan tried out some color shots with lingerie. His wife, Paula Carbone, is a famous designer at Van Raalte, so Alan was especially interested in this. Then the weeds inspired him, and he dug into the trunk of his car and came out with some slips and a caftan in silver lamé. I piled on the jewelry, and we got some shots that looked like Pharaoh's daughter down in the bulrushes looking for trouble. These shots turned out to be pictures I carried in my book for two years. Sometimes I will still show them—old as they are. It is the unexpected, hit-or-miss, instant impulse, these strange accidents, this surrealistic serendipity, out of which great photographs are born.

We had a beautiful lunch on the dunes. After lunch we went back to work. The commercial pictures you take for a specific purpose are always centered around the product that's being pushed; the model is always an accessory. Models and photographers need new test pictures as a showcase for themselves. We worked like dogs until the sun went down, and then we drove back to Manhattan weary but elated. When I got my prints the next week, I was floating. The big tragedy at Grand Central began to look like a big break. I didn't realize how pitiful my early pictures were until I saw the new ones—especially the exotic color shots of Pharaoh's daughter in the weeds.

Missing *la dolce vita* weekend at Mr. Fairchild's fabulous country estate had been perfect timing.

The thief who stole my portfolio in Grand Central had done me a big big favor. If that theft hadn't happened, I might have stupidly shown those tired pictures around for weeks and not gone to the effort and trouble of striking out in search of some new ones.

## CHAPTER 5

I had worked in a couple of TV commercials without false eyelashes. I made the rounds of my interviews without them. But I began to notice that even the receptionists passing as models were wearing them. When I saw some of the dikey bookers turning up in them, I began to feel naked without them, and I decided I'd better get in line. I bought a pair in the drugstore for six dollars and practically ruined them with glue the first time I tried to get them in place. One of the bookers at the Stewart agency tried to help me, but it really wasn't her department. She confessed she had a nearsighted, steel-handed roommate who helped her with the adhesive.

"Baby-pie," she said finally, "one day you'll just have to learn all there is to know about makeup. Why don't you blow five bucks for a session at the Make-Up Center?" Having just discovered that lashes, at six bucks a pair, can be a very expensive toy, I was ready, but I didn't know what the Center was.

She made an appointment for me at 150 West 55th Street. It turned out to be the closest thing in town to a private club for models and actresses. It is run by two Italian boys, Dick and Carlo La Torre. The walls of the reception room were crowded with autographed pictures of everybody who was ever anybody in the world of fashion and modeling. Little personal notes were scrawled over the signatures, such as, "To Dick, who gave me such beautiful eyes." I got the great feeling I had been admitted to this holy of holies, but when I looked around at all these beauties I couldn't help wondering if there would ever be room on the wall for me. When they let me register for my appointment and told me I was entitled as a working model to ten percent discount on everything, I felt as though I had passed one hurdle and was on the lower rung, at least, of the face-making and posing sisterhood.

Ingrid, the girl who took over, was a model herself. Between bookings she was a makeup consultant at the Center. She put a gown on me, skinned my hair back, and then she drew a map of my face. She worked in front of a mirror and explained what she was doing every step of the way. Carlo came in to oversee things and introduce himself, and he couldn't have been more charming and helpful. "Always remember brown pushes back and white brings out," he explained as Ingrid worked on my eyes.

Finally the moment came when they picked out the lashes. Then Carlo trimmed them for me. Then they showed me step by step how to put them on. Draw on your eyeliner first very thin. Curl your natural lashes out, then brush them with mascara so they will blend in from below. They never use the glue that usually comes with the lashes. I was glad to find out it wasn't just idiot me who had trouble with the stuff. They used nothing but a special adhesive called DUO made by a pharmaceutical house for attaching bandages to open wounds. When Ingrid and Carlo finished with me, I couldn't believe the mirror. I was ready to take on all the flint-eyed meat inspectors in town, including Miss Eileen Ford. But I was terrified that once I took this fabulous face off I would never be able to put it back together again. Carlo was sweet enough to guess how I felt. He made me promise that if I ever had any problems I'd just call them or run over and let them help me. If I ever got stuck on location in Tanganyika or Mozambique, I could just cable them and they'd airmail anything I needed. I felt I had a friend who could do more for me than the people at Chase Manhattan. The Make-Up Center became my second home.

As a parting shot, Carlo showed me a simple trick for keeping the curl in false lashes. Put the lashes up against an ordinary pencil and then wrap a piece of Saran Wrap around the pencil and the lashes. The Saran Wrap is self-adhesive. In the morning when you unwrap the lashes, *voilà,* a perfect 180-degree curl.

On the train back to New Haven that night I kept looking at my reflection in the window. When I got to my own mirror, I studied my new face as coldly as if it belonged to somebody else. Then I got out my portfolio and looked at my old pictures. Ingrid sure knew what she was doing. But how could I ever remember to do what she had done? Dammit, I'd just have to work on it just as I'd worked on everything else. Carefully I began taking off my face. First I took off the eyelashes. Then, step by step, I peeled off the mouth, the eyes, the shadings on the cheekbones, the white under my eyes. Then I laid out the map on my face that I'd put together in the morning. I was curling my new lashes around a pencil and wrapping them in Saran Wrap when David caught me in the act.

"Criminy, what's this you're up to now?" he exclaimed disgustedly. "If you knew how much better you look without those damn things, you'd flush them down the loo. Women with their hair in rollers are disgusting enough. But eyelashes in rollers—what pansy put you up to that?"

Oh, Lord, here we go again. What good will it do me if I get all done up like everybody else and lose my soulmate, my chauffeur, and the love of my life? I'll have to become a two-faced woman with one face for New York and another for New Haven. I can see myself now hiding behind some commuter's copy of *The New York Times,* glueing on lashes every morning en route to New York and peeling them off on the return trip.

Next morning I got up half an hour early to sweat it out in front of the mirror. I put on the new face. It wasn't perfect, but it was a good beginning. It took me a good twenty minutes to get the eyelashes finally on right. Everything was lovely until the train pulled into the station. I felt the lashes leaving me, and I was sure they were gone with the wind. Then I felt them scratching my sunglasses so I knew they were still there. I had a finger in one eye or another most of the day. But by mid-afternoon I knew there was no turning back. I went back to the Make-Up Center and splurged on another pair.

> *Born redheads are rare: the figure is something absurd like five percent. But the lure of red hair is far more primitive than the prosy mathematics of supply and demand.... Red hair can be any colour from marmalade to strong tea.... The hair can be tenderly and creatively encouraged to deepen from marmalade to bronze, or soften from orange to autumn leaf.... One of the minor but exceedingly gratifying triumphs of those romantic types in the chemistry labs is that any woman can become a believable redhead in twenty minutes. That's if her own hair is blond, gray, or light brown. A brunette needs a little more time. There are, significantly, many more red-haired beautiful people this year. There are more red-haired photographic models. . . .*
> —VOGUE, op.cit.

"Carolyn, are you still commuting from Connecticut?"

Whenever anyone in the business asked me that, I was stuck for an answer. I got tired of pretending to be just around the corner—playing games with my answering service. So one time when this casting agent asked me, I blurted out the truth.

"Yes, I am," I said. "Why?"

"Well," the man said, "I know a couple of kids with a great apartment on Park Avenue. One of them is leaving to get married. The other one is casting for a roommate. I thought you might be interested."

"Park Avenue?" I gasped. "How stiff is the rent?"

"Only two fifty-five."

The computer in my head began clicking. Two hundred and fifty-five dollars a month sounded like half the national debt. But when you split it in half it amounted to $127.50, which was about $4.25 a day. I was already spending more than five bucks a day commuting. If I was ever going to get anywhere, eventually I'd have to take the plunge. Events have a way of deciding things for you. I got the address and telephone number of the Park Avenue girls and called them, and they asked me to come over after work so we could meet and chat.

It was a new kind of casting session. I had never been in exactly that kind of spot before. About six o'clock I tripped over to this brand-new apartment house on Park Avenue. The location was fantastic—it was smack in the middle of everything—within walking distance of Seventh Avenue, most of the casting and talent agencies, the advertising agencies, and the big photographers' studios. It had a classy uniformed doorman. He took my name and buzzed the girls before he would let me near the elevator. The two elevator men looked me over and delivered me to the proper floor.

The two girls were waiting. It was a lovely apartment, near the back of the building and on the quiet side, high enough to avoid some of the street noises. It had a spacious living room, a huge bedroom, a small kitchen, a foyer and a luxurious bathroom and dressing area.

Linda had just gotten engaged to an intern. She was so busy thinking about her wedding that she left everything to her roommate, whom she called Clem—short for Clementina. She was tiny and Italian and taught school across the river in Brooklyn. There was a plus right there. She would be up and out of the apartment early every morning so I would have the bathroom to myself from eight until five. Having another model for a roommate would be impossible. There is no apartment in New York large enough to accommodate two models with all their collection of clothes, hair, makeup, and impedimenta.

Clem offered me a drink and we chatted. I liked her immensely, and if I could make it with anyone, I could make it with her. I hoped she was willing to try. I was relieved when she finally said, "Well, there's only one way to find out if we can stand each other. We'll just give it a try."

It was a big decision, but I decided to take the plunge. The next weekend dear old reliable David helped me schlepp all my things in from New Haven. The thought of being all those miles apart was a real wrench at first, but then fate produced another twist. Ten days later David was transferred to the New York area and he moved into Manhattan to share an apartment with a college chum. As long as we were within shouting distance of each other, the geography didn't much matter. We were both scraping and scrimping, hoarding our dollar bills to be able to meet the rent on the first of the month.

Fortunately, Clem and David liked each other, so at dinnertime it was often a threesome. David would come over with some groceries, Clem would pick up something at the bakery, and we would have a potluck meal. David spent so much time with us that Clem began to feel like a chaperon, but we always had a happy swinging time.

David and I were the big lovers, but who was the first one to get married? Little Clem. She eventually bagged herself a handsome Italian and moved off to Rome. I had the choice of doubling my rent or looking for another roommate. I had a few, and the less said about some of them the better. It took a few months before I was making enough as a model to be able to afford to pay that high old Park Avenue rent. The first day I laid out $255 a month without acute discomfort was like Independence Day.

I inherited the telephone number and the Park Avenue address. But even after I was living alone, I always carefully preserved the idea that I had a mythical roommate in the offing somewhere. It was a very handy way of cooling off rambunctious, oversexed gentlemen callers.

"I'd adore to ask you up for a drink, Mr. Snodgrass," I would say, "but my roommate is a schoolteacher and she has to get up so early." I wish I had a dollar for every time I told that lie.

In the jargon of college psychology texts, I was learning to handle rejection. When I showed up for a casting session or an interview with a casting agent, I played mind-reading games, trying to guess in advance how they would type me, what reason they would present for my not being "right." One day at the Rice-McHugh agency Ruth, the casting director, was studying my portfolio and brooding. I tried to beat her to the punch.

"Do you really think I look like the 'other woman'?" I said.

She laughed, then frowned, then looked at me and said, "No, I was wondering what you'd look like if you lightened your hair. Your hair photographs darker than it is in black-and-white. It's too severe for your face. A couple of other girls lightened their hair. You'd be surprised what a difference it makes with the cameras. Why don't you go over and see Richard at Derel Coiffures and have him take a look?"

Well, I thought, Ruth was at least *trying* to be constructive. The least I could do was see what the man said. So I went and he looked. He got a lot of business from that agency—more than he could handle. I knew I couldn't be a blonde—that wasn't my type at all.

"I can give you a French fluff," Richard said. "But it's always a gamble. It's a lightener, and your hair will come out with highlights. I don't know what color it will turn out to be. Probably somewhere in the red family. Your hair is reddish-brown."

I was scared stiff. I had never used any of the rinses or tints on the market—I had never touched my hair in my life. I'd gone to beauty parlors a few times to get a trim or have my hair washed and set, but I'd never spent more than five dollars at a sitting, and that was only for a special occasion. But Richard was very nice. I sort of felt he knew what he was doing. So I made an appointment for Saturday, and I went all agog. If I'd been getting a nose job or changing religions, it couldn't have been a more daring step.

Richard put this gook on my hair, and he stayed with me and held my hand. After a few minutes he washed my hair. I could see through the soap that it was a little bit lighter, but there was nothing really dramatic until it dried. It had highlights, but it wasn't anything anybody would notice except my mother. Maybe it might show up startlingly in photographs, but in the mirror it seemed hardly worth the trouble. Anyway, I had my feet wet now; I had taken the first step. I had the courage and the curiosity to go on from there. Richard suggested I try it for a week, and then if I wanted to take step number two, we would make a date.

I made my mind up before I left that I was coming back. Next Friday Richard left the gook on longer. When he washed it out, I could see very definite glimmers through the bubbles. After the rinse it was dark and wet, yet definitely red. When I came out from under the dryer, it was a beautiful shining copper color. I absolutely adore it. It changed the color of my skin. It made my eyes look huge and greener than ever.

Richard was pleased with himself. "You should have been a redhead long ago," he said. "You've got everything that goes with it."

"We have red hair in the family, anyway. Aunt Rose was a redhead. Why didn't I think of it before?"

"These things just have to happen," he said.

I couldn't wait for David to see it. I hoped he would like it, but there was no way to tell. The way he carried on about eyelashes and makeup, he might have a fit over what I'd done. We had a big jaunt planned for that weekend. David was meeting me at the airport, and then we were going to St. Louis for a big wedding. David had been tapped to be best man for his old college chum, Chuck, and I was going along for the ride. I had to get something new to set off my hair, so I went flying through the stores until I found the right suit in a smashing shade of aquamarine. I wanted to wear it to the airport to give my new mane its best possible frame, but I didn't dare.

So I stood there like a vision in a simple yellow dress, breathless, waiting for David. I saw him first, and I watched him looking for me. He spotted me, and then he did this explosive double-take, and then he came running toward me, like a Clairol commercial in reverse.

"Hon-eeeee!" he exclaimed. "What did you do?"

I couldn't tell if his reaction was positive or negative. He seemed to be in shock. If worst came to the worst, I could tell him it was a rinse somebody insisted on for some stupid job. He kept spinning me around and looking at me, and then he grabbed me in a big bear hug. He was a great one for bear hugs—real bone-crushers.

"Do you like it?" I finally was brave enough to ask.

"Like it? I love it. It makes you look different. It changes you completely, but I mean like... it works... it goes with you. Anybody can see that."

That did it. David was even more conservative than I was. He makes Bill Buckley look like a temporizer in some areas. We flew to St. Louis on cloud nine, but the really dramatic moment arrived the morning of the wedding. I worked on my hair for three hours, making sure it was perfect. I slipped into my aqua outfit and my bone shoes. I was ready when David called me from the hotel lobby to tell me to come down and meet his friends. It was an old-fashioned hotel with a staircase, so I could make an entrance. David and the groom-to-be were waiting below.

"You didn't tell me Carolyn was a redhead," the groom exploded when I came waltzing toward them. "Hey, how do I know I'm not marrying the wrong girl? Mary's a lovely blonde, but. . ."

David was proud as a peacock. I looked at him and winked. I had been whistled at all my life, but I knew in my bones right there that the dye pot could open up a whole new way of life.

We've all seen that commercial so many times. I know.

I reached the point where I expected king-size reactions from everyone who knew me when. On Monday I couldn't wait to show my face and my mane at the agency. After all, it was Ruth who'd started the whole thing. I waltzed in expecting screams of delight. I expected the girls to swoon. Not on your life. They barely looked at me. I had to ask them how they liked my hair.

"Oh, yeah," Ruth said. "You did what I suggested. It's nice. Now you've got to hustle test sessions like mad and get a whole set of new pictures."

My roommate more than made up for their blasé reception. She exploded in a real shout. "OK now. NOW you look gorgeous. NOW you're set. You look the way you should. It works. It goes with you. You didn't need that mousy-brown hair." And then she went to the corner drugstore and bought herself a box of Dawn.

My mother and sisters loved it. Daddy was the only one who disowned me. "That's not my daughter," he said.

But there was no turning back. By that time Red was my nickname.

If I heard anybody shouting or whispering that three-letter word, I knew they were talking about me.

One day I was flying down Third Avenue in the forties when I heard someone hollering, "Hey, Red, you've got gorgeous hair." I didn't pay the slightest attention until this man ran up to me and handed me his card. He was a photographer, and he had a studio nearby, and he had a very fancy hyphenated name.

"Look, baby," he said. "I don't usually flag girls down in the street, but I'm doing some shots on spec for Lennen & Newell for a new hair product, and we're looking for a redhead. What agency are you with?"

When I told him, he said, "You're new, aren't you?"

There's a good way to be new and a bad way to be new, so I hedged. When he persisted, I gave him my name and told him he could call the agency and make a date and I would come around for a go-see. I had the agency check him out, and he came out very legitimate. He was listed in all the right directories, so when he made an appointment I went around to his place.

As soon as I saw his layout I knew I should have known better. He had plenty of space, and his equipment was first-class, but the dressing room looked as if it hadn't been swept in fourteen years.

He seemed to be alone in the studio with nothing to do except heckle me. Since the appointment had been made for him to do color test shots of my head and shoulders, I was concentrating on my makeup. While I was fixing my mouth, he began lecturing me about the need for precision in putting my mouth on. He told me he had photographed the famous German model Wilhelmina in earlier days and what a steady-handed fanatic she was about getting exactly the right even lipline. Well, nobody tries to make a mess of herself. And sometimes it's a little easier if you're not being lectured while you're trying to give yourself a touch-up.

All the name-dropping in the world wouldn't impress me at that point unless Josephine the Plumber and a bevy of Comet models were to drop in and scrub his dirty sink.

"Hey," my hyphenated friend said, off on a new tack, "your agency does a lot of lingerie. Do you do lingerie?"

"Yes," I said, "I do." Then he scurried off into another corner of his dirty atelier and came back with this huge box of bras and girdles and negligees. "Find something in here that fits you and try it on."

He tossed out this suggestion ever so airily, and then he walked away. What kind of game *was* this? My appointment was for color head shots. I wasn't about to do any test shots in lingerie. Especially after I looked at his box of treasures. Every garment was filthy.

I stuck me head out the door. "Thorry, thir," I lisped, "your lingerie is much too dirty. If you want to shoot me in lingerie, you tell me when and I'll bring my own. I won't put these on."

"What do you mean—dirty?" he said indignantly. He walked in the dressing room and began forking through these filthy rags as if he were going to fire his imaginary wardrobe lady.

"When I saw you on the street, the thing I liked about you was that you really seemed to swing," he began whimpering. "You seemed very relaxed, the way you moved. But maybe you're not as relaxed as you seemed. Maybe you're a little bit inhibited."

"Yes. I am," I said. "I'm very inhibited about climbing into other people's dirty drawers."

"You already said that. You made your point, Red. But you don't have to be so bloody stiff-necked about it."

"I used to be a little stiff, but I'm not anymore."

"Well, let me tell you something. You'll never get anywhere, kid, until you learn to turn off this stiffness. I'd like to show you some girls who are top models today. And they're up there today because I helped them to free themselves—to bust loose in front of the lens."

He led me to the front of his studio where his cameras were set up. Out of his desk he pulled a tall pile of contact sheets. He dusted some of the dirt and soot off them before he dropped them into my lap. I was no judge of whether the girls were on top as models, but there is no doubt they looked relaxed. He had pictures of girls odalisquing on the floor, plunging through the air, whirling around a pole, primping and pirouetting in every possible pose. They were all models all right. I recognized the body movements and the stock poses. But something was missing. They were posed as if they were selling dresses, but they had no dresses on. They were poised as if they were selling lingerie, but they had no lingerie on. They were primping as if they were selling bras, but the bras were missing.

My hyphenated friend began pointing over my shoulder at these various naked ladies and giving out with explanatory narration.

"This girl has gone a long way since I freed her and showed her how to move. This one has been making pots of money since I got rid of her inhibitions and stiffness. Now you see," he commented dead seriously, "once you learn how to move like these girls move, then you can do

109

absolutely anything with clothes. It only takes a little imagination to be able to see how sensational any one of these girls would be in today's fashions. Yet these pictures are ageless."

Well, he didn't have to draw me a map. If he was the only man who could free me, I'm sorry, I'd rather try to make it as an inhibited slave. It was a reverse play. He calls you for head shots, then he invites you to try on his dirty lingerie. And then he frees you by letting you take the dirty stuff off. It's like the old one about being hit in the head with a hammer. It feels so good when it stops.

He saw he was getting nowhere so he finally settled down and began taking those head shots in color. I'm sure he didn't waste any film on me. He was saving that for ladies who wanted to be free.

I was in a continual swivet about clothes. I never seemed to have the right kind of dresses. For the big jobs, it's no problem. The photographer has a stylist who borrows fantastic clothes from name designers or wholesale houses in return for a credit. For the small jobs, you're on your own. Sometimes the photographer doesn't even have a stylist. Sometimes he'll pick up a dress for you. More often he'll ask you to bring in what you have, and he'll select something that works with the setup he has in mind. You come in with three suitcases, enough clothes for a trip around the world; you trot everything out, and nothing is right. The photographer wants something low-cut and dressy—or he wants something high-necked and demure. If you have the right style, the color is wrong.

It was only a small job—a trade advertisement for Nine Flags men's cologne. The photographer wanted something that looked like Christmas Eve, dark and simple and very dressy. Very Fifth Avenue Matron. Finally he said, "Tell you what you do. You go to a department store. Do you have a charge account anywhere?"

"Yes," I admitted. "I have one at Saks."

"Fine. May as well get the best. You go down in the morning and pick up a dress. Bring it in at eleven-thirty. We'll do the shooting at twelve. After lunch you can return the dress and tell them it doesn't fit."

I was shocked at the audacity of such an idea. My New England background was showing. No wonder I wasn't getting anywhere. I wasn't onto all these sharp New York tricks.

"What's the matter?" said the photographer. "Everybody does it."
"They do?" I said. It wasn't a national ad I was booked for. For that
you get a bonus of something like five hundred dollars. But it was
worth at least a hundred bucks. It was a hundred bucks I couldn't
afford to pass up. I was scared. But I was tempted, too. "OK," I said.

I didn't sleep much that night. I felt like an amateur shoplifter about
to go out on her first heist. If only Didier Grumbach were in town at the
Plaza with his Paris collection of Castillos and Venets. He was such a
doll, paying us extra for late showings and letting us order afternoon
tea on room service and hors d'oeuvres and drinks at five. One of the
models who worked with me showing his collections was a real crazy
Austrian-Italian nut. She wanted to go to a ball at the Plaza one night,
and Didier let her borrow this fantastic Castillo ball gown. He just
looked the other way when she put it in a box and walked off with it for
the evening. After all, it was a sample. If Didier were in town, I could
call him and ask him, and I was sure he would have let me borrow the
perfect frock. But this was all pipe-dreaming. I had to have a smashing
outfit by noon tomorrow, so in the end I screwed up my courage and
flitted into Saks as if I were Doris Duke.

The saleslady couldn't have been nicer. She trotted out some
beautiful copies of Paris and Rome originals. There was one that was
absolutely perfect at $210 plus tax, and exactly my size. I whipped out
my charge-plate and signed the slip as if I had been buying two-hun-
dred-dollar dresses all my life. Then I zoomed out of there and dashed
to the studio. I put my hair on, fixed my eyelashes, then slipped into the
$210 job. I wasn't taking any chances on removing any of the tags. I
tucked them inside the zipper where they wouldn't show. Then I wiped
off my feet. When I stepped onto the white seamless, I was a vision.
Just what he wanted.

"Perfect," the photographer said. I was happy he was happy. I
swooned over the nine bottles of cologne in a huge gift box for a couple
of shots, and then we took a break for coffee. Again I wasn't taking any
chances with the borrowed dress. I slipped it off, put it on a hanger with
a cellophane slipcover, and threw on my robe. I was just about to join
the crew for coffee when I spotted the reverse side of the Saks tag. There
in screaming purple letters—gleaming through the cellophane—it said
plain as day: NONRETURNABLE. I could feel the perspiration
collecting under my knees. Everybody does it, sure. But the gonifs in

this business at least know what they're doing. Now the stores were catching up with them. As soon as they see a lanky thing come in with hair flying and false eyelashes on, they know what she's up to and sweetly they direct her to this darling lady who shows her a few things from this special rack with the NONRETURNABLE tags on it. Why hadn't I looked? What made me think I could get away with it? I was so hungry to get this chic little job because I needed the money, and now it was going to cost me exactly $210 plus tax for a dress I didn't want and couldn't use.

I was so frantic I ran into the studio carrying the dress as if it were on fire. "Look, Bernie!" I was screaming. "The tag on this dress says NONRETURNABLE."

"So why did you take it?"

"I was in such a rush to get the right thing I didn't look. Oh, my God!"

"What did you pay for it?"

"Pay for it? It cost two hundred and ten dollars plus tax. I put it on my charge account."

"Well, then, all you have to do is take it back and think of a good excuse."

I was sick for the rest of the shooting, but I got through it somehow. I packed the dress back into its box not quite daring to wonder if it belonged to them or to me. I walked up Fifth Avenue as if I were headed for the Supreme Court. I was such a lousy liar I couldn't think of a single story that didn't collapse under its own silly weight. I thought of telling them the truth, but I was scared that if I did they might ask me whom I was working for and I might get Bernie in the soup along with me. Finally in the elevator I had a flash. It wasn't brilliant, but by the time I found the original saleslady I was in tears, and the tears at least were real. I told her I had picked out the dress as a present for my sister on her birthday. At least I had sisters and all my sisters had birthdays. I had been in such a rush I hadn't noticed it was nonreturnable. From then on it was blue sky as I babbled on about the girls in her office asking me to pick out something and they would all chip in together. We had this special birthday lunch and everything was peachy until she opened the box and she didn't like the dress.

"She didn't like it?" the saleslady said. Oh, my God, I thought, maybe she believes me. That feeling didn't last very long, because she then took me to the manager. I repeated the whole spiel, adding a few details about how strange my sister was and how I had forgotten and this severe black number was just the kind of thing she *should* wear and just the kind of thing I wanted her to wear, but, poor thing, she always wanted something a little too frilly and she was so turned off by the dress I was really upset, because the girls were all upset, and they were upset because I was upset.

Now the manager went into a huddle with the saleslady. He asked her if she had told me the dress was nonreturnable. I held my breath for the answer. "No, I must confess I didn't," she said.

Oh, you beautiful, beautiful woman, I thought. You honest true-blue beauty, you, you told the truth, and if Saks takes this dress back and gives me a credit slip, I'll never, never, ever, ever, do it again. When they gave me the credit slip, I bounced out of there as if I had just been acquitted of a murder. St. Patrick's Cathedral is right next door. I had never been in there in my life, but I went in and lit a candle for Mr. Saks. I took a vow I'd never do it again, and I never did.

A model is in the same spot as Eve in the Garden. Even before she needs a new fig leaf, she needs extra hair. A quick change of hairdo with a fall or a wig can often mean the difference between working steadily or not. The more hairpieces you have the more you can do to change your look. Wigs and falls are terribly expensive, and then unless you're an expert in quality you can really get yourself stung. Once you've hit the dye pot yourself, your extra hair has to match your dyed hair exactly. Some Asian or Japanese hair is OK for brunettes, but if you try to dye it, it turns into a messy purple and it's time and money down the drain.

So I kept after everyone I knew to be on the lookout for someplace I could get hair. It was finally a jeweler who volunteered that he had a friend who was a hair buyer. The hair buyers were all congregating in New York one week at the Statler Hilton for a hair show. I never dreamed there was such a thing as a hair buyer or a hair show. But someone has to trap furs, and someone has to buy hair. It doesn't get from the Balkans to Sixth Avenue without passing through a few middlemen on the way. I called the friend of my jeweler and told him I needed a good fall. He made arrangements for me to get in the show to see him. When he saw me and I told him my problem, he said, "I know

113

just the woman who can help you. My girl friend got two or three wigs from her. I expect her in tonight sometime. Why don't you stick around and wait?" I waited until eight-fifteen that night in the booth with him. The show was due to close at eight-thirty. I was ready to give it up as a lost cause when in she walked—a tiny woman in black pants, black boots, a fur coat cut like a coolie jacket, and a red Chinese hat. Her name was Sherle. She listened to my tale of woe and finally said, "Come on out to my studio someday and we'll see what we can do."

Her studio was an enterprise called The Wiggerie, Ltd., and it was in White Plains—about three quarters of an hour out of New York on the train.

Sherle is a real operator—she never does anything for less than three reasons. I went out to see her one afternoon, and by the time I arrived, we were practically in business together. She wanted some pictures of some of her wigs for the magazine *HairDo.* She needed a good photographer who wouldn't charge her an arm and a leg. I had done modeling for this magazine, so I got the photographer I knew to give her a special rate. I wore her pieces, and she got her pictures for a song, and I got myself a beautiful matching fall. It was genuine Hungarian hair of good quality that would have cost three hundred dollars if I'd had to walk in and buy it retail.

Sherle and I became bosom buddies right off the bat. She became my New York mother. She had a daughter about my age, Jan, a student at the University of Connecticut who had a keen interest in being a model, and Sherle knew what it takes to keep in shape to work as a model. Any time I needed anything special, an SOS to Sherle meant I had it the next morning.

When she had fashion shows at The Wiggerie for the ladies of Westchester County, I came out and modeled her hairpieces for her. When I needed a regal do when I was named Queen of a Japanese Motorcycle Show, Sherle lent it to me.

When Sherle got the commission to design a solid-gold thirty-five-thousand-dollar wig for the Neiman-Marcus catalog—for the woman who has everything—she spent weeks getting it ready. She tried every way to get me the job of wearing it in the Neiman-Marcus catalog. She was ready to resign when she found out they had photographed another girl in it. But when the wig was to be modeled live on the

Johnny Carson show at Christmastime, Sherle wouldn't allow anyone to model it but me.

Vito Palermo, a handsome Italian hair stylist, always did my hairpieces and wigs. A master at his craft, and what a hunk!!! He was Sherle's number one stylist when he could sneak out from his own shop to give Sherle a hand. Between them, they solved my hairpiece problems.

"Sorry, dear, you're too pretty for us," said the casting lady. "We're looking for plain Jane mama types today." I thanked her and was picking up my portfolio when I noticed her looking at my hands. "Do you do any hand work?" she asked.

I was ready for anything—Indian wrestling, a quilting party, or a crocheting contest. "I haven't had a chance yet, but I'd like to try," said game little me. I knew that Compton Advertising had oodles of soap accounts, but I didn't know that there was a whole raft of models who do nothing but stand in for those close-up photographs showing flawless hands.

"We're shooting a lot of things next week—I'd like to have one of our producers take a look at your hands." She buzzed someone and someone buzzed back, and the first thing I knew I was in the outer office of the associate producer in charge of the hand department. He looked me over from the elbows to my cuticles, and then he took me in and showed me to someone else. Even hands are pigeonholed into possible types. There is the housewifey hand with short nails and no polish. There is the teen-age hand with skinny fingers and natural polish. There is the horror character hand—all chapped and wrinkled and the redder the better—and there is the beauty hand with slim fingers, long nails, and supple wrists. They tagged me as having beauty hands and booked me to do a hand commercial for a glamour soap the following week. They explained to me that hand models don't get residuals; they get a buy-out—a waiver of royalty payments in favor of a fat flat initial fee. I didn't quibble. They had helped me to discover another little aspect of the modeling business that I hadn't encountered before.

The booking was three days away, and for those three days I had to pamper myself like Paderewski. At night I soaked my hands in cold cream and lotion and wore old gloves to bed. I begged off helping my roommate wash the dishes. I wore rubber gloves in the bathtub so I wouldn't oversoak. I did everything but walk around with both arms in a sling. When I arrived on the set at MPO on the appointed morning, I began to understand why hand and foot models are some of the biggest prima donnas in the business. They have to be. They're more like the stage mothers with little baby models in tow. Their precious hands are like disembodied spirits. They talk about them as if they were children or pets. Can you imagine being married to one of these girls? One of the beauty hand models told me her hands have never been touched by water in eleven years. She wears gloves every minute of the day and never uses any kind of soap—including the kind she was getting paid to fondle in front of the cameras. I learned a lot watching the other girls work, so that when my time came I was able to give the clients just what they wanted. When you're a hand model, you feel as if you were deaf and dumb and wrapped up in a straitjacket. You have to do all your emoting with your hands.

I did several good soap commercials as a hand model, and it gave me lots of confidence, knowing I had added another string to my bow. You never know when you're going to be able to use these little tricks you've picked up. It was only a few weeks later that I got a booking for some Christmas catalog work. I was scheduled to do several pages of jewelry and sweaters. I was working away with the photographer, Al Rotonde, knocking off page after page like a real pro, when there was a sudden crisis in the studio. Al had two pages of gloves to shoot. It was somebody's idea to cut corners and use the stylist for the glove shots. "My God," Al complained, "she has hands like a bunch of bananas." I didn't say a thing. Between shots, while Al was readying a new setup I just began emoting in an imaginary three-act drama with my hands. "Lemme see that again," Al said. "We'll try you."

They threw me several pairs of gloves in my size and a red and green Christmas ball. They propped me up on a piece of white seamless mounted on a table. At first it was difficult—much more difficult than making love to a bar of soap. Posing with one glove is easy, but when you use both hands, you have to practice to turn your wrists, so the fingers fall naturally. Every fold in the glove has to be just right, and you have to show off ten fingers, the seaming, and the trimming in one tiny bit of precious catalog space. After a rough beginning I got into the swing of it. "That's great, kid," Al admitted finally. "You've got the hang of it. We'll use you from now on as a glove model." Six weeks before I hadn't known there was any such animal.

I reached such a point of proficiency that I was ready to test for that commercial that shows your fingers doing the walking through the Yellow Pages of your telephone book.

"What kinda body you got, baby?" this big joker asked me. At first I was startled. He was pretty crude. I knew he wasn't blind; he had been ogling me for fifteen minutes. It was obvious I was standard: two arms, two legs, two of the usuals. I just gave him the freeze.

"No, I'm serious," he laughed. "I'm doing a bubble bath thing, and I'd like to see your book."

"OK," I said. It was lunchtime at this studio in New York where we were shooting an Alcoa commercial. I was very unhappy about being cast as an extra. Frank Gerard, the producer—called F.G.—was a huge man, six feet two, with a horrible thick neck and a horrible little potbelly. When we were off camera, he was like a bull in a doll shop, always fooling around and fiddling with the girls, always finding some excuse to paw them or touch them. I explained that I didn't have my book with me, but could I bring it another day?

"Come into the office," he said. "I'll show you the kind of thing I've got in mind."

He had this huge, important-looking office down the hall from the studio. On the walls were a whole series of color shots of girls lolling in bathtubs. "We usually go on location to do these jobs," he said. "One time we rented a house in Palm Beach and flew everybody down there. The kind of zingy marble palazzo they used for a bathroom—hell, you couldn't build it on a stage no matter how big a budget you had." When I looked closely at the photos, I could see what he meant. "I like you," he insisted. "I think you'd be great. But I gotta see your book. I couldn't sell you to the client or fly you to Palm Springs until I was sure your back is good. For these bathtubs shots you gotta have a very sexy spine."

He started running his fingers up and down my back like a chiropractor looking for a slipped disk.

"My back is OK," I said, walking away. "Nothing but a few tiny beauty marks."

"Well, then," he beamed, "what are we waiting for?" Now he picked me bodily off the floor, and when he put me down, he moved in to give me a big sloppy smooch. I wanted to bring my knee up gently and plant it squarely under his pot, but I didn't want to blow the commercial on the first encounter. After all, this seemed to be his manner with all the girls. Maybe this was just one of the things you had to put up with. In New York perfectly strange men started in calling a perfectly strange girl sweetie and honey and pussy and God knows what else. So a smooch meant about as much as a handshake. I kept telling myself not to act like a prudish New England schoolmarm. Just because he was the type that turned me off as a man didn't mean he wasn't a good craftsman or wasn't important in the business. So I untangled myself as gracefully as I could.

"Why don't you come by here Friday and bring your book?" he said.

"What time?"

"I'll be shooting until we finish. I don't want to keep you waiting. So why don't you come near the end of the day?"

I agreed without thinking twice. I got there at five, and I suddenly guessed what the game was when I saw people leaving and heard everyone saying goodnight. He waited until the place was empty before he came into the reception room. I had my book open on the secretary's desk. Before he glanced at it, he had me in his arms, chewing at my hair and clawing my back. This was too much for my New England manners. I got very bold and very uppity.

"I'm not here for that, F.G.," I announced. "If the job in Palm Springs includes this kind of extracurricular activity, I'm sorry. I'm just not interested."

He seemed genuinely shocked when I picked up my book and marched out of there. I had learned one thing. When a big, important slob like F.G. asks you casually to drop by at the end of the day, watch it. Maybe other girls were wise enough to know what that meant. From now on I would be wise too. Screwing doesn't always mean you'll get the job.

St. Patrick's Day, 1967—that was the day the mad mod look hit New York as far as I was concerned. A few days before, Virginia called me from Models Service with a job she knew I would want to latch onto. In the beginning I'd had to drop in at the office every day to pick up my assignments. But now I was a veteran. My rates had gone up, and I had clients asking for me by name, so Virginia called me whenever she had anything she knew I would enjoy.

This job sounded sensational. A big organization that coordinated fashion shows had been commissioned to give a big blast at the hot new discotheque Arthur. The ex-Mrs. Richard Burton had just married a young rock 'n' roll singer from there, and it was all in the papers, and Arthur was the place to be if you knew anyone who could get you in. I had been there a couple of times, and it was really a swinging place if your eardrums could hold out against the blast.

For this job they wanted ten or fifteen girls—tall high-fashion types—to model the kinky new mod outfits that were being copied from Carnaby Street. It would be half fashion show and half nightclub performance. There would be fittings and rehearsals, and everything was going to be done right. Having fittings for special clothes means you make more money. For the time they're fitting you you get paid half your regular rates. Each girl was fitted with a whole raft of outfits complete with accessories—jewelry, belts, chains, and props. I got a huge helmet to wear with one of my outfits.

When we arrived for rehearsals, all our clothes were hung in the dressing room on special racks with our names on them. The director put us through our paces while the rock music split the sound barrier. He encouraged us to kick the usual haughty showroom manner and let the music send us. We stopped and did little bits of dancing business. We improvised, and whatever they liked they kept in and told us to do it full out for the show. We were booked from four to seven. After the mini floor show and fashion show, complete with an imported comedian and his blond foil, the band played for dancing until nine. Then everyone had to clear out for Arthur's regular business. I told David about it, and we made a date for him to pick me up at seven-thirty for dinner.

The opening night was a real stunner. The WABC-TV cameras and the fashion celebrities in the audience turned it into a real event. It was the most beautifully produced show I had ever appeared in, and I was all excited. Everything went off without a hitch. Almost, that is. I made my big entrance in my kinky outfit with my mod helmet and went into my dance. Suddenly the place sounded like a burlesque house in Newark, N. J. A bunch of real rude and rowdy men at a front table began cheering and shouting and calling me by name. "More, Carolyn, more!" they shouted. All our names were in the program, but none of the other girls had inspired this kind of response. Finally I heard a familiar voice, and when the light caught me just right, I saw David at the front table with his whole gang from J. P. Stevens textile company. How he wangled a ringside table he always refused to tell me. After the show I fixed up David's pals by persuading four other girls to go out on the town with us. We covered every place on the East Side from Pete's Tavern to Elaine's. David had deserted IBM for J. P. Stevens. He could sell ice cubes to Eskimos, so now with him peddling fabric and me pushing mod clothes, we were practically partners.

You gotta have a gimmick—another axiom from burlesque. Well, the helmet turned out to be my gimmick. My picture in that mod, mod headgear made *Women's Wear Daily,* and I got fan mail on it all the way from Vietnam.

Claudine had an elfin face like Audrey Hepburn's, but she was tiny and blond. She was part French and part Austrian, and she had an accent that made everything she said seem either funny or profound. She had been in New York only a year. We met one day when Virginia at Models Service sent me out on a job modeling for a house that imported beautiful French ready-to-wear knit dresses and suits. Claudine had taken a permanent job at this place as a house model. But in the peak season with so many buyers in town they needed a relief model, so I was hired for the week. Claudine was so attractive and so winning that I couldn't understand why she had tied herself down to a regular job in the garment district. She had tried to do print work, but she felt she couldn't take any chances on irregular bookings, so she settled for her regular $150 a week and was thrilled to get it. It was twice what she could make in Paris working at the most famous *maisons de couture* there.

When she told me she was married, I was even more baffled. Most girls who are married or living with guys don't have to worry about getting the rent together the first of every month. One advantage in being a married model OR a kept woman is you can afford to hold out, to keep making the rounds, to invest your time seeing every photographer in town in the hope of getting that one big break that will start things rolling.

Claudine and I got to be real buddies. We spent a lot of time together comparing notes and gossiping. She filled me full of Paris, and I told her all about Vermont. We had another thing in common. She was a ski freak, too, and when I heard that, I invited her to go with me to Middlebury some weekend so I could show her the American Alps we had in our back yard. Claudine seemed not too sure about going. Her husband, she explained, was an artist and he was not at all keen on outdoor sports. Besides, she couldn't take chances. Suppose she fell and broke a leg—her husband would be miserable. "It's your leg," I told her. "Besides, I've been skiing for ten years and I've never so much as pulled a tendon."

Claudine was tempted, but I could never get a commitment out of her. One day when things were quiet she took a funny-looking little machine out of her tote bag and parked it on the table in our dressing room. Out came some little white cigarette papers and some tobacco. It didn't smell like pot. I sat there wondering what she was doing. I saw finally that she was rolling cigarettes and packing them in a little tin box and carefully counting them. Now it was perfectly clear what she was doing. The only question was why.

"They put saltpeter in the paper of American cigarettes to make them burn faster. My husband doesn't like it," she explained.

I had heard jokes about the Army putting saltpeter in soldiers' food in order to suppress their sexual urges. I never knew whether it was true or not. And I never knew a soldier well enough to ask him. It was much too provocative a subject to discuss with a man. Well, I thought, these Frenchmen are supposed to be great lovers. Maybe that's the way they keep their reputations. No detail is too small to be overlooked. But if there is saltpeter in American cigarettes, why not buy French cigarettes? I explained to Claudine that there was a place in the Fifties where you could get cigarettes of all nations.

"Yes, I know," she said. "But they are so expensive. Even a French cigarette that is cheap in Paris is over here *très chere.*"

Well, I had heard the French were frugal, but this seemed to be carrying it a bit far. I had it all figured until I discovered that Claudine's husband was not French at all. He was American. I had a picture of her rushing off to Ninth Avenue after work, buying fresh vegetables and cooking a real French meal for her husband because he demanded it and he was entitled to it. But rushing home to cook for an American

121

husband after standing on her feet for eight hours in the garment district—have a heart, man. Maybe her husband was American, but he must have been educated in France. Sometimes these Americans who go French turn out to be more Parisian than the natives.

"No," said Claudine, "we met here in New York. He has never been to Paris. He is from Oklahoma." The way she pronounced it, you could tell she thought the Indians and the cowboys were still there.

"I have to roll the cigarettes for him because he must have them and he has no time to do it because he must work without interference."

I could understand that, but what kind of work did he do?

After dinner I could see Claudine lighting the butts for him, but who performed this ceremony while he was working? What did he do that meant taking time out to roll a cigarette might break the spell?

"He is an artist," said Claudine. "He paints beautifully. One day he will be very famous."

Oh, sure, of this I had no doubt. Any guy from Oklahoma who could get an adorable French girl like this one to go out working all day for him while he sat at home thinking about what he was going to paint—he was famous already as far as I was concerned.

"Today I must roll his cigarettes for tomorrow so he does not have to interrupt his work," said Claudine, rolling away, as happy as a little geisha.

"That louse," I started to say, and then I swallowed hard.

Trying to keep a man happy—maybe that's happier than being kept.

# CHAPTER 6

I once owned every record Barbra Streisand ever made. Later I gave them all to the Salvation Army. In between I met her, so to speak.

It was a hot day in July—a very slow month in modeling—when I got a call from a talent agent: Columbia Pictures would soon be on location in New York doing outdoor scenes in New Jersey for *Funny Girl.* There would be a cattle call early Monday morning to pick ten girls to play bit parts as Ziegfeld Follies Girls. Eight days' work—good money and what have you got to lose? "They're looking for super figures, good legs, baby, so wear the tightest, shortest little number you own. Two of the girls will be cast as day players with special business, at more money—maybe you'll get a crack at that."

Monday morning at the Columbia office I showed up for my appointment, and of course the producer was late, so droves of girls were piled up waiting—actresses, models, showgirls—a real mob scene. Since I was all done up, anyway, I decided to stick it out and wait my turn. Finally I received an audience. One man looked at my portfolio of pictures and another man looked at me. It was all over in a minute and thank-you-very-much-Miss-Kenmore, and I was sure that was the end of that until the agent called me the next day to say they wanted me to play a Follies Girl.

"Am I one of the ten or one of the two?" I asked him.

"Oh, the two girls who get to do the special bits of business were picked from up top somewhere—the casting people had nothing to say about that."

That figured. But even to register as one of ten in that mob scene was something. The agent was pleased with himself and delighted to give me my marching orders. The next day I reported to the Eaves Costume Company for fittings. After all that to-do about having to have legs like Lana Turner, the costumers, of course, fitted us out in the long wool coats and dresses that hung to the floor in the style of

1913. They fitted me with gigantic feathered hats and told me to bring along all the extra hair I owned. All bit players were instructed to report at the Circle Line pier at the foot of 42nd Street in Manhattan for transportation by water to the location—an antique railroad station on the Jersey shore of New York Harbor, the last of its kind that had not been demolished. It was misty and foggy that morning when the bit players and the extras reported at the pier—enough people to remake *Gone With the Wind.*

When we got to the station, the basement had been rigged up as a dressing room and makeup parlor. Ten girls who had worked on studio scenes had come from California, and they got most of the attention from the hairdressers and the makeup men. The new girls from New York were only going to be used for scenery, so we had to fend for ourselves. When we'd finished getting our faces on, they gave us a quick once-over. Then we sat and we waited. And we waited. By 9 A.M. the temperature had gone zooming up into the eighties. We were soaking with perspiration in our long dresses, fur-trimmed coats, and Queen Mary hats. Finally a real train pulled up on the tracks and we went to work. We spent three days getting on and off that train.

Crowds of bystanders were lined up across the tracks watching the excitement. Barbra Streisand's air-conditioned trailer dressing room was parked near the station, but she didn't appear till the fourth day, and then she arrived by limousine with her entourage. The three days of shooting were the prelude to a very simple scene. The Follies Girls get off the train followed by the star and her chum, played by Anne Francis. They have a few lines together, and this is a cue for Miss Streisand to go into her song and dance, "Don't Rain on My Parade." Director William Wyler called for places. All we Follies Girls were in place. Anne Francis was in place. When the lights hit us, the temperature zoomed another ten degrees. Our costumes were stifling and our makeup was getting gooey. Anne Francis stood there in place under the hot lights alone for one minute, two minutes, and the star didn't appear. She was off on the side, near her trailer dressing room. A Negro maid stood next to her holding an electric fan against her face. She just wasn't tuned in to what was supposed to be happening. Anne Francis just stood there. Then she began tapping her foot. Finally she threw her hands in the air and stomped off the set. The director tried to soothe her. She told him they could tear up her contract. She had had it. The whole company just stood there, and the crew stood there, waiting at five thousand dollars a minute, and the star didn't pay the slightest attention to what was going on. She was stuffing her face with pastrami or chocolate éclairs and ruining her makeup so it would have to be redone. Then the director would have to go on bended knee to her and invite her to join the party. And by the time he got the two girls back on the set under the lights, there was ice all over the place until the moment the camera turned and they went into character. Once the director called cut, the ice reformed.

The director, the choreographer, the entire crew were working like dogs to make the star look good in her first picture, and she treated them like ants trying to get into her lunch. The word was out that Miss Streisand had finally looked over the Ziegfeld Follies Girls and anybody she considered too pretty was getting reshuffled into the back row. I had never seen a woman so bold, so crude, so uncouth, and so unfeminine in my entire life. After three days on the set with her, I could never again stand the sound of her voice. On the last day of shooting, everybody was a little giddy, happy that it would soon be over, when the location was enlivened by the arrival of Tad Morrison, a big public relations man. He made the rounds of all the girls, with a big smile and a glad hand. He took time to take me aside and tell me how gorgeous I was and ask me if I wouldn't consider coming to his house that night for a little party he was giving for the cast and some of the studio bigwigs from California. Jack Warner would be there, and Tad hoped I could make it. Of course, I was thrilled to be singled out for so much attention, so I took his name and address and promised I'd be there.

Later in the day in the dressing room all the Follies Girls were a-twitter. "Tad invited me to his party." It turned out it was a very intimate little party to which he had invited everybody. He didn't use the public address system—that's all.

That night on the boat back to New York all the girls were chattering about the party. The California girls were all staying at the Sheraton Motor Inn right on the Hudson River, a stone's throw from where the boat docked. The New York girls had to fly home in cabs and get themselves together.

The Morrison town house in the East Fifties was lit up like a Christmas tree when I arrived a few hours later. The buffet looked like something off a film set, the bars were staffed with so many maids and bartenders that every time you turned, someone was trying to thrust a drink into your hand. And at least six deep in every direction, suntanned and manicured, massaged, mudpacked, and cologned, it was like a convention of all the dirty old men in town.

All the New York girls who had worked on the picture were presented to Mr. Warner and all the other VIPs. There were at least ten men for every girl, so safety in numbers was the rule. We were doing exactly what we had done all day on the picture—a line of girls strung out to look like scenery. The DOMs were sniffing our perfume and lighting our cigarettes and finding us places to sit where we could cross our legs and show off our outfits. The party was very low-key and polite and decorous when suddenly all the DOMs rushed from one side of the drawing room to the other, as if they had been called to man the lifeboats. Somebody whistled as the door opened and in stalked seven of the California girls from the picture. We sat there in our severe, sophisticated, stark little monochromatic and black outfits from Para-phenalia, and in come the California Amazons in Jax yellow and Jax orange and Jax magenta—with cutouts under the arms, across the navel, over the hip. There wasn't a bra or a slip or a pair of panties or panty hose on any of them. Everything they had was let out, cut out, pushed out, hanging out. Their little Jax nothing dresses were cut out deep on the hip, revealing huge disks of tanned skin advertising the fact that pants had gone out of style. The girls were all in their twenties and amply stacked, stripped for action, with bare legs, no makeup, and hair flying. It was the summer sex Olympics—the Wild Swinging West versus the Uptight New York look.

All the big-bellied DOMs were like kids at a peep show—eyes darting from cutout to cutout, eagerly making book on which bosom would be first to slip out of the dock. It was no contest. The New York girls, left to sniff one another's perfume and light one another's cigarettes, retired in disarray to the buffet.

It was eight-thirty on the dot when the doorman buzzed me.

"Your car is here, Miss Kenmore."

"Thanks, Sam, I'll be right down.

I had already given myself the once-over three times, and I'd had five whole minutes in the think tank, so I grabbed a light coat and my purse and dashed for the elevator. The party ought to be fun. This rich, rich publisher had a fabulous town house on 67th Street and he was sending a car for me. I still had qualms about going to cocktail parties alone, but Grant was a dear man and he wanted so much to help me. He couldn't stand the thought of me trudging from agency to studio and back again on my go-sees. He was very cynical and felt most of the really great breaks were wired in advance. "This is a come-and-be-seen party for you, Carolyn," he had told me. "The place will be crawling with important people, and you can only do yourself splendid." I hoped he was right. There were sure to be a lot of DOMs there, and I hoped I could tactfully stay out of their range.

The elevator man got me downstairs express. There wasn't a soul in the lobby as I walked through the front door. I stood there looking for a big black limousine. Well, I thought, maybe he'd gotten there early and had to park around the corner, so I scanned the street again looking for the chauffeur. Absolutely no chauffeur. I was about to ask the elevator man what had happened to the doorman when I saw this brand-new black Thunderbird double-parked in the street with an attractive gentleman in the driver's seat. Oh, well, Grant *had* said he was sending the car. He hadn't specifically said he was sending the limousine. Maybe there was a shortage of limousines on the weekend and he'd had to rent a T-bird. It was strange, though, that the chauffeur didn't wear a hat. But some chauffeurs are funny. They hate those hats. Some of them get their kicks out of thinking the jazzy car belongs to them.

The door of the T-bird was open so I hopped in. "Good evening," I smiled. Suddenly something didn't feel right. I could tell from the clothes this man wore that he was no chauffeur. He absolutely reeked of the most expensive cologne, and he was wearing touches of bronze makeup under his eyes. He looked as though he had just stepped out of some beauty salon. I knew Avis was trying harder than Hertz, but this was absurd. Anyway, I kept smiling and waited for him to make the first move.

"Were you a blonde as recently as night before last?" he inquired politely.

"I have never, ever, been a blonde," I said. "Even the hair I left home is red."

He looked puzzled and said, "Well, are you 10G?"

"No," I replied automatically, "I'm 12F."

"Well, I'm waiting for 10G, and I was told she'd be a blonde."

"I'm sorry," I said, opening the door. "The doorman buzzed me and told me my car was waiting. I assumed you were it. I don't see another limousine in sight, do you?"

I was halfway to the curb when it hit me. The girl who lived in 10G *was* a blonde. The boys on the back elevator once told me she was a model, too. But nobody in the building had ever seen her schlepping her portfolio. She was always getting packages from Saks and Bergdorf, but I'd never seen her carrying anything but her purse. Aha, Carolyn, this must be her other profession. The whole deal was settled on the phone, and her gentleman caller has nothing to go on except her apartment number and the color of her wig.

I just stood there at the curb wondering what to do. "I'm sorry," I shouted as a kind of afterthought. This seemed to make him even more nervous and embarrassed. There was nothing to be embarrassed about.

"Wait a minute," he shouted. "Did you say you were expecting a limousine?"

"A friend sent a car to pick me up at eight-thirty. That's all I know. If you'll excuse me, I'm going to have the doorman get to the bottom of this."

"I only mention this because now I remember I did see a chauffeur-driven Cadillac drive up. A girl came out of the building and got in. They drove away."

With that this long black Cadillac swung around the corner and pulled up behind the Thunderbird. This dignified gray-haired chauffeur was at the wheel, and beside him in the front seat was this big blonde with her fancy pouffy last year's overblown hairdo and her silver mink stole. If you're going to be dressed like West End Avenue, you'd better sit in the back of that long black thing. Up front was certainly not her image at all. She looked like a retired Samba professor from Arthur Murray's moonlighting as a driving instructor.

"I think there's been a mistake," I laughed. "Your date digs Cadillacs. She's not the outdoor type."

The dignified gray-haired chauffeur jumped out of the car. But before he could get around to open the door for the big blonde, Madam had sprung herself. As we exchanged cars we traded stares.

"Things got a little confused tonight," she said, fluffing her stole.

"Yes," I laughed. "Our doorman is slipping."

"You live on the twelfth floor. You just moved in, didn't you?"

"I live in 12F, but I've been here for months."

"I'm sorry about this mix-up, but sometimes things are meant to happen. Maybe we should get together. Why don't you stop by next week? I'd love to talk to you." She was casing me every second, and I was casing her back. My chauffeur opened the door for me, and Madam hopped into the T-bird.

Zap! Smack! Bang! When the door slammed the idea hit me. She thinks we're sisters under the skin. Or under the coverlet, to be more exact. She's doing so well she probably has an overload of clients. She's shopping for another operation. Merger is on her mind.

I've got her number, and she thinks she's got mine.

"Who am I and where am I going?" I asked myself as I climbed into this twenty-three-hundred-dollar green Castillo ball gown. I was still scrounging and scratching to make ends meet, taking any assignment that came along and trying to get my portfolio built up so that I didn't have to explain that I was just a beginner. At that point a twenty-three-hundred-dollar Paris gown can just overwhelm you if you're not careful. I was one of four girls sent over by Models Service to this elegant suite at the Plaza where this elegant Frenchman, Monsieur M., was privately presenting the newest designs of Castillo, Patou, Madame Rochas, and Phillipe Venet to selected buyers from the big important stores like Saks and Bergdorf. Modeling a complete Paris collection for a single frozen-faced buyer can be like doing a whole comedy routine to an empty house. I found it helped me to feel comfortable and terribly offhand with these expensive clothes if I imagined I was the Empress of Iran showing off to her cousin from the country or something. Just leaping, swishing, and slinking around like a twenty-five-dollar-an-hour model from Vermont didn't seem to make much sense. So with each gown I gave a performance. You never know whom you may be playing to. Every time I zipped myself up, I gave it everything I had. When we finished modeling forty costumes in as many minutes, I felt as pooped as if I had just done a matinee as Lady Macbeth. Two of the girls ducked out for coffee. I just put my feet up and lit a cigarette.

"Are you an actress?" Betty suddenly asked me. She was a tall blonde from Finland. I had once done another job with her in the garment district.

"Well, I have been. I'd like to be. Why?"

"Well," she said, "there's this company I once worked for in a film. They're casting for the lead in a new picture. They want someone new."

"Well, I'm new all right, but I hoped it wouldn't show."

Betty laughed as she dove into her tote bag and fished out her address book. "Copy this down and send them a picture and a resume. What have you got to lose?"

I knew I was too new to know an important lead from an unimportant lead, so I tracked down everything and followed through on every contact like a very eager little beaver. I began to suspect there would have to be a whole string of little breaks before I would ever get near any big break. So that night when I got home I dug out my favorite glossy and a smoothly typed resume and addressed them to Stellar Film Company, Madison Avenue, the address Betty had given me. I put the envelope on the floor by the door so I wouldn't forget to mail it in the morning. After looking at it for half an hour, I slipped on my coat and trotted to the mailbox with it myself. They're probably getting a hundred photos a day, I told myself. If I mail it tonight, they'll get it early in the deluge. I was tempted to splurge on a special-delivery stamp, but I decided that would be too pushy. I just mailed it and forgot about it. I was absolutely stunned to get a  call the next day from the film company. They wanted to interview me.

I was there on the dot with my portfolio. The producer seemed to be at least sixty, with a foreign accent which I suspected to be Greek. He looked the way old-style Hollywood producers are supposed to look. He was very charming and well-mannered, except that all short men will do anything—but anything, including wearing a phony plaster cast on their leg—to avoid getting up when a tall girl walks into the room. He looked at my portfolio, and then he apologized because the scripts were not yet available so he couldn't ask me to do a reading. I was a bit relieved at that until he suggested going ahead anyway. "I would like to see you do something. Just a short improvisation. Let's see now," he muttered as he looked at my resume. "You're a girl . . ."

My first thought was that perhaps he was blind and going on the sound of my voice. Then he picked up a copy of *The New York Times* and began scanning the front page. He seemed to get something out of the headlines. I wished then he had picked on the *Daily News*. The *News* has only one story on page one, and often it's a juicy murder— something to get your teeth into. "You're a girl. You're a young girl," he kept repeating. "And you come into this room, and you go over there to the mirror, and while you're fixing your hair, you notice someone slips a letter under that door over there. You go over and pick it up and open it, and you read that your boyfriend has been killed in Vietnam and you react to that. That's it."

I was too numb to speak. I had known a few girls whose boyfriends had been killed in Vietnam but nobody I knew would be dumb enough to write a stupid letter like that and have it shoved under the door. Shut up, Carolyn. You're not being auditioned as a technical adviser. He just wants to see you emote and weep and carry on. I looked around his office to see if there was anything there to work with, something I could smash. I got up and started to fix my hair. Next time I go on an interview for a film, I'll come prepared with a scene, I thought. Something I've worked with. Something I already know. Don't blame this poor little man. If you had come prepared, this wouldn't have happened. I turned and looked casually at this imaginary letter. I tore it open. Who was it from? Why couldn't it be a telegram? But if it were a telegram, that would already prepare me for bad news. What was my boyfriend's name? I wanted to let out a terrifying shriek, but I couldn't think of a name. Wait a minute. It's David. David is dead. I tried to imagine it. I really tried. I forgot I was in this office. I was home, and this was a special-delivery letter, and the doorman had slipped it under my door because I wasn't dressed. Suddenly I was in tears, real tears. But it was all wasted because there were no cameras and the producer was in the other corner of the room—blind as a bat, probably.

"Not bad at all, Miss Kenmore," the producer said finally. When I turned to look at him, I could barely see him through my tears. Now he was wearing glasses. "I had a little something different in mind, so let's try it again."

I had the feeling we were getting nowhere, but I gave the retake everything I had. I imagined David with one side of his beautiful face blown completely away, and the picture was so vivid it scared me to death. That reminded me of all the girls I knew who were going through

131

the same horrible thing, and I wept for them, too. Once I got started, I cried my face into an unholy mess.

"Better," he muttered. "Much better. Terrific, as a matter of fact. Now I have a book here I want you to take home with you and study until next week when the scripts will be ready. Then we'll have a regular reading. It's a very dramatic part I have in mind for you."

The book was Stanislavski's classic, *An Actor Prepares.* It looked so old it must have been a first edition. Well, I thought, if I did as well as he suggests, maybe *I* can ask a few questions. So while I was putting my face back together, I asked him what kind of film it was going to be.

"It'll be a low-budget sleeper like *David and Lisa.*"

Oh, well, I thought, if anybody was making a high-budget film they wouldn't tell you. It would take private detectives to find that out. I told him I was already a member of the Screen Actors Guild and I couldn't work unless it was under the Guild. He assured me it would be an SAG contract.

"It's a very dramatic role. A very unusual story. We expect to shoot on location on Long Island for four or five weeks. Betty has already been signed for one of the leads."

"Oh, she has?" I said. "Isn't that wonderful for her! It was Betty who suggested I send you my picture and resume."

"Yes," he said. "You've got a great little friend in Betty. She wouldn't let me rest until I gave you an interview."

I was at that stage where I could see my name in lights again. "Introducing Carolyn Kenmore." "Where will this picture be shown?"

"In some of the best art theaters in the country," the producer said. I was so dumb I didn't know what an art theater was. In Vermont we had only one kind of movie theater. Frank Labshere slept behind the screen, and every three days he put up new names on the marquee. The S's usually went up backwards, and no matter how many times the manager complained, Tyrone Power always came out Tiron. The town got used to it.

I must have looked a little blank at that point because the producer explained that art theaters are places like the Baronet and the Coronet on Third Avenue and the Little Carnegie on 57th Street in New York. Oh, well, I thought, even if the movie doesn't play Middlebury, maybe my folks can go to Boston or Albany to see it.

When I got home, I tried to read Mr. Stanislavski, but it was very rough going. I couldn't imagine that anything in that book could get me ready for my next audition. In a couple of days the producer called me. He was very nice. The scripts were ready, and he was sending one over to me by special messenger. "I want you to study it over the weekend and call me when you're ready for a reading. Remember you're reading for the part of Jill."

It seemed to take hours for the messenger to arrive. I was dying to read the script, but David was picking me up at five-thirty and I couldn't ask him to wait. The script arrived seconds before I flew out the door, so I just stuffed it in my bag.

We were driving to the Hamptons to spend a quiet weekend.

The script was very impressive-looking. It was bound in beautiful black imitation leather with the film company's name on it in gold letters. The title *Endless Love* was no great shakes as a title, but it was probably just a working title, and there'd be lots of time for them to get a better one.

"What's this?" said David, picking it up. It was the first film script either of us had ever seen. He was fascinated.

"My script," I said, so very casually. "I have to study it. They expect me to give a full reading next week. You may have to help me. You know, cue me."

He picked it up and began reading. It wasn't long before I heard those low moans as if he were dying somewhere in Vietnam without any morphine.

"Carolyn, have you read this thing?" he hollered.

"I haven't had a chance to."

"What are you doing with a thing like this?"

"What's the matter? I told you I had this interview and they want me to read for this part."

"Which part?"

"The part of Jill."

"Oh, brother!" David yelped. He threw the script at me, and I began reading. Jill was this voluptuous, sensuous tiger-lady model. This mousy lady stylist from the ad agency goes mad every time she sees her fantastic body. Jill is AC-DC, but she tortures this other lady by playing hide-and-seek with her fantastic body while they're working in this photographer's studio. Then she invites this poor Minnie Mouse to her fabulous place on Fire Island for the weekend so she can torture

133

her some more. They have a big scene on the beach where Minnie Mouse unhooks the strap of Jill's bathing suit and smears Noxema on her sunburn and practically comes apart with unrequited and unfulfilled passion. Jill lures her boyfriend out from the city, of course—she can torture two people as cheap as one, considering the rent she's paying for this Fire Island château. When Jill takes off on her water skis with her boyfriend, Minnie Mouse has forty fits. That night people are crawling in and out of each other's beds, and the next morning Miss Mouse turns out to be a raging lesbian—but of course she's suppressed it all these years, but she can't stand it any longer. Jill is driving her to drink. The boyfriend tries to get her off the booze and shoves some pills down her tender little throat to get her primed for the stupendous orgy scene. The orgy goes on for hours, and when little Miss Mouse realizes what she has done, she runs into the kitchen and gets the bread knife. While Jill is lying naked and stoned on a couch, Miss Mouse lunges the bread knife into her.

It was the most stupid and disgusting trash I'd ever read. The story was a slim excuse to string together endless nude scenes of two girls pawing and heaving at each other. The Stanislavski tome, the Madison Avenue office, the letter from Vietnam—all this was just window dressing. The producer was just a dirty old man making dirty new movies. No wonder he had Betty doing his scouting for him. If an agency sent you out on an interview like that and they handed you a filthy script, you'd know the whole thing was shady. When I thought of myself weeping and swooning in his office over my dead lover in Vietnam, I felt like the fool of all time. What a waste of mascara!

When it's a legitimate job you're dying to get, they can keep you on the string for weeks. When it's something disgusting and shady, they're after you like the FBI. Monday morning early this DOM called me. He wanted to arrange a reading that very evening with Betty. Their lawyer was preparing the contracts. They wanted to sign the three leads before the end of the week. There would be a five-hundred-dollar advance once I signed my name to the contract. He was sure I could do it, and Betty was sure I could, too. Finally he asked me if I'd read the script.

I tried to be cool and diplomatic. "I have to be honest, Mr. Prapandopolous. I just couldn't play this kind of part."

I should have been insulted, but he had the gall to act insulted. He lectured me as if he were Cecil B. DeMille. "This is the true test of an actress, playing parts of this caliber. You don't seem to realize what a great opportunity we're offering you." He rattled on about the script being so great that they were adding to the budget. He was bringing in a special cameraman from Amsterdam who had done some fantastic beach scenes in another epic. "You just ask Betty about him. She worked with him in Europe," he said. Aha, I thought, I'll bet she did. Finally he said, "If you're really concerned about the subject matter of the script, we can arrange it so you don't have to use your real name."

That did it. If you let them talk long enough, eventually they hang themselves. There was no more pretending.

"I wouldn't dream of working in a movie I was ashamed of, " I said. He told me I was taking the wrong attitude. But he still thought I was bargaining for more money. When he raised the advance to seven hundred and fifty, I couldn't help thinking how beautiful that lovely round figure would look in my ratty square checkbook. But he wouldn't take no for an answer. I sent back the script and the Stanislavski book so he would have no further excuse to call me. Nothing stopped the man. He called me every night that week. I reached the point of dreading to pick up the telephone. And if a working model is afraid to answer her phone, she might as well be dead.

Finally he made the mistake of calling late one evening when David was there. David heard me muttering and stammering, so he grabbed the phone right out of my hand. "Mr. Prapandopolous, sir," he began very coolly in his juiciest Dartmouth accent, "this is Miss Kenmore's personal manager. We regret it very much, but we cannot allow her to do films of this category for any amount of money. I have discussed the entire matter with the Screen Actors Guild, and I feel it would be to your distinct advantage not to bother Miss Kenmore any further. Thank you, sir, and goodnight."

"Why, David," I exclaimed when he'd hung up, "you sounded more like the headmaster of a very chic prep school than an agent, but you were very convincing. I'll bet you scared him to death."

"I read the Stanislavski book he gave you," he laughed. And that was the end of that. Almost a year later I bounced into the apartment elevator one night and here was this tall blonde absolutely dripping with caramel-colored mink. By the time I realized it was Betty she had stepped into the foyer where this DOM was waiting for her. He was a good five inches shorter than she, so she walked ahead and he lagged behind. They walked in single file like Jacqueline Kennedy does with Onassis.

By now, of course, lesbian movies are old hat and Betty is probably a big star on 42nd Street. I wonder whose name *she's* using.

We were all stripped down to our brassieres, standing in line like a bunch of freshmen waiting for chest X-rays. But the man inspecting bosoms was a director, not a doctor. We were in the semi-finals of the selection of eight girls who were to be extras in a beach party extravaganza commercial for Maidenform bras.

"What about these scars, dear?" he was saying to the girl in front of me as he inspected her cleavage.

"I was in a bad auto accident," she said. He yanked her bra to one side and then gave her that don't-call-us-we'll-call-you smile. She walked out, and now it was my turn. I had no insecurity in the bosom department. I had to quit wearing sweaters when I was thirteen because all the boys at school called me Chesty. I was a perfect 34 B, and if I couldn't make the Maidenform finals, I couldn't make anything.

Suddenly I noticed the casting director wasn't even looking at me. He was holding his head as if he had seen two too many and had his eye on the door. "Jesus on top of Jesus," he moaned to the girl with the clipboard, "that kid's tits felt like stale bagels. She's full of silicone and got the goddamnedest scars. The doctor who did that job should be strung up somewhere by his own nipples."

Finally he was looking at me. "Great," he said. "You'll do fine, Red." They explained to me that eight girls were all being hired as product extras. We would be paired off with eight fellows when we went on location, and it would be up to the director to decide who got what kind of special business to do. I couldn't make less than one hundred and thirty-five bucks, and if lightning struck, I might get my chest or my face within camera range and stand some chance of getting a residual. The shooting was scheduled for the following week at Jones Beach on the Atlantic Ocean, about an hour and a half from Manhattan. The lucky eight girls were fitted with little striped sailor jerseys and tight white duck pants. It would be simple and outdoorsy, and this meant no extra hairpieces or extraordinary makeup. Besides, we were told, the location unit would include a hairdresser, a makeup man, and a wardrobe woman.

That night we left the studio in a chartered bus, our beach party seemed to be really rushing the season. I took along a good warm coat. The men had all been cast at separate sessions so we never got a chance to look at them until we got on the bus. One of them was Bob Ames, one of New York's top models. He had been around for years, and his face was as handsome as it was familiar. Certainly he had been booked for a principal. Whoever got paired off with him would certainly be in line for residuals.

After we'd been on the road for an hour, it began to get dark and the bus driver finally admitted he was lost and couldn't find Jones Beach. The crew was restive, and the mix-up gave them an excuse to agitate for a dinner stop. They managed to find a fancy restaurant, and all of us piled off. Since the client was footing the bill, everyone ordered food and drinks as if there were no tomorrow. We started off with booze and shrimp, then booze and steak, then champagne and desert, and then more booze for the road. The crew began tucking bottles of wine into their equipment in preparation for what looked like a long, cold, clammy beach party.

When we found the beach, the crew started huge beach fires and began setting up poles for limbo dancing. The camera was going to be set up very low so that when the girls came snaking under the pole doing the limbo with their partners, their Maidenform bras would stand out like Vesuvius and Kilimanjaro. The geniuses who thought the whole thing up had thought of everything except the music. The music was going to be recorded and dubbed later. You'd think someone would have brought along a few calypso tapes or something to help us get into the mood. But no, that would have been too simple. All we had to dance to was a tiny transistor radio. And you could hardly hear that over the sound of the surf.

It was getting colder by the minute. We had no place to dress expect the tiny john in the back of the bus that smelled like an open can of Drain-O. Our little jerseys and snaky tight white ducks were clammy as we snuggled into them. While we stood there shivering, all perfect 34 B's, the director picked out two girls as principals. A lucky little blonde was paired off with Bob Ames, and immediately the hairdresser and the makeup man began giving her the star treatment. The red-headed Miss Kenmore was an also-ran. I had to do my own makeup sitting in the driver's seat, using the rear-view mirror. The director got the shots he

137

wanted of all of us sitting around the campfire, but when it came to the limbo sequences he was in trouble. Little Miss Blonde whom he'd picked as his leading lady froze up as soon as the cameras got on her. She had trouble getting into the mood. She complained she couldn't hear the music, and when they turned the transistor radio up as loud as it could go, what came in was a news bulletin or some noisy disc jockey chattering away. She and Bob Ames were supposed to snake under the limbo pole; this was the key scene in the commercial. They tried everything, but she couldn't do it. "Just pretend I'm not here," the director was pleading. "Keep dancing and doing things with your body. Just smile and twist and forget all the people around you. There's nobody here but you."

She must have been hanging around with Actors Studio people or something because she was carrying on as if she were Duse. "Maybe a little jolt of wine would loosen her up," one of the crew suggested. So a couple of us girls took her into the bus and began pouring wine down her gullet.

Our makeup was getting gooky from the sea spray, and our hair was beginning to look like great globs of glue. We wanted to get it over with and get out of there. The wine seemed to do the trick. By the time we brought her back to the director, she was all giggly and girly. She was playful and abandoned, throwing sand around and ready to dance around the fire nude. The director quickly got us all in place. Bob Ames took her by the hand to help her snake under the limbo poles. The cameraman had everything set to bring out the natural line of her Maidenform bra when she suddenly announced she was dizzy and would have to lie down. Somebody grabbed my coat and huddled her into it. At that point she announced she was going to be sick. I put my arm around her as if I were a visiting nurse, then I took my coat and got back on the bus. The director had picked his little star. Now let him cope with her.

"Where do they get them from?" the extras were complaining. "The more trouble they cause, the more work they get."

"What kind of pills is she on?" someone else wanted to know.

Finally the director had no choice. He had wasted a full hour trying to get one simple shot of Little Miss Upchuck pushing her Maidenform bra under the limbo pole. He had to give someone else a chance. He put another girl and me through the paces; we snaked through under the

limbo pole, and in ten minutes the whole stupid commercial was
wrapped up, the crew began breaking up the set, and the rest of us were
back on that mangy bus.

Little Miss Upchuck played Camille all the way back to town. But as
soon as the Manhattan air hit her, she came suddenly back to life.
When Bob Ames offered to drop a couple of us girls off in midtown on
his way home to New Jersey, she suddenly crashed the party. That was
a jinx right there. When we unloaded, Bob went to get his car in the
parking lot next to the studio. It now was 3 A.M. The parking lot had
closed and the keys to his car had been impounded. He was in a swivet
because he had to get home and back to Manhattan by eight the next
morning because he had another booking.

"I feel terrible," said Little Miss Upchuck. "I feel it's all my fault.
You can stay at my place."

"Thanks very much," he said gallantly, "but I have someone I can
call. Let's all go have some coffee."

She couldn't take the hint. We found a joint open on Third Avenue. I
was tired and I wanted to retire from this little group but Bob wouldn't
let me. He hung on to me for dear life as if I were the Scoutmaster and
he were a Cub.

Little Miss Upchuck was only about seventeen, and she was acting
like one of those little groupies that follow rock 'n' roll groups around,
swooning and going limp in their hotel lobbies. She was all over Bob.
She knew she was irresistible, and she couldn't understand what was
taking all this time. She was ready for the scene.

Bob made what I guessed was a dummy phone call, and then said to
me sotto voce, "I don't want to take this on. Haven't you got a couch at
your place?"

"Sure," I said. "And I have a roommate, too. Shall I tell the blonde or
will you tell her?"

So we broke it to her gently and somehow got her into a cab.

"You don't know what I went through," Bob said when her cab had
disappeared. She had been after him from the instant the director
paired them off together. The entire drama on location had been her
idea of making herself sexy and alluring.

"Where do they get them from?" he wanted to know.

It was three-thirty in the morning. I knew I was from Vermont, but
that's about all I did know. So I took him back to the apartment with

me, and he was deliriously happy when he saw the living room sofa and I threw him a blanket. We both collapsed. He had a booking at 8 A.M. and my roommate had to get up before seven in order to start judo exercises with her class at P.S. 183 in Oceanhill-Brownsville.

The next morning I found a thank-you note from him on top of the john in the bathroom. Bob was a wonderful guy to work with and one of the nicest gentlemen in the business. It was just my luck that I never ran into him again.

Every picture has a life of its own. Whenever you do a test session, you may put one or two of the best ones in your portfolio, but the others go their own way, and where they end up you'd be surprised. One day in the mail I got a check from a photographer I'd done a test session for months before. His agent had presented some of the results to a big company that publishes oodles of magazines. You send back the release form and you get your money, and then weeks later you may find your old face staring at you from a newsstand on the cover of *True Love.*

Dell Publishing Company publishes piles of magazines, and they are constantly casting and shooting and looking for faces that look like new faces. They sent for me one day and wanted me to do a whole series of shots in a black leotard for an exercise book. But exclusivity reared its ugly head. I was always being tagged as the athletic type, and I had already done about 150 shots for the official exercise book for women of the President's Council on Physical Fitness published by Simon & Schuster. That was still around, with President Johnson on the back cover and me on the front. So that was the end of that particular bright idea. But Dell has a number of art directors. I had already done many shots for their hairdo magazine, and now they sent me into another department. The art director looked at my book and then sent me over to Carnegie Hall. In the Carnegie Hall Studio Building there happens to be a nest of photographers who specialize in book covers and record jacket photos. I had already done half a dozen paperback book covers for the photographer Morgan Kane—I wore a tight green dress and piles of red hair for a book about Las Vegas; I once posed in a filmy negligee in an African safari setting, and I did a cover for one of the nurse novels, *Nurse on Trial,* wearing a tight white uniform. I was ready for more of the same.

140

The photographer they sent me to was a marvelously funny little Italian man called Vincent with a multisyllabic last name.

"I got something coming up you'd be great for," Vincent said after he took a gander at my book. "It'll be a two-shot—a girl and a guy. You'll be wearing some kind of negligee. I'll pick one up tomorrow. I got an idea what kind I want. I'll call your agency and give them the time."

Next morning when I arrived at Vincent's, he had a black velvet backdrop set up and in the middle of the studio was this rumpled double bed. Vincent worked like a house afire. He introduced me to the male model and then he threw me this slinky negligee. When I'd put it on, combed out my hair, touched up my makeup, and gotten back on the set, the male model was stripped to the waist. He practically couldn't talk—he was so busy holding his stomach in. "We had another coupla kids in this bed already this morning," Vincent boasted as he adjusted his lights and began rumpling the sheets.

The art director and the photographer went into a huddle. The scenario called for me to be an aggressive type trying to get this man into the sheets with her. They tried me lying down and grabbing at him, but there was nothing for me to tug on but his watchband. So they put his shirt back on and tried me clawing at that. That didn't seem to work, so finally they had Joe standing looking off into the distance. I knelt on the bed with my negligee slipping off my shoulders while I yanked at his arm. Vincent had no time for mood music. He was too busy saving time and cutting corners. When he got the positions he wanted, he worked on getting the right facial expressions. We were acting without a script. I didn't have the slightest idea who I was or what I was supposed to be thinking. Vincent knew what he wanted, and when he got it he was sure it was right.

That was just the beginning. Tomorrow he wanted to take me on location. He booked me to meet him on the ten o'clock train to Newark. He told me to bring along my tote bag and carry a coat. The trick to this sort of location job is to choose an hour when the commuters are out of the way. If a stranger walks into the shot, it means the photographer has to pay him for signing a release and that throws the budget out of kilter. Vincent took several shots on the train, but they didn't work, so he decided to get a sad and lonely shot of me standing alone on the platform. He liked that one so well that he

141

booked me for two other location jobs. He rented a sports car, and we went to Long Island, where he took some shots of my boyfriend trying to murder me by running over me in his Porsche. Then one afternoon he took me and another girl model to a hotel he used for location jobs. This time we had to furnish our own wardrobes. I had to have a tight-fitting slinky dress on. She played the little wife from the suburbs in a Peck & Peck suit. Vincent wanted a shot of her walking in on me and catching me with her husband. Vincent used me so many times within the next few weeks that I was swiftly burned up as far as the romance magazines were concerned. I never bothered to look at any of the pictures. They were not the kind of things you display in your portfolio. It's just a quick way to make money while you're struggling for the rent every month.

A few weeks later I got a call from my sister Elinor, all excited.

"Carolyn," she said, "I found a story about you in *Modern Romances*. We're sure it's you. Isn't it?"

"I don't know. I haven't seen it."

"You haven't *seen* it? It's a huge picture of you in this sexy nightgown with this half-naked man. It's very dramatic."

I tried to explain to her that it was just another modeling job. Vincent had taken so many pictures that I had no idea which one she was talking about.

"You *know*," said Elinor. "'A Pill Made My Husband Frigid and Almost Wrecked Our Marriage.'"

In those days an extra in a TV commercial got a flat $37.50 a day. The advertising agencies which did the casting never paid any ten percent commissions to the talent agencies. The bookkeeping would cost them more than the $3.75 commission. So they kept a master list of various types and did their casting direct. Once you have been interviewed at an ad agency for a part as a principal, they usually put your name on one of the extra lists automatically. Whenever they needed bodies, they would call you. If you happened to need $37.50, you would be happy they did. But after playing extra three or four times, I saw how easy it would be to get permanently cast in extra roles. It could become just another rut. So when the casting ladies from the ad agencies would call me, no matter how badly I needed that $37.50, I would say no.

There is another kind of role in the hierarchy of the nobodies in TV commercials. This is called a "product extra." Recognizability in the final commercial is what makes you a principal. Extras are unrecognizable and part of the scenery. In TV, as in movies, bodies are cheaper than union-painted scenery or rented props. The product extra is someone—no matter how unrecognizable—who gets to touch the product in the course of a TV commercial. This entitles you to what is called a buy-out and is worth between $150 and $200 a day. A special bit of business, like caressing a bottle of shampoo, making love to a bar of soap, or getting to touch a glass of beer—this makes you a product extra. So I drew a line for myself. I would do product extra roles, but I wouldn't do straight extra. And I was holding out for principal parts in the commercials. That's where the money and the prestige and the residuals are. Unless the talent agencies assured me the casting call was for a principal role, I would refuse to go to the advertising agency to be looked over.

Advertisers and their clients have a dream-image of the kind of people they want publicly associated with their products. They decide what girls should go steady with what boys; they decide what visual types should be married, how many children they should have, and then they proceed to find the children, the aunts and uncles, the cousins, and the grandparents. So casting for couples is more complicated and tricky than casting for a bunch of pretty girls. The talent agency sends over a raft of pictures to the advertising agency. The casting people scramble them around and try to decide who looks as if they would be married to whom. Then the likely couples are assembled live for the final rituals of matchmaking.

One day I got a call giving me the glad news that I had been picked for a principal role in a Schlitz beer commercial. I was to be one of the young marrieds from suburbia who go bowling together every Tuesday evening. It would be a simple deal, no script, no lines, just look pretty and swoon over the beer. The final matchmaking would take place the next afternoon at four o'clock at the studios of Wylde Films. Naturally I was terribly excited. There seemed to be only one final hurdle between me and some residuals.

It is never quite as simple as the agency tells you, however. When I got to the studio the next afternoon, there were at least five girls there and six or seven men. After we signed in, we were paired off and were ushered into the inner sanctum in twos. Nobody ever tells you anything, and what they do tell you is subject to instant change without notice. So you are still playing Madison Avenue roulette right down to the last moment. The girls all seemed to be in their twenties, but the men ranged in age from twenty-five to forty. Some girls were paired off with more mature men—slightly tanned and graying at the temples. They paired me off with a young man I'd never met before—one of the youngest-looking chaps in the place. From this you get the message that they are trying to spread the appeal of Schlitz beer to cover the generation gap. Just when I was about to feel secure about being cast young, they surprised me by sending me back into the inner sanctum with a gray-haired man to see how I looked as an older man's darling. After an hour of milling around, everybody says thank you very much, and you leave without knowing whether you're in or out.

Everything is definitely tentative. It always takes a telephone call to put you out of your misery.

"You made it, Carolyn baby," the agent chanted. "They picked two couples, and you're the young one." The residuals were so close I could taste them.

The logistics involved in this simple little commercial were too stupendous to be believed. A huge bus left New York at seven o'clock in the morning so the entire cast could be in place and ready to shoot when the agency people and the client arrived at nine. In addition to the two principal couples, there were a dozen extras. Every model carried enough luggage for a trip to Bermuda. They told us to bring along extras of everything—skirts and blouses, sports clothes and low-heeled shoes. Some of the extras brought along carryalls so they would look like principals. The wardrobe lady brought along a couple of huge valises. The makeup man had all his paraphernalia. There were two hairdressers with all their impedimenta. The cameras and the crew of about ten people went out ahead of the players to set things up.

We unloaded at this huge bowling alley in New Jersey, and the hairdressers and the makeup men went to work. This was the first time I had really been fussed over and treated like a star. The wardrobe lady brooded over my neckline; the hairdresser tried on all my hair and half of his before deciding on one particular hairdo. Every hair was in place by nine o'clock when the director began to give us our places.

It turned out the real star of the commercial was a man who hadn't even been on the bus at all. He was a champion bowler who was going to do some fancy turns. Our job was to "oh" and "ah" and come alive with astonishment in some stunning reaction shots. The director placed the other couple first. The man was about thirty-five and the girl was done up to look like his wife. The director indicated the place for us—right behind them, on another banquette.

"Carolyn and John, I want you right in there," he said, indicating the place where the lights were hottest and directly in camera range.

The extras were milling around, standing on one foot and then another, upstaging one another like mad, maneuvering to catch the director's eye, hoping to get close enough to the product so they might touch it. That little old bottle of beer was like the Holy Grail. Touching it while cameras were turning was worth a hundred bucks. So all the apparently innocent and aimless maneuvering and meandering had a meaning all its own. But the director is always as aware of his budget as the extras are. His job is to make sure that accidents don't happen. I always figured that if he wants a glass of beer in your hand he's going to put it there. If he doesn't want a glass of beer in your hand, he's going to remove it—even if you were desperate enough to sleep with the propman the night before.

Finally all the principals and the extras were in place. The cameraman measured our distance from the camera with tapes; the lighting was adjusted, and the director gave us the action. Andy, the bowling champion, threw a couple of zingers down the alley, and we exploded with admiration.

At that point the client arrived with the art director and an entire entourage. The director went into a huddle with them, so he gave everybody a ten-minute break. The hairdresser began fussing over me. The makeup man checked the tip of my nose. It began to look as though I would appear in profile in the principal shot, so he had to keep my nose properly dusted—not too matte, not too shiny. Then the director gave us the signal, and we took our places again. Andy, the star bowler, was in place, waiting for his cue to toss another zinger. He waited and we waited. Finally the director spoke up. "Carolyn and John, I want you to change places with Ellen and Raymond."

Change places! After spending a full hour getting us in place, now they were going to change things. And who were Ellen and Raymond? That wasn't the other principal couple. Those weren't their names at all. Well, John got up. When the director barks, you move. I got up with him. The lights were so blinding we couldn't see what was going on until we moved. As we moved out of position, a couple of extras were moved into our spot. Ellen and Raymond were Negroes. I had noticed them on the bus that morning, but no one had introduced us and I didn't know their names.

Being a principal in a beer commercial doesn't take very much acting ability. But getting demoted to an extra in front of an entire cast and crew and pretending convincingly not to care—that takes talent. For the rest of the day I had to do my best acting out of camera range. The residuals had been so close! Now I was back to being one of THEM—the hardy band of extras trying too hard to get to be faces in the crowd.

Television commercials had been 99 44/100 percent lily-white for so long. Anybody who knew anything knew it couldn't go on like that forever. The famous Double Mint twins had already been converted to blackfaces in a new commercial that was showing on TV. But after a hundred years of segregation, why did Schiltz beer have to integrate right in the middle of my first big break? And why did I have to stand there with a silly smile on my face, laughing and applauding while it happened? Now the director was talking softly to Ellen, telling her to smile and move her hands the way he had told me to. Now the makeup man was fussing over her and ignoring me. The hairdresser had worked on my hair for half an hour, but now it didn't matter. Now they had him working on Ellen, too. The lighting men were having fits. The lighting setup that was right for four white people just didn't work right for two people who were beige and two who were dark brown. While this was going on, I had to ask myself all the old questions. How would you like it if your sister married a Negro? That was a silly question. That was my sister's business. Ask them. Everybody in the family was married but me. How would you like it if a Negro family moved into your block? In New York it couldn't possibly matter.

The question nobody ever asked out loud is: How would you like it if you lost your job to a Negro? The only honest answer I could give myself is that I didn't like it at all. It hurt. It really hurt. It wasn't just losing the break I needed to get started. It wasn't just the money. It was all those things and none of them. In college I had never carried any political banners. I had never gone on any of those picketing and marching civil rights junkets into the South trying to tell other people how to behave. The whole question had never really touched me until this very minute. There was something wrong right here. When I looked at Ellen, sitting under the lights where I had just been playing star until an instant ago, I tried to look at it from her point of view. She had probably waited longer for this break than I had. It was probably as embarrassing to her to be put in the front row because she was black as it had been for me to leave it. Once more it wasn't what had been done—it was the way they had done it.

The lunch break gave everybody time to rehash the little real-life drama that had just taken place amid the fakery of commercial TV. John, the male model I had been paired with, was no beginner. He was an established model who had done plenty of principal parts on TV, and he was furious at being reduced to extra status. "Don't worry, Carolyn, nobody will see us the way they have us placed." The extras made things worse by trying to console me, telling me how unfair it had all been. Ordinarily extras and principals keep their distance—even during lunch breaks. Now they were moving in on me. Just to make things worse, Raymond, the male Negro model, started carrying on in the restaurant as if he had just been elected to Congress. He was playing Mr. Irresistible, name-dropping all over the place, telling us all the shows he had done as an actor, and making it very clear he rarely condescended to do a TV commercial. "Who needs it?" was his whole attitude. Poor Ellen was left to herself, like a new girl in town.

New York looked pretty grim to me on that gruesome bus ride back to town. I knew the model racket was a tough nut to crack at any time. Today I had learned something new. There were going to be a lot of jobs around that I wasn't going to get because I wasn't the right color. When you're out of Schlitz, as the commercial says, you're out of beer. And I was out—definitely. I told the agency what had happened, and they arranged for me to get paid as a principal. But you can't put a canceled check in your portfolio. That doesn't impress anybody.

"Hey, Carolyn, Rheingold is casting girls for an Irish commercial, so I thought I'd give you a tinkle. You're Irish, aren't you?"
Irish is practically the only thing I knew for sure I'm not. I'm

Hungarian, French, English, maybe a little Indian, but I had learned to say yes to everything. "Well, I'm not completely Irish," I replied, which was true enough.

The sweet man who called me had one of those voices that melts margarine. He did narrations for oodles of commercials. I had met him when I was an extra on the first commercial I'd ever done. He liked me and was always trying to help.

"Never mind," he said. "With your red hair I think you've got a chance. Write down the name of this agent who's handling it. Tell him I sent you. Tell him you're Irish, and let me know what happens."

Miss Rheingold was dead, and the big New York beer company was off on a new ethnic kick. One commercial was pitched at the Italians; another at the Arabs; another at the Germans, and so on, and the tag was, "We must be doing something right."

Hanns Wolters, the agent my friend John sent me to, had the job of digging up photogenic Italian grandmas, Arabian belly dancers, and Irish colleens. Hanns took one look at my red hair and sent me over to Doyle, Dane, Bernbach, which handled the Rheingold account. There were a dozen girls in the office milling around. When I signed the register, I began to think Kenmore didn't look very impressive after the Murphys and the O'Tooles and the Doyles and the O'Malleys. What if it was a speaking part they wanted me for and they expected me to give it the old Blarney? Well, I thought, I'd better ask. If they gave me a script, I could look at it, and if they were looking for brogues, I could beat a fast retreat. I was in no mood to be unmasked as a fraud.

"Is there a script?" I asked the girl with the clipboard.

"No, this is just a preliminary," she said, whatever *that* meant. Before I had time to figure it out, they ushered me into a room where three men sat behind a table. One looked through my book. One looked through me, and the third one began firing questions.

"Kenmore," he said. "Were you born in Ireland?"

"No, sir," I said. "I'm second generation."

"What part of Ireland did your parents come from?" he snapped.

Suddenly I couldn't think of the name of a single spot in the old sod. Oh, yes, I could!

"Dublin," I said.

One more question and I would have been dead. That one word seemed like the biggest lie I had ever told in my life. I was so tense I could feel perspiration running down my back. Now I noticed the man was writing something on a sheet of paper. He turned it around, pointed to a blank space at the bottom, and handed me a pen. Oh, Lord, it's probably a legal affidavit, I thought. If they make me sign anything, I'll put down Grandma Kenmore as my mother. At least she came from the Isle of Man. I'll put down her phone number in Middlebury, and if I telephone her beforehand, maybe she'll have time enough to practice an Irish brogue. She has a beautiful operatic voice—I'll tell her if she gets a long-distance call to break into a couple of choruses of "Mother Machree." If I get through this one, I'll never drink anything but Rheingold as long as I live, as a penance for telling such a big fib.

I didn't even look at the paper. I just closed my eyes and signed so afterward I'd be telling the truth when I said I hadn't read it.

"Will you be available next week for shooting?" the man asked.

Next week was an absolute yawning blank.

"I'm sure I can fit it in," I said grandly.

"Thank you very much," he said, and I trotted out.

The very next afternoon Hanns called to say, "You got it, you got it!" He was much happier than I was. It seemed awful to me that the first real lie I had ever told in this business was about to pay off. I'd probably be punished by being typecast as an Irish colleen. I knew there was no future in that.

Hanns told me where to report and when. I thought eleven o'clock was rather late to start shooting a commercial, but he assured me that experience had shown they couldn't develop the proper convivial spirit until the actors got a chance to taste the product, and not everybody can start drinking beer right after breakfast.

"Got any green dresses?" Hanns asked.

"Show me a redhead who doesn't," I said.

"That's a good girl. Bring all of them," said Hanns.

Some of the extras seemed to know there would be free beer aplenty, for when I got to this huge colorful old bar uptown on the East Side, it was packed and the Rheingold was flowing. The Irish music was going a mile a minute, and everybody was feeding me beer. The producer liked the first dress I tried on. The other principals made me feel like a real foreigner. They all had brogues so thick I could barely understand them. When they asked me where I was from, I couldn't say anything else but Dublin. The director showed us our places and introduced various members of the family. Grandpa and Grandma were going back to Ireland on a holiday, and the entire clan had gathered to give them a send-off bash. I was the granddaughter. All the drinking had to be done off camera—the director made a big point of that. While the camera is on you, you can touch the beer glass, you can hold it up in a toast, you can get your mouth set to wrap around it, but actual imbibing is not permitted by FCC regulations. Everybody agrees that this is insane, of course, but it's a remnant of Prohibition. At least that meant it would save wear and tear on my makeup. I wouldn't constantly have to be running to the makeshift dressing room to make repairs and check to see that there was no foam on my foundation. I smiled most of the afternoon until the director finally got what he wanted and they wrapped it up. The party was still going strong when I left.

I was so excited I called David, and he came in to pick me up. We were going out on the town to celebrate my principal part in a big TV commercial. Sure, it wasn't a national one. Most beer things are regional and shown only in the area where the beer is marketed. But the next time some bull dike lady told me I looked like a homewrecker I had the evidence that somebody at least had cast me for a sweet fake little Irish colleen. With the luck of the Irish still upon us, David decided to take me to the famous P. J. Clarke's bar on Third Avenue. When we walked in, the bartender greeted me like a celebrity. "Well," he said, "if it isn't our sweet little Irish colleen!" Then I tumbled. Phil had played bartender at the Rheingold party that afternoon.

Everybody in Middlebury, Vermont, saw me in that commercial because they ran it between innings at the Mets games. Nobody ever twitted me about passing for Irish. They didn't believe any of it for a minute. They just thought I was an actress playing a part. If I could fool the big-city-slicker ad men, it was something to Middlebury's credit. Nobody really takes commercials as seriously as the people who make them.

A strange name, an unfamiliar telephone number. When I rang my answering service at the end of a rush-rush day and got one of those, it was like a mysterious surprise package, gorgeously gift-wrapped. I couldn't wait to find out what was in it for me. I was at *that* stage.

"Joe Perle wants to see you sometime tomorrow, Miss Kenmore."

Joe Perle. Joe Perle? The name seemed to ring some kind of bell, but I couldn't find him in any of my directories. I tried looking in *The Madison Avenue Handbook,* but it was absolutely no sale. I finally found him in the telephone book with an office listing on Madison Avenue. Before I called him back, I talked to Woody at the answering service.

"Of course I've heard of him, sweetie. He's a big agent, very big for films and TV. If he heard about you and called you cold, that could only be marvelous. Squeeze him in for a quick go-see."

I tried to be cool when I called him back. I was panting with curiosity. So I tried to act weary.

"Tomorrow looks like an absolute hell day, Mr. Perle. May I call you in the morning if I find some free time?"

"I would strongly advise that you do that there," said Mr. Perle.

"That there?" I'd never heard anybody say "that there" in all my months in New York. He must be powerful if he dared to talk like that. He could be an absolute illiterate, or it could be some new groovy way of talking I wasn't into yet.

"All right. I'll definitely call you tomorrow, Mr. Perle."

"If you're that busy, maybe I could give you a ting-a-ling at the end of the day." That sounded to me like the beginning of an end run to ask for my home telephone number. I wasn't giving anyone my home number, so I fenced. "No matter what happens, I'll give you a ring early tomorrow," I promised.

Next morning I woke up scheming. I was going to arrange the confrontation with Mr. Perle, that was for sure. The only question was what should I wear. I wondered what I had been featuring when he had spotted me and where. Should I come in tall, centrifugal, and breathless, with hair flying in all directions and chains clanking and pants sweeping the floor, or should I pull myself together and be tucked in, grand and serene? If I was going to be serene, I'd have to rush by before lunch. If I only knew which pictures he'd seen, if I could only guess which Carolyn he *expected,* I could work against it and come in doing another number. At least change my hair. Change your act or back to the woods!

Carolyn, quit doing your Miss Hamlet thing. You've got miles of red hair, stick out your endlessly long neck, flare both nostrils in your stubby nose, bat your fringed eyes, shut your kissy mouth, and rely on your fabulous bones. Wear the first thing that comes into your head and then forget about it. He called you. He wants what he saw somewhere. You're not selling—you're *buying.*

"Mr. Perle," I panted, "I'll drop by at two-thirty."

I couldn't believe there were any walk-ups left in that classy block on Madison Avenue where Mr. Perle had his office. But there it was, and a tiny card on the bell said one flight up. After schlepping my portfolio and my tote bag since 10 A.M., I found it hard to be carefree about climbing those stairs. Constantly I had to remind myself that my tote bag weighed a ton. I kept switching it from the right arm to the left. One set of biceps I didn't need.

His name was on the door in small, dignified letters. Something told me to knock. There was no use making a flashy entrance with hair flying and wasting the entire effect on some glassy-eyed receptionist. So I knocked.

"Come on in," someone shouted. I was sure it was his voice. "The door's opened," he hollered. I walked in.

Indirect lighting is all very nice, but the place was dark as a tunnel. The dirty Venetian blinds let in thin slits of sunlight. The man hugging the telephone behind the huge desk was fat and bald. Yesterday one could say he needed a shave. Today one could only guess that he was thinking of growing a beard. Sideburns anyway.

"Mr. Perle, I'm Carolyn Kenmore."

He clamped one fat fist over the phone and said, "Have a seat. I been anxious to meet you." I squatted on one of the wooden chairs near his desk and leaned my heavy leather portfolio against the dingy green sofa.

"Yeah. Yeah, yeah," he kept growling into the phone.

A coffee table was piled with old issues of *Vogue* and *Harper's Bazaar.* Piles of models' composites were strewn across the sofa. Glossy pictures of models in every conceivable pose were piled on his desk. On the wall were some very sultry ladies, pouting the way models used to in the late fifties, with dark lipstick looking as though it had been applied with a soup spoon. Some of them looked vaguely familiar. Most of them were autographed with a flourish, "To Joe." If I were a cleaning woman, I wouldn't know where to begin. The rug looked as though it hadn't been cleaned since World War II. You could write your name in the dust on the antique black leather tufted sofa. As my eyes adjusted to the darkness, I could see that Mr. Perle had many chins. He was even bald on the back of his neck. The only coverage he had was a thin strip that dipped under the back of his skull, between the ears. That was coal-black. His new sideburns were show-white. "Does he or doesn't he?" was hardly the question.

Suddenly he slammed down the phone and picked up my portfolio. He began turning the cellophane pages like a symphony conductor directing an overture at Lincoln Center. Then he let out little grunts and groans of what I took to be appreciation.

"This here one's a gas," he grunted. "Who done it?"

When I mentioned the famous photographer's name, Mr. Perle exploded with what I took to be indignation.

"This here girl I handle told me he shoots models in the nude."

"If he didn't, he wouldn't be working," I laughed. "Everything is nudity these days. *Vogue* is getting to look more like *Playboy* every issue. Haven't you noticed?"

"Nah, I don't mean that there," said Mr. Perle. "I mean I heard when he shoots pictures, *he* don't wear nothing, neither."

I tried to look surprised. "I never heard that," I smiled. "Maybe I haven't been around long enough to be taken into his confidence."

"You're a cool one, Carolyn," he said. "I like that."

I wasn't going to tell HIM I knew what everybody knew—that this photographer *does* have a thing about wearing nothing but his boots and his beard and his love beads sometimes when he is searching for the moment of truth with his lens. He likes to think he sets models aflame with the sudden sight of his bare body. I had heard about it, true. I had also seen it when he tried it on me. It was as much a legend of the modeling business as Dean Martin's drinking was on TV or the frieze of nude hippies in the first act curtain of *Hair*.

Mr. Perle finally put down my portfolio and leaned across his desk. He dropped names all over the place and sputtered out in great detail little stories of top models he handled and how he had spotted them in lucrative TV commercials and wangled contracts for them to do their first films.

"You got a great thing going for you, Carolyn. But you can't do print work forever, and it's time now you should be making the move toward films."

"I've already done one film, Mr. Perle," I reminded him.

"And you didn't get a contract out of it?"

"It hasn't been released yet, as far as I know."

"Look here, Carolyn," he lectured me. "Before I go any further with you, I want to make one thing clear. You know what this business is all about, don't you? You gotta swing. You can't wait around until a film is released. Who you gonna swing with then—the film critic of *The New York Times*? She's a woman, fer chrissakes. The girls I represent are up for lead parts, and they only have to take care of one guy. Nothing done on speculation. Absolutely none of that. You got a signed deal for the job before you ball anyone. I don't believe in all this running around in public, this here dating and dinners and trips. It's all a waste of time. You get marked lousy and the guy runs risks they don't write insurance for, and for what? I'm here to make sure my girls don't waste their time. A beautiful girl needs to do certain things to get ahead in this world. But she can't afford to waste a lot of time doing it to the wrong people, you know what I mean? That's why she needs adequate representation."

Finally he stopped his intense recital and waited for me to say something. I guess I was shocked to find I wasn't shocked. In an office like that from a man like that, what could you expect? I looked at the pictures on the wall. I reacted to the names of the models he mentioned. Did they or didn't they? Dear Doris Day, did you have to or didn't you? He was waiting for me to react.

Finally I said, "Yes, Mr. Perle, I know what the business is all about. It's no big secret."

"Call me Joe," he said, leaning across his desk again.

"But the girls don't always get the parts. They end up at the bottom of the heap instead of the top. I've seen it happen."

His bloated body began squirming in the high-backed chair. Maybe he thought he had a live one.

"Look, honey," he replied. "I hope you haven't got any problems. About sex, I mean. I hope you haven't got any hang-ups. If you don't, you got it made. You got the looks and the know-how to make it big. All you need is a little direction. I can help you there. But you gotta do what I suggest. I'll never lead you astray, and I can save you from having to put out to every assistant director and guys like that there. . . . How about it?"

I had drawn him out this far. I was going to see it through.

"No, Mr. Perle, I don't think I have any hang-ups as far as sex is concerned...."

"Well, then," he said, "it would be a pleasure to handle you. I could get you started tomorrow."

"Tomorrow?" I said. "You see I already have an agency representing me, and this is something I'd have to think about. It's not something I could rush into overnight."

"What's to think about? I'm not asking you to sign any *paper*. We can have a handshake deal. I sent plenty of girls on their way with nothing but a handshake.... I'm not one for papers and lawyers and things like that there. There's just one thing I have to make sure about. This hang-up thing. Right at the beginning, in order so's I know what kind of an impression a girl is going to make on an important man I'm sending her to, I make it a policy of making it with every client. Only once, right at the beginning. We do it, we ball together, get it over with, and never mention it again. I feel it's important in order to have a close and swinging relationship, businesswise."

Jeepers creepers, is this really the way it is? Is Joe Perle the name of the game? I'd have to study at the Actors Studio for at least five years before I could let him touch me. If THIS is the way to fame and fortune, movies and TV, it's a fate worse than debt.

"Well, what do you say?" said Mr. Perle, his dirty, chubby hand fingering my photograph. "Ya got ten minutes?"

Ten minutes? I had blown my cool. I knew it showed. I wanted to laugh at myself, but I was afraid I'd throw up. "I—just can't," I stammered, knowing I had said the wrong thing, but I couldn't help it.

"What do you mean, you *can't*?" he exploded belligerently.

I began to mumble about my inability to fit it into my schedule. I improvised a routine about being due on Park Avenue South for a shooting in twenty minutes. I heard myself saying I didn't have enough time, as if that were the issue. TEN MINUTES. I hated myself for being afraid to offend him, and I tried to think of a way out of there. "Anyway, I can't," I said finally.

"What do you mean, you can't?" Joe said defiantly. "Is there something physically *wrong* with you, fer chrissakes?"

Unbelievable as it was, the vanity of Mr. Joe Perle gave me my clue. I always knew men were vainer than women. But this was vanity in spades.

"Yes, Mr. Perle, you see my doctor said to be really safe I shouldn't . . . at least not until I've had a final examination. . . ." I tried to imagine how Julie Andrews would demurely break the news that she had an unmentionable social disease, and I hoped this big bloated horror would be vain enough to believe me.

"Oh, well, fer chrissakes," said Mr. Perle, "in that case we'll have to take this up later. Tell your doctor I hope he gets you straight pretty soon. This can slow you up considerably. I can't send you out for the big stuff until he gives us the all-clear, now can I?"

I shook my head like Mary Poppins and wished I could fly out of there. I reached for my portfolio. Maybe I should send it to the cleaner's.

Joe Perle stood up and reached for my hand. A handshake I took to mean no hard feelings. Maybe I could send my whole outfit to the cleaner's.

If my daddy could see me now, Madison Avenue would soon look like Nagasaki. If the Great Rinaldo had chased one New York date into the Vermont woods for buying his daughter a hamburger, what would he do with a grubby pimp like this one?

I had to smile when I thought of it. As I drew back my hand, it seemed Mr. Perle was standing in a hole or something. He was at least six inches shorter than I was, which added up to a bare five feet two. He probably stayed behind the desk so nobody could get a look at his spike heels.

"Give me a call when your doctor gives you the all-clear, Carolyn," Joe shouted as I beat my retreat.

Sure, sure, Mr. Perle. Doomsday plus two.

While I was passing for an Irish Miss Rheingold on Channel 2, I got the news that I was being paged to play an Indian maiden like Minnehaha. The more faces you have in this business, the further you can go and the longer you can last. The more range and variety you can show in the portfolio you peddle, the wider the net you can cast for jobs. If you get typecast too much too soon, they use you up. This is a big trap for beginners.

The agency called to say that they had been asked to send over pictures of girls who could pass for Indians, and out of the eighteen sent over, the only girl the client asked to see in person was Kenmore.

This was before the hippies went into buskin, beads, and headbands and made them a new fashion. I couldn't wait to look at myself. It had never occurred to me to think I could pass as Hiawatha's sister. But maybe there was a little Algonquin in there somewhere from the French-Canadian forebears of the Great Rinaldo. Could be. If they pressed me for my geneology as they had for the Rheingold job, I would trot out my French-Canadian family tree.

Anxiously I took down the details. Mr. Barron was the contact at OED Film Productions. "*Film* productions?" I asked.

"Oh, yes," said the agency calmly. "This is for a part in a new Hollywood movie." I tried to control myself, but the Hollywood fantasy is still so overpowering that in two seconds I had visions of Daddy and Mother walking into Grauman's Chinese Theater with me at the premiere. I tried to concentrate on my address book to get the name and address and the time right, but all I could see were neon lights discreetly saying under the title: INTRODUCING CAROLYN KEN-MORE.

I knew it was bad luck to count on anything even for an instant. I was fighting my fantasies as if they were demons. But how many days could a girl be asked to keep something like this to herself? I decided I would tell no one but David.

The day of the interview I was in torment over what to wear. If they already visualized me as an Indian, there was no need to rub it in. I decided to go for the young-thing look in a casual sweater and skirt. I tied a Saint Laurent scarf around my head in a hundred different ways before I finally settled on one. The French touch was as close as I would come to being suggestive. The part might be an Inca girl or an Aztec princess. After all, Indian was about as specific a word as American.

Mr. Barron was a tall, handsome man, beautifully dressed and distinguished-looking. He was all business, and that was a pleasure. He put me at ease instantly by telling me I looked better than my pictures. He was very straightforward. He told me casting sessions and tests were also being held in California, but he had been asked to test anyone he found in New York who was new and different-looking. He gave me a script but told me not to worry about memorizing lines. For the test we would improvise. It was a quality they were after that was more important than the words.

"How do you feel about horses?" he asked, as if it were an important part of the deal. I was relieved to be able to tell him truthfully that I had been riding since I was knee-high. "That's great because we'll shoot the test with just you and the horse. How about your hair? Do you have any long hair to make into braids?"

All I had was an extra switch, but I was sure I could figure out some way to do it. I knew the boys at the Make-Up Center would rally round. "We'll go out to one of the stables outside New York," Mr. Barron said. "You'll need dark makeup, some braids. Bring along some shirts and levis and a jacket."

This would be my first screen test. It was happening right under my nose, and I still couldn't believe it. Some of my elation must have showed because Mr. Barron reminded me, "This is only a test, you know. The Coast still has the final say. We'll just keep our fingers crossed. I'll be in touch with your agency about the time and location. We should be able to do the whole thing in one day."

That day I needed the full thirty-pound weight of my tote bag and the seven pounds of my portfolio to keep my feet on the ground. I couldn't wait to call David and tell him. Having to get together those braids was a godsend. It gave me something to do with my hands. I dragged out my sad and only auburn switch and tried braiding it fourteen ways. The more I tried the more I looked like a Hungarian yenta rather than a Hopi princess. I read the script, and when I got to the part where the Indian girl was supposed to burst into tears at the loss of her favorite spotted horse, I cried up a storm. I knew I could do it. I called up the Make-Up Center and decided I would splurge and rent the best Indian braids in town for the day. This was no place to save money. I could live on gelatin for a week. Carlo at the Make-Up Center was marvelously helpful. He told me to bring over my switch and they would have one of their girls braid it for me. If it didn't work, they would lend me the best hair they had. I was bursting to tell them how important it was, but I didn't. I'd never forget the people who helped me, I told myself. I'd invite the whole Make-Up Center crew to the premiere.

I bought pots of dark makeup and socked them into my bag. I picked out about six shirts in various shades and all the levis I owned. I had my bag packed for three days before D day finally arrived.

Mr. Barron picked me up at the Make-Up Center. Hazel had done a beautiful job on the braids, weaving them into my hair so that they seemed to be my very own.

We wheeled through the Tunnel into New Jersey—Mr. Barron, the sound man, the cameraman, and myself in a station wagon full of cameras, lights, and other equipment. Mr. Barron told me he had decided to shoot the test himself. I felt I was in good hands.

When we got to this beautiful stable in New Jersey, Mr. Barron introduced me to the horse while the crew was setting up. The horse was a beautiful Appaloosa. He was playing the title role in the picture, anyway. In comparison, mine was a very small part. I caught myself laughing. My first movie break turns out to be a love scene with a horse. I laughed at the thought of my encounter with Joe Perle in his sleazy ratrap office on Madison Avenue. Imagine if some young thing like me had been giddy enough to believe Mr. Perle! Suppose she had a strong enough stomach to ball this hideous little man, and then went on balling everybody he told her to ball, and then when she finally got on the set, the *horse* didn't like her!

They set up a makeshift dressing room for me in the stable. I put my makeup on in the station wagon, using the rear-view mirror. I put on about six layers, but when we got into the noon sunlight it was washed out on camera, so I had to put on even more. The cameras were set up in the ring near the stable. I rode in a circle for several takes. Then they filmed me riding into camera looking sad and woebegone. Then we did one setup in the hills with me riding at a canter, gay and carefree. All this was without sound. Mr. Barron was happy, and I was so happy that I could have played *Peter Pan* without wires. Next came the acid test—two-shots of me and the horse saying a tearful good-bye. We nuzzled each other against a railing, and I made up my own lines as I talked to the horse. Everything went beautifully, but when the tears were supposed to come, nothing happened. I had wept when I heard about the test. I had wept when I first read this scene in the script. Now I was dry-eyed as a prison matron. I tried to think of the most horrible thing that had ever happened to me. I thought of Grandpa Joe dying. I thought of Mr. Brusso, the tailor in Middlebury, jumping off the bridge into Otter Creek. I thought of that horrible sex maniac luring me onto the lumber pile in Frog Alley when I was saved from a fate worse than death by my snow suit suspenders. Then I realized the saddest thing that ever happened in my life was happening this very minute. Hollywood was waiting for me to burst into tears, and I couldn't. I was furious with myself. Absolutely livid.

Mr. Barron was prepared. He took it all very calmly. He took the glycerin out of his pocket and applied it discreetly to the corners of both my eyes with an eyedropper. I had so many layers of makeup on that the horse could have spit on me and I wouldn't have felt a thing. The horse was weeping and nuzzling my chest so affectionately he was making horrible sounds which the microphone hidden inside my jacket was picking up. Mr. Barron was putting more glycerin drops on me but before he could get the camera turning again, the strong sunlight and arc lights dried up my ersatz tears.

Mr. Barron finally shouted at me, wild with pleasure. I was crying because I couldn't cry, but I didn't know what I was doing. I was crying because I thought I was letting Mr. Barron down, and he was shouting with glee because he was catching the real tears with the camera, but I was too numb with frustration and too caked with makeup to feel anything.

We had been working more than four hours when Mr. Barron wrapped it up. When I said good-bye to that darling horse, I was ready to burst into tears again. We had a beautiful lunch, and then we drove back to town. I refused to take off the makeup and the braids. David was coming over right after work, and I wanted him to see me in my Hollywood getup. I was so elated I was floating on little pink clouds. Mr. Barron told me he was going to edit the film that very night and rush it off to the Coast on the earliest possible plane. He promised me that David and I could see it later.

I tried to convince myself that the test had been horrible and I didn't have a chance. I knew it would be at least ten days of *Waiting for Godot,* and I couldn't stand the suspense. I pretended that the whole thing had been a fantasy, but the borrowed braids were too real. I decided to return them to the Make-Up Center as a kind of gesture, evidence that I expected nothing to happen.

After a week Mr. Barron called me to say that the West Coast bigwigs were all on location and hadn't had a chance to screen the test yet. Horrors, the waiting began all over again! David was a darling. He never once asked me if I had heard anything. He knew he would be the second one to know.

Finally a phone call from Mr. Barron took me out of my misery. Even before he said he had bad news for me, I knew. "They loved the test, Carolyn, and they loved you, but they decided on a girl who had just made a big picture with Tony Richardson. The producer asked me to tell you to keep plugging and your chance will come along one day. Honestly he did."

Suddenly I felt sorry for Mr. Barron. He felt worse about it than I did.

"You've got to hang on and keep plugging. The test was terrific. Really."

It wasn't that I didn't believe him. I wanted to see for myself. When I told him so, he arranged a screening and David and I went over alone. I was glad I had the nerve to face it. I felt better afterward. It really was good. I felt everyone had been very honest and aboveboard with me. I was lucky to have been tested at all. Someday the test would pay off.

When you're working in print or testing for commercials, the people are rarely this gentle and considerate. After traipsing to as many as three auditions, you never know. They never tell you anything. Some faceless men somewhere make the decision, and the only one they ever call is the girl who got the job.

A year later when the movie opened, David and I went to see it together. It still had the same title, *The Appaloosa.* Marlon Brando was the star. If they had told me that in the beginning, I could have told them I was too tall for him.

They also used a different horse. My beautiful horse from New Jersey didn't get the job either.

"You're the Rheingold girl, aren't you? You should be a mermaid for us." We were both waiting for the elevator in Rockefeller Center when this sleek-looking older man introduced himself to me and handed me his card. It was right after I had been interviewed on TV between innings of the Mets game as a Rheingold colleen, and for a few days I was a minor celebrity. I was used to being hailed in the street.

His card gave his name and his corporate title with one of the big soap and cosmetic companies, but he had the MC brand all over him—married commuter. I knew he was angling to invite me to lunch. For MCs, lunch seems to be the center of their day. My guess was that he would ask me to stop by his office one day with my book around eleven-thirty. And of course he did. He started showing me sketches and advertising layouts, and he pretended to be looking at my portfolio, but I knew it was all just a game. The important pictures were all on his desk—the wife, the four kids, the swimming pool.

"Don't make me any promises," I told him. "Just give me a little sample bottle of nail polish right now—something I can take home with me."

"I suppose you girls get tired of big grandiose pitches." He laughed. "What are you doing for lunch?"

"I knew you were going to ask me, so I didn't make a date."

He had his secretary call for a table, and we arrived at this swanky restaurant—Brussels—in the East Fifties. He drank too much and talked too much about how unhappy he was, displaying all the classic symptoms of the MC. He was an attractive man with a very smooth manner and fun to be with. But he wasted so much energy trying to give freshness and conviction to the story of his malaise which all came out like lines from a movie. It was a movie I'd seen so many times. But apparently he had never seen it at all. After lunch he wanted to know when he could see me again.

"Do I have to pretend I can advance your career?" he asked.

I told him I had two telephone numbers. If he wanted to book me as a mermaid, he could call the agency. If he had something else in mind, he could call my answering service. I had two other private numbers, but those were not for MCs. When he called my service, I didn't call him back. When he called the agency, I did. He wanted me to have lunch with him again, same fancy restaurant. When I met him he was at the bar.

"I'm a little tired of the people in this place," he said. "I know a quieter place uptown a way." I had a booking at three, and I didn't like to wander too far from midtown, but he promised he would get me to my appointment on time. He had a private taxi waiting—one of those black VIP cars with uniformed chauffeur and two-way radio that wait for you and pick you up by appointment. The chauffeur drove us to a block of houses in the East Seventies near Second Avenue.

"This doesn't look like a restaurant to me," I said.

"It isn't. It's a sort of private club." He seemed to enjoy watching me watch the mystery unfold. We got off the elevator, and he opened the door with his own key. It was only a two-room apartment, but it was a veritable married commuter's dream. The hi-fi was playing softly. A table was set for two with the wine out and the bar ready. A little Chinese in a beige Mao jacket took my coat and started mixing martinis.

"Did you borrow this from a friend, is it yours, or is this one of the fringe benefits you get from the company?" I asked him.

"It's all mine. Do I have to pretend I work here?" he asked me.

"Certainly not," I replied.

"It's my funch place," he said.

"Funch?"

"Brunch is a breakfast and lunch combined. Well, funch is.... come on, let's dance."

Jerry confessed he was thrashing around on the loose these days because a long-standing extramarital affair he had been having had just broken up.

"What happened?" I asked him.

"She got a divorce," he said. That's the way MCs are. They like to play in their own league. Once a lady is free even to *think* about getting married, it's all over for an MC. I knew his Chinese servant would never intrude with the won ton soup as long as we were dancing, so I broke that up, pretending to be starved.

"When I first came to Manhattan, I stayed with three girls in the village who had less space than you have. And you don't use it for anything but funches. No wonder there's such an apartment shortage in New York," I complained.

"I have a set of keys for you any time you want them," Jerry replied.

"Do I have to pretend I'd be good for you?"

We had a great Chinese lunch, and he got me to my booking as he'd promised. He never quit calling me. Every month, as regular as a gas bill, I would get a message from Jerry inviting me up for funch. On my first jaunt I got wise to the life style of married commuters. Not anymore.

# CHAPTER 7

In the beginning I was naïve enough to think I needed an agency in order to get the top jobs and make the big money. I discovered the hard way that sometimes you have to get the jobs and make the money before you can get an agency to condescend to represent you.

I had done a lot of very good jobs. I had a good portfolio built up to prove it. Still, I was having better luck with the casting people direct than I was having with the high-powered ladies who run the big model agencies. It was the art director at Grey Advertising who suggested, "Why don't you go see Willy?"

Wilhelmina had been a top model herself, and she had recently retired and opened her own office. She was one of the first foreign models to make it big over here in the late fifties and early sixties. She had come from Germany via Chicago and had the usual reputation for being very thorough and a good businesswoman.

"One of her bookers keeps calling me all the time wanting to send me girls," the art director said. "I'll call her and ask her to make an appointment for you." I was delighted that he liked my work enough to want to go out of his way to help me. I talked to Wilhelmina's office and made the appointment for late in the afternoon.

Wilhelmina had a very smart office on Madison Avenue in the Fifties. Stephanie, the booker, looked me over first. Then she took my book into the inner sanctum. It's always the portfolio they look at first. They want to see you on film first, then live.

Honestly, I wasn't expecting anything much to happen. I was having more luck with men than with women. The art director at Grey Advertising was too important for them to be anything but nice. For all they knew, I might be somebody special in his life. I expected them to be very cordial and polite, and then after about three weeks I would still be wondering what the upshot would be.

Now Wilhelmina wanted to see me. She was not what I'd expected at all. I had seen many of her pictures. I noticed she didn't keep any old ones around the office.

She was very tall, very thin, with fabulous bones. Not pretty— elegant. With her hair skinned back tight, her face was scattered with cold sores. Everyone has off days, and this was hers. She was very conscious of these blemishes and explained immediately that her dermatologist was on his way up to look at them and she expected him any minute.

"You have a very nice book," she began. I was tired of hearing that, and wanted to say so what, but there was something about her that was very nice and extremely sweet. I felt no hostility at all from her as I had felt from many ladies. She didn't treat me as if I reminded her of someone who had stolen her boyfriend. She didn't nag me about looking like the "other woman." She seemed like a real pro. At the same time she made me feel comfortable. She could have been cold-blooded and haughty like Eileen Ford and some of the others. But she wasn't. She was simple and direct.

"I want you to meet my husband," she said suddenly.

"What have we here?" Bruce, Wilhelmina's husband, asked as he began flipping through my portfolio. It is one mark of people who are new in the business— expecially men—that they insist on talking about you as if you were a filet mignon on a plate.

"Not bad in the looks department," he started. "She might be good for lingerie. If we use you in lingerie, you'll have to knock off a few pounds, though. It's a nice face and the makeup is good, but we'll have to do something with that hair. Before we do anything drastic, we'll get a few more test shots to beef up your book. That will give us some idea of which way to move. Have you met Dovima and Camilla?"

I didn't know whether they were products or clients or what. My blank look must have told him so—he volunteered to introduce me to their two cohorts. Dovima was a staggeringly beautiful woman—dark hair, fantastic figure, and an indefinable aura of glamour about her. She had been one of the top models of all time, but I was too stupid to have known her by name. Camilla was not the ex-model type at all. She wore a plain hairdo and glasses. She was slim, attractive, with a different kind of aura about her: she knew her business and she knew the model business backward and forward. She had been a booker at the Ford

165

agency for years and had gone to Wilhelmina when she'd started her agency.

It had been so easy I couldn't believe there weren't any more hurdles. Was I really in? I wasn't sure until I called up my friend from Grey.

"Yes, they liked you," he assured me. "You're in." Wilhelmina hadn't asked me to sign any agreement or anything, but that wasn't too strange. That usually happens when you take another step up the ladder and get really in demand. Then some agents get nervous and want the security of your signature on the dotted line.

I was too superstitious about counting my blessings before they hatched, but the next evening Dovima called me with a list of ten appointments for my first Monday. I had nine photographers for go-sees and an ad agency on my list. Finally I could believe it.

On Monday morning bright and early I started out with a new spring in my gait. I was one of the girls—Wilhelmina's girls. That very first day I ran into other Wilhelmina girls as I was making my rounds. It was like being members of the same sorority at college—we had something in common. And the icy aloofness and the cutthroat competition seemed a little subdued. I had to check in with Dovima at least three times a day by telephone—early morning, at noon, and then again at the end of the business day. Sometimes Dovima would call me when I was out on a go-see or a booking. Communication is a vital part of the business when you're with an agency. If someone needs you or wants you in a sudden crisis, Dovima consults a little chart with your name on it on the booking board in front of her. In a cellophane envelope with your name is a list of your appointments for the day. If there was a cancellation or an addition, Dovima would call me on the job. The telephone was our umbilical cord, and Dovima was more like a sorority house mother than a boss. I'll never forget the first time Dovima called me while I was having a test session with a photographer. She had lined up a slew of test sessions with top photographers in order to have new pictures of me to make up a brand-new composite.

"Call Dovima at the agency," the photographer's secretary broke in.

"How is Dovima these days?" the photographer asked me. "I've talked to her a couple of times, but I haven't seen her in years." It turned out he had grown up with her and had seen her become a legend in the business. I felt terribly stupid not to have known how famous she had been in her time. Just the mention of her name was enough to spin this photographer back on the time track. He began telling stories about her when she had been in her prime. I was all ears. It isn't every day you discover someone who knew your sorority house mother way back when and is willing to spin endless yarns about her glamorous, fabulous past.

Then there seemed suddenly something very sad about it. If I had been the toast of two continents, I think I would have quit when I was ahead. I wouldn't want to hang around the business working as a booker, spending all day at the booking board, telephoning green young things like me and telling them what kind of bras to wear. It was wonderful for us to be able to take advantage of her experience and her expertise, but how must it be for her?

"Look," said the photographer suddenly. "Here is Dovima at her peak." He had dug out one of those colored stand-up displays for a beauty product, the kind that decorate a whole window in a good drugstore. The brunette wore a fabulous red velvet gown, she had a diamond tiara in her hair, and she held a huge candelabra that probably once had had lights that flickered on and off. Looking the other way was another model, a blonde in a long page boy, looking very Grecian and very draped in a big cloud of deep purple nothing. The photographer had dug the poster out of his prop room. We stood looking at it as I was getting dressed.

"It's sensational," I said. "How long ago did you do that?"

"It's not mine," he said. "I only wish it were. It's a classic. That Dovima was really something." I honestly hadn't recognized her as the lady in red velvet. When I looked again, I could see that it was the same beautiful face. I didn't ask how many years it had been. Dovima still had great poise and beauty. I couldn't help admiring her. I hoped I'd be as resilient.

What this business can do to you if you let it get you! It really shook me. I know the bells toll for everybody, whether they're in the modeling business or any other, but I could hear that old clock ticking double time for me.

"Yeah," said the photographer. "In this racket you got to make it fast or it's over before anything's really happened."

"I wonder if Dovima has one of these posters. Maybe I should send it over to her."

167

"Oh," I said, "she probably has dozens of them."

A few days later, in the booking office, I saw the fabulous poster again. Obviously, the photographer had sent it over to Dovima. Camilla was squinting at it and then she was looking at Dovima. I wondered what Dovima was thinking.

"What ever happened to the blonde?" Camilla finally broke the long silence.

"I don't know," said Dovima. "She really knew how to handle herself well for a girl with heavy legs."

This was one-upmanship in spades. Dovima's legs were still fantastic. In the long regal red gown in the poster they were completely covered up. Now she had them out there, slim and sheer and gleaming—enough to make any man's head turn.

"God, I'm looking for a redhead. I gotta take four girls. I've got two brunettes from Wilhelmina already and a nice little English blonde from Stewart." I was back on the block. It was here-I-am-baby time. You have to know you look good. That's the only security you've got. If that's not enough for you, you'll never make it. My portfolio was zipped open on the desk. The secretary had begun looking at my book, and then she had said, "Wait a minute. Lemme call Hal in to look at you."

Hal was Hal Reiff, the photographer. He had been around since before my time and had a big reputation, but I had never worked for him before. Dovima had sent me to his studios on my second week of rounds.

"You look great in a bathing suit," he said, scanning my portfolio, never looking at me. I was wearing a little girl suit that day, but I had a bathing suit in my carryall. I wondered if he would want me to change. He kept staring at my portfolio while he gave me a rundown on the job. "We'll be doing two jobs in one," he said. "We'll be shooting a lot of bathing suits on location in Puerto Rico, St. Thomas, and Montego Bay, and then in between we'll be working every day on the ship shooting in black and white and color for their brochure. You'll need tons of clothes of all kinds—lots of evening things, sports togs. Linda will be going along as stylist, and I'll be taking one assistant who'll be doubling as a model, and one male model. I'll need you for two weeks starting November eleventh. We'll get back just in time for Thanksgiving. My wife is going along and the art director and his wife. You'll be great. Let's call Dovima up right now. Might as well get this whole thing settled."

I couldn't believe my ears. My second week out as one of Wilhelmina's girls and already I had bagged a cruise booking. This is one of the dream jobs. You get a flat weekly rate, which isn't up to what you might make working by the day, but the fringe benefits are fantastic. You get to play in between. You get to get out of dirty old New York at the beginning of the winter—no taxis or buses or subways or rush-rush-rush for two solid weeks—and you have a fancy all-expenses-paid vacation. And Hal Reiff was booking me this very minute.

"Look," he was saying to the agency. "I've got Carolyn Kenmore over here now. I want to book her for the November eleventh cruise. She's available, isn't she?" I knew I was, but he had to get it officially. Usually after hearing about one of these fantastic deals, you have to chase around until the art director sees you, and then he sends you to the client, and then you have to go home and wait, and two weeks later suddenly you're saying to yourself, "I wonder who got that cruise booking?"

But to get it and hear it confirmed in front of your eyes in three minutes flat—this was unbelievable. I was sailing. I dashed to the nearest phone to call David. He had been through enough ups and downs with me to send a man to the seminary. He tried to tell me not to get too excited until I actually had my foot on the gangplank, and I had to explain to him that nothing could go wrong because of the way it had happened.

I decided I wouldn't call the agency—I'd stop by. I was glad I did. Dovima was so happy. "Hal Reiff has booked you for the cruise." Everybody in the office knew already, and so did I, but this made it even more official. And I had only a week to beg, borrow, or steal the trunks and trunks of clothes I would need. A formal dinner every night for fourteen nights meant fourteen evening gowns right there. It was going to take some doing.

I sent out an immediate call for help to all my friends in the garment district. I called Sherle at The Wiggerie in White Plains. She was so excited about it that she drove into New York that very evening with two huge garment bags full of summer things, all fresh from the cleaner's. She had a daughter who was just my size. She brought a tray of jewelry, and she lent me at least six expensive hairpieces. In a couple of days the tickets arrived by special messenger. I had never been on an oceangoing vessel in my whole life, and I couldn't wait.

The night before we sailed I was up until three o'clock packing. Sherle drove down from White Plains to help me get myself together. She combed and set all the hairpieces and carefully installed them in the wig boxes. All that hair was going to be my salvation. I knew we would be changing four or five times a day, and there would be no time in between to send any hair to the cleaner's.

The Greek liner was docked at the foot of West 42nd Street, just a short jerk in a cab from my apartment. You forget Manhattan is an island until you have occasion to step right out of a taxi onto an oceangoing liner. Two other Wilhelmina girls were already there, and we swooned when we saw the accommodations. Huge outside cabins on the main deck about six steps away from the swimming pool. Marsha, my cabin mate, had been up all night packing, too.

People were strolling on deck with their friends. Parties were in progress everywhere, so we took a stroll around the liner. As soon as we showed our legs on deck, a guy with a camera asked if he could take our picture. He posed each of us individually and wrote down our names and addresses. When I got home, I had a bushel of love letters from strange men, which I couldn't explain until my doorman told me my photo had been in the *Daily News,* complete with name and address.

Our entire little group had accommodations within partying distance of one another, and the purser booked us all at two tables in the dining room. We had an extra stateroom for our gowns and props and impedimenta. Linda, the stylist, took over and began picking and choosing among our things, setting up scenarios for the shooting. As soon as Hal Reiff and his wife arrived, we went to work. We had to get completely done up and pose in the card room.

Right from the first setup we became a permanent floating floor show for the passengers. The brochure had to show off every corner of the ship, and every time we changed the background, we had to make a complete change of outfit, from shoes to hairpieces.

Then for dinner, which was the real thing and not a pose at all, we had to make still another change. The waiters were all handsome Italians. They seemed very shy, but they knew how to flirt effectively halfway across the dining room even though they were apparently totally involved in transporting tremendous trays loaded with silver tureens. I knew about eleven words in Italian, but two of them were "*bella rosa*," so when I heard them, I knew I had a live one. When we docked in San Juan, Puerto Rico, we went ashore in a regular safari for a full working day of shooting bathing suits on the beaches and against the architectural landmarks of the island. That night at dinner my handsome waiter slipped me a note. His English was mangled irresistibly. He and three of his friends were inviting the four models to sneak off with them that night to the Geronimo Hotel which featured gambling, floor shows, and fun. Bella Rosa had to be the ringleader and mother hen. All the girls wanted to go. We didn't want to go alone. The waiters were better-looking than any of the men on board, so what did we have to lose? I spent three of the best summers of my life slinging hash and waiting table in summer resorts from Maine to New Jersey—certainly I was no one to stick up my nose at a fellow worker, just because he happened to come from Genoa and look like Vittorio Gassman. Our Cinderella boys had to work until nine, but once dinner was over, they were out of there in a flash, dressed sharper than their cousins in New York and greeting us with clouds of cologne. When we got to the Geronimo, it was like a waiters' convention. Every waiter from every ship in port was there. And every American girl cruising the islands who had snagged herself a handsome Italian counted herself lucky. One of our group hit it lucky, and the champagne flowed. The MC dreamed up a dance contest, and naturally that was heaven for my itchy feet. I had been posing all day, so I felt like busting loose with the Bugaloo or anything else the orchestra was ready for. When the MC saw our false eyelashes and our getups, he dug we were models, so he began restyling his little attraction. He wanted us to parade around and take little bows during the dance contests. The other girls were shy, especially the little English girl.

"I could never do a thing like that," she said.

"That's because you've never worked in the garment district like I have," I told her. "You've done nothing but print." We declined his offer to have an impromptu fashion show, but I went into the dance contest with a vengeance. I did a turn with the MC, and in the middle of it he turned me loose. I knew he wanted a little dress parade, so I swished around past the tables, working the fabric in my dress.

171

Everyone applauded like mad, and I won the contest, and the prize was a huge bottle of champagne for our table. I drank a quiet toast to Cecelia Newman and the girls at Models Service. If I had bypassed the garment district and gone directly into print work like so many girls, I would never have developed the *chutspah* it takes to do ramp work.

Stefano, my lover boy from Genoa, was not one for the new athletic dances that keep boys and girls doing their separate thing on the floor. He was a cheek-to-cheek dancer of the old school, and suddenly I discovered that that had its charms, too. I had to keep reminding myself that he certainly had a wife and several bambinos back in Genoa and probably cousins by the dozen in the *Homeric* crew. Suddenly it was one-thirty and we had to get back to the ship before it sailed at 2 A.M. We didn't even know how far we had strayed. But like a company of Marines breaking camp, the Italian waiters all gathered their confreres together, took a quick head count, and commandeered a fleet of taxis, so that all of us somehow got back to the pier five minutes before the ship was ready to take off. It seemed a breathtakingly close call that first night, but we began to suspect it happened with great regularity. Every waiter knew every Caribbean island like the back of his hand.

At the pier we girls had to traipse up the gangplank into first class unescorted. And our escorts had to take the tiny gangplank into the below-deck quarters for the crew.

By the third day we had our work schedule down pat. We worked mornings in shorts and culottes playing shuffleboard. Then we changed into different outfits for a round of volleyball. In the afternoon we were shooting by the pool in next season's sample bathing suits. In the evening we got redone to pose in the lounge and in special setups in the dining room before we sat down to our regular dinner. When we docked at the Virgin Islands, we went on another safari with more bathing suits to find more locations. We were so busy being photographed that we never got a chance to take any snapshots on our own. We had to do all our souvenir hunting in a fast two hours and then get back to the ship for dinner. The waiters kept their tropical complexions bronzed by sun-bathing in the bow in a little compound.

Our foursome was down in front waving to us when we boarded the ship. They were preening and peacocking around among their compatriots. They were the kings because they had snagged the models.

There were some very nice American men aboard, but by the time they found us, we were already sewed up. They were much too slow for the guys from Genoa. It was Romeo and Juliet all over again. Because of the caste barriers between us, it was much more fun having to plot and scheme and break the rules to party with our Latin lovers. At dinner we kept finding little notes in our napkins and under our plates. We decided to arrange a party in our prop room. Stewards walked the companionways at all hours to protect the cruising ladies from intrusions by amorous members of the crew. But the waiters knew all the back stairways and the secret passages. They kept their mess jackets on, and one after the other arrived with trays piled with goodies—sandwiches, pastry, cookies—anything they could steal from the ship's stores. When the party was over, we girls had to play decoy and engage the patrolling stewards in conversation so our boyfriends could escape back to the scullery. During the day we never got to see them. We were either shooting on the boat or on location ashore. Our friends always tried to finagle to get upstairs to the decks or card rooms or lounge rooms while we were doing our number, but their colleagues were in no mood to trade off.

Whenever we asked for our waiters during the day, the reply would always be: "Stefano and Mario look like hell today. You girls have been keeping them up. Too early!"

At Montego Bay the waiters got to go ashore. As soon as we were finished posing at the Half Moon, they would whisk us off to the straw market and other tourist hangouts. They bought beads for us and presented them to us with great ceremony. That day we really missed the last boat and they had to send the tender back to collect us.

But that was small potatoes. Everybody was happy. Hal Reiff, our photographer, was delighted with the way his work was going. The art director was happy. There was absolutely no bitchery going on among us girls. We worked together as if we had been friends for years. We were always on time, and we never got behind with our schedule.

Amateur night, of course, is the climax of the cruise, and the social director had been casting all week for his amateur floor show. Someone had to represent the Wilhelmina contingent, so naturally, after I had won the dance contest at the Geronimo, the other girls started acting like stage mothers. They retired gracefully and began to push my talents onto the social director. Where I got the nerve from I'm not sure. But

173

when he asked me to dance, I replied with great aplomb that I would prefer to sing. He already had more singers than he could use. The art director's wife had been a professional singer before her marriage, so she had already been booked for a spot on the bill. Although I had been taking vocal lessons for years, it was like going to the gym for me. I studied voice in order to improve my poise and my speaking voice. But I had auditioned for everything else at one time or another, from pornographic movies to Hiawatha's sister, so what did I have to lose? There was a young American on board who played the piano, and he went with me to the audition in the lounge. Of course, I wanted to sing our song—David's and mine—"The Girl from Ipanema." I knew my key was D. I sang, and it didn't come out too bad. I was booked for a place on the bill.

The floor show was all set to go on after the second dinner seating. Suddenly I had no appetite. The waiters all thought I was ill. They were right too. I had a paralyzing case of stage fright combined with a touch of *mal de mer.* My throat was dry. I knew right then I could never be a performer on stage or in nightclubs. Since I couldn't eat, I went back to the stateroom to get ready. I thought maybe having something to do would calm the butterflies. I had practically exhausted my wardrobe. There was virtually nothing I hadn't worn except a gorgeous full-length tropical flowered silk dress with slits up the sides. Well, I thought, that will do. If I'm going to sing flat, I'd better look good and round in a few places. I put on about three hairpieces, so I looked about eight feet tall. Then I borrowed a huge pair of chandelier drop earrings from Marsha's vault. When I came down to meet the social director, the art director's wife was already doing her number. She had a beautiful trained voice, and she used all her tremolos in singing her aria. Then I heard the social director at the microphone promising the people that one of the models who had graced the cruise was going to sing. When he mentioned my name, a roar burst out from the crowd. It was our group—my cheering section of stage mothers egging me on.

As soon as I heard the music, I felt better. The band was in fantastic form. They gave me a real bossa nova beat with plenty of time to make a long walk to the center of the stage. The lights were so bright I couldn't see anything but darkness around me. The entire dining room was hushed and waiting. Not a cup rattled. Not a piece of ice tinkled. Absolute quiet. The first few notes sounded like somebody else. I couldn't believe it. The band sounded so great they would have made anybody seem good. Suddenly I enjoyed being up there. I liked it. I loved it. When I came to the end of the chorus, I repeated the phrase three times, more softly every time, and while the band kept up the insinuating bossa nova rhythm, I sneaked off the stage.

Well, my cheering section really tore it up. The MC begged me to come on and do an encore. But I was too smart for that. I knew enough to quit when I was ahead. I took two or three bows as if I were selling my dress, and then I retreated. Later I joined my gang at our table. We were all rewarded with champagne, and then the social director presented me with a huge crystal ash tray. I felt as though I had won an Academy Award—for supporting player, at least.

On the last night out, nobody slept. No work was done. Everyone was happy. The drama began at the final dinner course. While champagne corks popped, the lights went out, the violins and guitars came on like a Gypsy funeral, and then a whole platoon of waiters entered on cue with tray after tray with flaming baked Alaskas. They circled in the middle of the dance floor, they crossed and they flounced around while the band went into a chorus of "Hello Dolly." Then the partying began in earnest. Some American friends gave a party for us in their double suite. We also had another party going in our prop room for our guys from Genoa. We had to commute between the two. This went on until five-thirty, which was the witching hour for the waiters. They had to disappear like Cinderella and be ready to serve breakfast at six. The passengers had to switch from champagne to ham and eggs and then be packed, dressed, and ready to face the customs inspectors at eight. Everybody had bought so much extra booze in the islands— much more than they were allowed to bring in duty-free—that they were determined to bring in the maximum amount of alcohol concealed in their bloodstream. One needed to be a little typsy. The end of a beautiful two-week holiday would have been too impossibly sad to contemplate without some kind of anesthetic.

Christmas in Vermont is a joy, in California it's a joke, in New York it's a horror. Models are all low men on the media totem pole. They have to establish their existence, remind people they're alive and kicking by giving gifts to the people all the way to the top. It starts with their agencies. One agency I worked for had the real Scroogey custom of sending out a letter to all models on their lists suggesting that they contribute an hour's booking fee—fifty or sixty dollars—to the Christmas kitty to be distributed to the bookers at the agency. Of course, it's only a suggestion, but right after Christmas come the days of January clearance at the agency—the time when models are dropped right and left to make room for new faces from here and abroad—so the meaning of the suggestion is horribly clear. Put up or shut up. So scores of models have to shell out so the head of the agency does not have to give a Christmas bonus to his office employees. It's also unfair to the new girls who have been with the agency only a few weeks. They're asked to contribute as much as the regulars who have been on the roster all year.

Another agency gives little presents to the models. But even the presents cause emotional havoc with the girls. Some get on the A list and get a mod watch; others get the shakes when they get only a little bottle of cologne and realize they've been given a B rating.

Sometimes the agencies have parties—ranging from little sit-down black-tie dinners for important photographers, art directors, casting directors, and fashion coordinators to big mob scenes when they take a night club for the night and invite everybody in the business. If a girl is invited to a sit-down dinner with the *important* people, she knows she's in for a Merry Christmas; if she gets a notice to show up at a mob scene, this means she may be on the way out when the January clearance rolls around. Most of the models give presents to their good accounts—the photographers who gave them repeat bookings, or the casting directors who were especially nice to them in the past year. Booze is always the safest bet. One year I had a lucky connection who had a father who ran a liquor store in Queens. I got a sensational bargain on those six-bottle packs. When I arrived at Wilhelmina's office with one, Bruce Cooper greeted me with the crack: "What did you do—rob a bank?"

At Christmastime the photographers, too, have to pass Christmas gifts up the totem pole. They have to establish *their* existence by giving presents to the art directors and the account executives at the advertising agencies.

The art directors and the account executives in turn give gifts to the clients in the big corporations and conglomerates. When it comes to the corporations and the conglomerates, I'm not sure what happens.

Maybe they don't have to give to anyone but the politicians and the gods.

Them that's got shall get—as far as Christmas gifts are concerned. By the time you've covered yourself from every direction and blown your budget out of kilter, covering every eventuality, there are the elevator men and doormen and postmen and garbage men and the boys at the garage.

When you're finally exhausted from all this, you can't wait to get back to a beautiful white Christmas in Middlebury, Vermont. You want to get there before the snow blocks the highway, so you try to sneak off a few days ahead of holiday time. You go to the garage where they keep your car. And under the windshield wiper is a lovely red-and-green card covered with holly and mistletoe. You open it, and it says sweetly:

> Hark, the herald angels sing.
> Merry Christmas—Final Notice.

"Please, God, *don't* let me be sick in this jumpsuit. If I schlepp it back tomorrow with *one* spot of puke on it, Chester will never lend me another thread." When I walked into the ladies' room at Raffles, I could hear this drunken wail from the cute little cabinet designed by Cecil Beaton. If I hadn't had to go so badly myself, I would have turned around and split. If there's anything I can't tolerate, it's a drunk of any kind. To make things worse, the attendant thought she was a friend of mine. She was ready to give Miss Upchuck back her quarter and turn her over to me. It was almost quitting time for the maid—she was counting the seconds until she could get the Mad Ave bus uptown. Nowadays everybody and his brother gets done up hoping to be mistaken for a model. It takes one to tell one. I knew Miss Upchuck was a realie, and she knew the same thing about me. When she came lunging out of the toilet with her zippers open and no bra on, all bars were down. She started talking a blue streak to me as if we had been working together on a job all afternoon.

"If *only* I'd taken that Pucci print, on that the puke would never show," she muttered as she inspected the brown crepe microscopically for a telltale sign. "Hey, look me over, will you, buddy?" she begged me. "If there's a dreck on it, that's the last straw."

"It's all in your mind," I told her. "I can't see anything on the suit."

She dragged herself into the corner under the lamp and made me look again. I tried to tell her she had nothing to worry about.

"Thanks, buddy," she said. "Thanks a lump. Who you with?"

I told her I was with my boyfriend and his boss. Raffles was one of the new private East Side clubs nobody could get into unless his host was a member. I'd never been there before. I didn't know too many people who belonged.

"Naw, naw," she said. "What headsheet are you on?"

I told her I was with Wilhelmina.

"If you can't lick 'em, join 'em," she said bitterly. "These Communist cunts from Europe. Eileen just brought over fifty more of them. I starved myself for six weeks. I spent three hundred dollars going to the thin doctor and lost eleven goddam pounds. Look at me. Look. If you find an ounce of fat on me, I'll eat it."

She had a beautiful figure, but she just wasn't built to be a freaky high-fashion model. She was younger than I was, but her eyes were glassy and she had a frightening cough.

"I knew it was coming," she whispered. "I wasn't making six hundred a week anymore. Two weeks before Christmas I didn't work a day. I got so frantic I went to the thin doctor. Then they dropped me anyway. I got the ax this afternoon. They don't *want* me. Sidney doesn't understand what that *means.* He says it's not the end of the world, but what the hell does he know? When Eileen Ford drops you, you can hear that thud all over town."

She had to be terribly tight to talk that way. It was a frightening time of the year in the model business. Right after the first of the year the accountants get to work on the books and the head sheets are passed into the front office. The girls who haven't been making the top money they used to make get red crayon marks next to their telephone numbers. The boss ladies breeze off to Paris and Rome and Berlin in search of new girls. It's out with the old and in with the new faces. Things that are usually whispered about in hush-hush tones were spilling out all over the rest room because it takes one to be able to tell one. No wonder she had been drinking. There was no telling when she would stop. And after that would come the pills. If she had been going to one of the diet doctors, she probably had enough pills at home to do herself in. I wondered if she lived alone. I tried to think of something I could do. If I gave her my phone number and I had a crazy drunken lady calling me after the bars closed, I'd have nobody to blame but myself. If I did nothing and then read about something horrible happening in the papers, I'd feel like hardhearted Hannah.

"Where do you live?" I asked her as she was putting on a new mouth.

"I live with my boyfriend," she said. I felt like saying, "Thank God for Sidney."

"Don't get all psyched up about Eileen dropping you," I said. "Maybe you're not cut out for high-fashion junk. Some other agency might be better for you."

"Yeah, sure, uh-huh," she said. "That's exactly what the bitch had the nerve to tell me after I'd lost eleven pounds just for her."

"Eileen Ford once told me I wasn't pretty enough for her. It almost killed me, but I didn't resign from the human race," I confessed.

Finally she smiled. It was my cue to get out of there.

"Watch Willy," she shouted to me as a parting shot. "I hear she got a whole boatload of European bitches she's bringing over."

If a man isn't tall enough to be a New York policeman, he's shorter than I am. That doesn't bother me. But it seems to bother the hell out of them—especially if they are rich and successful and important and powerful and want everybody to know it. It's always the mini-man who ends up saying, "Lie down, I want to talk to you." He can't rest until he can get you someplace in the horizontal where his mother's prenatal calcium deficiency won't show. For the man who has everything, a model seems to be fair game. If men can buy everything they see advertised in the slick magazines, why not the girls who go along with it?

Every time an important photographer gives an important party at his studio and invites all the models on his list, it's sort of *de rigueur* that you show. As soon as word gets out that the models will all be there, it becomes a kind of mecca for all the rich runts in town. The photographer invites all his clients and the clients bring along their short friends from out of town. The art directors from the agencies have to keep in tune with what's happening, so they all show up, and everyone seems to bring along another mini-friend. The music is blasting away in the deserted streets along Park Avenue South, and that seems to attract little visitors. I sometimes think cabdrivers get the message. Whenever they spot a succession of models arriving singly or in pairs, they spread the word in the hope of getting an extra tip from the mini-men in the street. By the time you arrive, the picture is always the same. A whole bunch of hairy models are staring at one another over the sea of thinning male hair in between. The booze is flowing and the music is blasting. It's like the subway rush hour except everybody has a drink in his hand instead of a strap and every girl is leaning over smiling at every man and constantly saying, "What did you say?"

I had a leather dress on that night and I was dancing with a TV commercial producer when he got the signal from his boss that his boss had a client who was dying to meet me. The client came up almost to my earrings. I smiled as we were introduced.

"Ohhhh," he said, eyeing my exposed navel, "you look like Barbara Ellen." I thought maybe he was talking about his daughter. But the music was blasting so loud I couldn't be sure.

"Most navels look alike," I laughed. "Who is Barbara Ellen? What does she do?" Now the account exec got into it. He smiled at me as if I had just won the man of the week on *Dating Game* and he didn't want to see me blow my big break. "He said you look like *Barbarella*—you know, Jane Fonda in the movie—and that's not bad, is it?" Now he was winking at me and nudging. "Oh, this is a great guy. This Fred is one of the sweetest guys I've ever done business with. We've had our little ups and down together at the agency, but we've always stayed friends. We've even balled together—that's how close Fred and I are." I don't know whom that was supposed to impress. I pretended the music had drowned out what he said. I guess he could feel the ice. He nudged me and answered, "Fred's a big automobile account. One of the biggest."

"How nice," I said.

"Yeah," he said. "We get to go on a lot of location jobs together."

"I'll bet you do." On location the heat is really on. You're out in Arizona someplace with a big residual staring you in the face, and they break it to you gently that the client is really smitten with your looks. He's thinking of using you throughout the whole campaign. Just letting him drop by your motel can mean as much as $50,000 in the bank. I knew that whole routine. I'd heard about that gambit.

I know a girl who was flown to Acapulco to do a fabulous cigarette commercial. Nobody told her she had to be available for the client

180

twenty-four hours a day. When she spent the night with a Mexican high diver, they shipped her back to New York as if she had violated her SAG contract or contracted a social disease. She lost her job and her residuals.

Now the account exec was moving in and rearranging the choreography for escorting me home. Since his client had eyes for me, Pete was supposed to disappear.

"Pete has to catch a train," the account exec explained to the client who was drooling for his reward. "I promised him we'd see the little lady gets home all right."

Pete looked sheepish and surely felt like an ass. The client beamed. They expected me to be thrilled to bits. Crotch politics is the name of the game, and my name was Miss Pussy Pawn.

"You be smart, Carolyn," the account exec advised me. "Pete's a nice chap, but he can't do anything for you alongside what Fred here can do."

Short men never want to dance. They always want to eat. When they talk about taking you out for a "bite to eat," this means they have found an excuse to use that old expense account to show how important they are. It never matters that you're not interested in seeing a whole side of beef spilling over a plate at two o'clock in the morning. If these little men feel like being seen with you in some of their restaurant haunts, there's no way out.

Tonight it was going to be Gatti's, Fred decided. The account executive looked at his watch and thought they closed at two o'clock. This became a challenge to Fred's standing as a regular. We wheeled up to Gatti's, and he kept his limousine waiting. The place was virtually empty, and there was no one to impress except the maître d. He immediately began bowing and scraping. Fred began ordering blind without ever looking at the menu. He wanted his special salad and his special wine and his special shrimp and some of those little tiny things with the cheese on top.

"See," said the account exec as Fred wended his way to the men's room. "I told you he's the greatest. We've even balled together."

"You told me that," I commented. "Have you got a thing for that? I think it's sort of perverted, really."

"Are you sick or something?" the account exec lectured me. "Don't you know there are a lot of girls in this business who'd give their eyeteeth to be sitting where you're sitting tonight? Here with Fred." He hadn't heard a thing I said to him. He hadn't gotten a single message. Nothing mattered except that Fred had spotted me in my leather dress and gotten all excited. The account exec had the job of getting Fred everything he wanted.

"Look, Carolyn, you live in town, right?"

"Right," I said.

"After we leave here, I'm gonna split. Then you take him up to your place for a drink. You play your cards right and aha, va va va voom. . . ."

"Yes, and suppose I play my cards right—what's in the cards for me?"

They always get very defensive if you ask for the tiniest detail about this great big break they have in mind for you. "Don't get smart with Fred now," said the exec. "Fred doesn't like to be pinned down when we're partying." I don't like to be pinned down either, but since my karate lessons, no mini-man could scare me very much.

Fred came back from the john like a man just off desert patrol, dying of dehydration. He began to drink Scotch and wine in alternate gulps. Fred was furious that I wasn't drinking as fast as he was. I had to remind them I had a schedule for tomorrow and next week and next month, and bags under my eyes were something I couldn't use, thank you very much.

Then the two men began regaling each other with stories of their past exploits. They were like two kids in a locker room. Suddenly I wasn't even there. They began tossing names of models around as if they were tank town tarts. At least two of them were girls I knew. Several I knew by reputation.

I finally said, "Look, fellows, I thought women were supposed to be the gossips. You can talk about girls when you're alone. I don't want to hear about it."

Fred looked at me as if I had used the wrong fork. If all these girls were running after them, what did they need with one more? If they could talk this loosely and disgustingly about other girls in the business in front of me, what would restrain them tomorrow night from telling tall tales about me? The special salad hadn't appeared yet, so Fred left to go into a huddle with the maître d. Now the exec went into his automatic routine, telling me for the eleventh time how powerful Fred was and what he could do for me by just lifting his little finger.

"Have you ever seen his office?" he wanted to know.

"I never met the man before in my life, remember?"

"No wonder you're acting so dumb, Kenmore," said the exec. "You should see his office. A whole suite he has for himself, with three color TVs built in the wall. He has one whole wall like a control tower just for media review. A concealed built-in screen. A private dining room. A bathroom and massage table and a sauna. You'll never run into this little guy on *your* rounds, baby. When he has to flag off to Detroit or LA, one of his secretaries buzzes for the corporation jet. He lives right, Carolyn baby. If you saw his setup, you'd plotz. You haven't seen many setups like his. You stick with Fred, baby. If he likes you, you're halfway there."

It was no use asking halfway where? It had settled into a routine. Whenever I seemed insufficiently impressed, Fred would wander off while his buddy pumped me full of hot air. Then Fred would come back and sit down as if to say, "Well, now that that misunderstanding has been cleared up and you know how important I am, let us proceed."

The feast arrived and the waiters swooped around under the watchful eye of the maître d, who did everything except eat the food for the two boys. Ever since my summers as a waitress, I have had a horror of wasted food. It actually makes me ill to see a bunch of drunks order a huge dinner. The cook sweats to fix it just right, the waiters and waitresses hustle to serve it hot, and by that time the customers are so boozed up they can't even taste it. The food goes back to the kitchen virtually untouched. I know that waste is common in this country, but wasting food still strikes me as a hideous mortal sin for which one day we will all be punished.

And yet I couldn't eat what the waiters served me. I tasted the salad and the shrimp and the special doodads, and I had a sip of wine. Nobody but the waiters seemed to mind. The supper wasn't for eating, anyway. It was to impress me that Fred was such an important customer that even when he walked into the restaurant within minutes of closing time for the kitchen, he could issue commands and expect to have them obeyed. Fred needed to prove to himself that he was a success.

I hoped the waiters were hungry, and not just for money. Our trio couldn't eat a third of what the great man had ordered. Of course, he had to overtip. And he had to do it in a way that would impress me. The maître d practically bowed to the floor as we swept out of there in single file. When you're with short men, you always walk like the Indians.

The limousine didn't seem to be waiting, and I wondered what that meant. We started walking. My friend, the executive, was anxious to disappear. But he didn't dare vanish until he was certain that I would invite Fred up to my apartment for a nightcap. I wasn't going to make it easy for him. So they started another conversation designed for me to overhear. It was all about a girl named Nita and how shocked she had been when she got to keep every cent of the $50,000 she had earned doing a TV commercial for Fred last year. That didn't strike me as anything to write home about, and I said so. Dumb little me. I said, "If she got it direct and not through an agent, why should she have to pay anything to anybody?"

"You must be jesting," said the account executive. "You think these girls get to keep all that money? Looka here, kid, you'd be surprised to know how many girls have to agree to kick back twenty, thirty, forty percent of their residuals before they ever get to sign a deal."

I had heard of all kinds of kickbacks and payola, but this I'd never heard. "Do you mean to say before you even get a job you have to agree to split with somebody?"

The two men laughed as if I were the greenest thing in town. Who would you split with? The casting director, the art director, the account executive, the client—who?

They just kept laughing. Finally Fred assured me I had a right to my ideals. He was idealistic, too. He felt the same way I did. He wouldn't tolerate payola, and he made sure that every girl who worked on his account got every cent the union said she was entitled to. If he got so much as a hint or a whiff of payola being extracted from any of his girls, he called them right up to his office and straightened the whole thing out. Heads might roll, but virtue always triumphed in the end. Nobody ever lost any money.

It was the first time Fred and I had achieved what you might call a meeting of minds on any subject, and the executive was as happy as a poodle. He felt this was the right note, the perfect note on which to disappear. He gave me the wink and the nudge and told me he hoped everything would work out for me just great, just great. He knew it would if he and Fred had anything to say about it.

Then he left. Suddenly Fred seemed very nice. He asked me if I minded if he walked me to my place. He said he often got so bored with riding around in the limousine by himself that he got out and walked. Especially at night when the streets were deserted. Especially after such a fabulous high-cholesterol supper as they always made for him at Gatti's.

What the hell, I thought to myself, maybe he's not such a bad fellow after all. You can't generalize about any group of people—even mini-men. There are always the exceptions that prove the rule. Fred began talking quite rationally about an interview he wanted to set up for me with his media director. He carefully wrote down my name and the name of my agency. He gave me a sketchy rundown on what I would be required to do. He was thrilled to know I was a good driver. The campaign they were planning needed a girl who could navigate through some spectacular scenery. There would be lots of zooming, so they couldn't use a double. Being a Midwesterner, he was surprised at how helpless so many beautiful girls were when it came to handling a car on rough terrain. He wasn't asking for a hot-rod specialist, but it was nice to know I qualified for the action. We were getting down to business when we reached my apartment, so it would have been less than polite if I hadn't invited him up for a drink.

Fred was so effusive with the doorman and the elevator man that I was scared he was going to offer them a tip. When we arrived at the apartment, I went to the bar and asked him what he would like. He asked for a Scotch, so I got out the ice and gave him one on the rocks. He was talking a blue streak about automobiles until I handed him his drink. He broke a sentence right in the middle, put down the drink, and said, "Goddamit, you knew what you were doing when you put on that dress, didn't you?"

I had heard about leather freaks. I didn't think the dress was all that inflammatory, but then you never know.

"It's the first thing like this I ever bought. You know, whatever's new, a model has to have one in her arsenal."

"I get excited just from the feel of it," he said. Oh, well, I could remember the old days when men were inflamed by the color of your eyes or the smoothness of your skin. But getting the hots from a hunk of cowhide somehow didn't seem quite kosher. He had his little arms around me and was giving me a big sloppy kiss. He tasted like a pizzeria, but before I could untangle myself, he was chomping on my mouth and ears.

I made a mental note of details of my last karate lesson, and when he let go, I crossed the room to fix myself a drink. I didn't want the evening to be a total loss. Maybe there was some way of getting rid of him gracefully without blowing the interview tomorrow with his media director. While I stood at the bar, he looked at me and said, "Why don't you take it off?"

"You like this dress so much you want to take it home?" I countered, trying to keep everything light and laughable.

Suddenly he was mean and angry, and he started crawling all over me with Russian hands and Roman fingers.

"What are you after, anyway, Fred?" I laughed. "Me or the dress?"

"I wanna go to bed with you," he said.

"When?"

"When, for God's sake! I got no time to play around, I'm a busy man. I can't drag you out to dinner three nights a week. I'm never in town three nights in one week."

"Well," I said, "I think you're nice and all that. But I'd like to know you a lot better before—we get into the bed scene."

"Listen, Red," he barked. "I got no time for games." He walked to the window, and when he turned, it was as if he were another man, disgusted and through. "Every time I meet a good-looking model, I ask her to go to bed with me. I don't want you. I don't need you. What the hell do I need you for? I just wanna know how far you'll go to get a job. I want to know how far everybody will go. I want to know it about waiters, and I want to know about restaurant owners, and I want to know about pimps from the ad agencies, and I want to know about pretty young girls who walk around with their bare stomachs in leather dresses, their tits hanging out and their tushies out there asking for it. You wanna be a big-deal model, you want your ass on TV, you want your fifty thousand a year in residuals, and you don't want to sweat for it. You don't even want to take your dress off for it. Listen, Red, I'm giving nobody a thing for free. Not anymore. It cost me plenty to get where I am. And I'm not giving anybody anything. Let them go through the same shit I went through—every bit of it."

He picked up his drink, downed another slug, and then he looked at me as if to say, "Oh, honey, you're so stupid you're pitiful. You had the whole world within grabbing distance, and you blew it. Forever and ever."

And then he marched across my living room and went crazy mad insane cuckoo because he couldn't get the door open. I let him struggle with it, and then I put him out of his misery. I opened the door for him. He didn't even say goodnight.

I couldn't wait for Saturday to retreat to Livingston, New Jersey, to spend a real homey day in suburbia with my sister Paula, my brother-in-law Dick, their son Tommy, and their little girl Barbara.

# CHAPTER 8

Somehow I knew the jig was up when Dovima started to cry. January clearance time had come and gone, but I was on ice at the Wilhelmina agency, and I knew it. I wasn't getting the bookings, and I wasn't getting sent out on rounds. Wilhelmina's new head sheet featured about seventy new girls from Europe. They were getting the play. It had reached the point where lots of American models had fled to Europe where they and their American accents would be exotic and cute.

Finally Dovima had asked me to come in. It was all in her eyes, and I wondered what I could do to make it easier for her. "We feel, Carolyn, that perhaps you'd do better at another agency," she began, and then the tears came. Cold formalities went out the window as Dovima continued, "God, Carolyn, I don't want to see you go. I don't think we've begun to touch your potential yet. There are so many more things I wanted to do...." She had the agency head sheet in her hand, and she pointed to some of the faces and said, "Look, here's a girl who hasn't made fifty dollars in five months...."

"And they're keeping her and letting me go. Why?"

I knew by then you don't get any answers by asking questions. Dovima and Camilla and Stephanie had been wonderful to me. We had done such great things at the beginning, and yet ... Suddenly I understood that Dovima was only doing what she had been told to do.

Then Bruce Cooper came bounding into the office shouting like Simon Legree. "Look, you know how much it costs for this woman here to waste her time trying to push you? You gotta do better than you did, kid, that's all. We've got our life savings invested in this operation, and if we send a girl out on three test sessions, she damn well better be able to get a booking out of one. You gotta do better than you've been doing, kid."

Again it wasn't what he said—it was his manner. It was the same crude showbiz manner he so often displayed when one encountered him in the office. "Well, who patted you on the ass today?" was his usual opener. And that was the springboard to some other vulgarity. He had never run an agency on his own. He had come from TV. His connections in television were his stock-in-trade. The three-way scene frightened me at first, and then as usual I got angry.

"Perhaps it will be better if I leave," I said as quietly as I could manage. When people are shouting, the only way to attract attention is to lower your voice.

"Maybe we can call some other agencies for you...."

"No, thank you," I said. Baby, I was thinking, I can't use a recommendation from you. It would take a saint of a man to surmount the spot Mr. Cooper was in. Too many people called him Mr. Wilhelmina, and that seemed to make it necessary for him to prove he was boss over something or somebody. I tried to stay out of his way as best I could. Inner agency politics can be lethal. If you're going to play that game, you have to be cleverer than I was.

The turnover at the agencies after the first of the year is unbelievable. And the business was changing right under our feet. High-fashion print work represented prestige. But you could go broke from being chic, so agencies that started out doing nothing but print now had to branch out and have a department to handle TV. Agencies that started out doing casting for TV now were trying to break into print in order to diversify and to garner some of that *haut monde* prestige. The scope of the media was international now. In print it was completely international, and the vogue for exoticism and accents had caught on in TV. In the endless and exhausting search for something new to grab the consumer, ad agencies were trying everything. Being pretty wasn't enough. Sometimes you needed to be ugly and a character actress to boot. In print work all the models looked alike, from Helsinki to Hong Kong. When you saw an ad for a typical American family, you had to be in the business to know that Papa came from Paris, Mama came from Hamburg, and the children might have come from the four corners of the U.S.A. Everyone was searching for a formula for survival in the sea of media in which we little fishes were swimming around. And the only formula that worked was no formula. Instinct—that's all you had to go on.

The time always comes, as it came to me that afternoon I knew I was

finished at Wilhelmina, when you think maybe you've had it. This is
the end of the line. Quit while you're ahead. Pick up your marbles, get
married, and kiss the girls good-bye.

I walked home that afternoon feeling very down. Rejection at first
sight is one thing. Eileen Ford gave me that. But being accepted and
getting a smashing start and then boom—it's all over—that was
something else. I had been made to feel that I had failed. That's what
hurt so much.

The more I thought about it the more depressed I got. My roommate
Clem didn't understand it. David didn't understand it at all. To them the
whole model racket was phony and crazy and insane. They saw no
rhyme or reason in it. You were up one day and down the next. They
couldn't seem to understand what being dropped by Wilhelmina meant.
It was—as the drunken girl in the Raffles ladies' room had said—a thud
that could be heard all over town. Or your ego was bruised to the point
where you *imagined* this was happening.

I finally summoned the courage to phone Reg von Cuÿlenburg. I told
him what had happened, and he dropped everything and came over to
the house. He held my hand for almost three hours and finally sold me
a little positive thinking. He told me the same thing that Cecelia
Newman had once told me: it wasn't what had happened that mattered
—it was how I felt about it. If I felt I had failed, then I had failed. If I
felt something else was involved and I had not really had a fair shake,
then that was something else.

So I finally accepted the incident at its worst.

Carolyn, I told myself, you have failed.

Once it was out in the open, it was like a horrible class in math or
something. What do you do about it?

Well, you try again.

I knew I had to work harder and make myself a better model. That's
all. That's plenty. But that's it.


"What's all that *brown* around your eyes? God of the Himalayas,
where do they *get* them from? What's all that dryness under your eyes?
Eeech... what funeral director did you study makeup with, dear?
Bosoms died with Miss Mansfield, sweetie—what kind of airfoam have
you got in there? Can't you flatten it down? What's that? What in
Christendom is that? Bunchies, for God's sake. You look like a boy.

Well, I can't blame you for wearing those bunchies, darling—anything, absolutely anything so they won't notice your hair. Your hair is hideous."

He was a real screaming pansy, the kind that loves to tear girls apart. I could hear him yelling from his posh inner sanctum. Whenever he had a fight with his flat-chested little roommate from the South of France, he would get even by shrieking at some girls. If you hadn't been briefed beforehand, he could have you in shreds in thirty seconds flat. I'd been through it once, so I knew what to expect. Nothing surprised me now.

When this little Miss Thing came out of the model agency, she was in tears, gazing with an awesome sense of discovery at her pelvis. Her pants were a little tight, and she protruded where girls don't usually protrude. Some girls are just built that way. In anything but skintight pants it wouldn't show. I've known photographers doing bathing suit shots who thought it was terribly groovy. The only way to cover it up is to get fat. She was a handsome girl, but she was literally in pieces.

"He won't be able to see any more girls today," the receptionist announced to me. I knew that meant he had already had his morning orgasm after destroying three or four girls so he didn't need anyone else to pick on. He couldn't scare me for a minute. I tossed Miss Thing a Kleenex, and we went out for coffee together. "Don't waste any juice crying. He loves to get you upset. That's the way he gets his kicks."

"I wouldn't mind so much if he had one constructive suggestion to offer. He didn't even look at my book," she moaned.

"He can't hurt you unless you let him. And he can do lots for you if he happens to be in the mood."

"If he hates women, why is he running a model agency?"

"You don't have to be mad for girls to want to push them around."

"It's so confusing. And so discouraging, don't you think so? Can I ask you another question?"

"Why not?"

"If you know about his tantrums, why do you come to see him?"

"Because my agency dropped me, and I'm looking around."

"Me, too," she said.

It was the first time I'd admitted to anyone I didn't know that I'd been dropped. Maybe it made her feel just a little bit less lonely. I know it did me. . . .

191

"You know, Carolyn," Stephanie said, "I think it's the hair. There's something not quite right about your hair."

Stephanie had been the first booker I'd met at Wilhelmina's. She had left there about the same time I had and gone over to another agency. Dovima told me about it on the sly and suggested I go see her. Stephanie and I had seen each other a hundred times, but when I met her at her new job, she looked at me as if I had been imported from Düsseldorf and was just off the plane. "I think I'll send you over to Eddie Senz."

As usual, I didn't know who he was. Stephanie briefed me. He had been the master of makeup at Warner Bros. in Hollywood for years. Bette Davis still goes to him, and he did the TV makeup for Mrs. Johnson when she was First Lady and sometimes for the Johnson girls.

The survival of a model ultimately depends on refining the endless flow of criticism she gets from all sides. I had learned to dissect my face and body and hair as coldly as if it were a dress I was trying on. You have to. You have to keep eyes and ears open and then decide whom to hearken to and whom to ignore. I decided to go on Stephanie's hunch. She made an appointment for me and a couple of other girls with Mr. Senz. I went in fully made up, and he sat me down in a barber chair and just looked at me. He was quiet as a brain surgeon for about five minutes as he cased me from every angle. Then he called in Ruby Gordon to look at my hair. Ruby is a fantastic character. He used to be a famous trumpeter with big-name bands some years ago. He had an accident on the road with his car, smashed up his mouth and teeth, and ruined his lip. So he found himself a new career. Everything there was to know about coloring and taking care of hair Ruby seemed to know. A lot of famous actresses and movie stars would fly in from California or from location in Europe just so Ruby could do their hair.

"Do you think you can do anything with it, Ruby?" Eddie asked.

Ruby was confident. He began to discuss formulas like a biochemist. He said my hair had been overprocessed. A double chemical process had been used on my locks where a single one would suffice.

Then came the hair stylist's turn. He wanted me to keep the long-haired look. He said it was absolutely right for me. I'm lucky in that my hair is straight to begin with. Some girls have to iron their hair on an ironing board or use chemicals to get it as straight as mine. What he wanted to do was restyle the front a little bit.

Ruby's voodoo came first. He put a long robe on me and went to work. He warned me not to expect any miracles the first time around. He said it might take two or three tries before he was able to balance exactly the right shade. We kept a small lock of hair as it was. When the new color came up, the difference was unbelievable. Then Jack, the hair stylist, went to work. He cut my bangs a new way in order to give me more height on top. Then on either side of my face he cut my hair so that instead of falling absolutely straight, it fell away naturally as a frame for my face. Then he set my hair and dried it. Before combing it out, they turned me over to Eddie Senz's assistant, who removed all my makeup and cleansed my face completely. Now I was ready for the maestro.

With all the great artists there is no mystery. Eddie explained everything he was doing while he was doing it and told me why he was doing it. He gave me a drawing of my face and encouraged me to take copious notes as we went along. The first thing he attacked was my eyebrows. He plucked my brows and gave me a completely different look. He said I had been wearing them too close to my nose. He moved them back to get rid of the menacing "other woman" look and lifted them higher on the outside to take advantage of the natural arch on my forehead.

My nose is wide at the top, so he put dark foundation on either side to push it back, a white liquid to open up the ends and sides. The liquid he used was a lightener for under eyes and brows. The tissues around the eyes tend to dry out more quickly, so anything powdery gives you a strange look. The shiny look is always better. He used very little foundation on the rest of my face. But it was a nice soft peachy pink—a true pink with no blue in it.

My eyes are exceptionally wide apart, which makes them easier to handle, from a makeup point of view, than having them too close together. I have a prominent brow bone, so he used lots of white just under the brow bone because white brings out and dark pushes back. He tempered it with a soft blue or green. He decided I needed a depth line between my eyelid and my brow bone. But the trick is to find the natural definition line and then accent that. This has the effect of enlarging the eye when it is opened. My eyes are almond-shaped, almost semi-Oriental-looking, and Eddie showed me how to make them rounder. He put on a very thin eyeliner before he put my lashes on, not after, as so many amateurs do. First he used an eyelash curler on my natural lashes, then he added brown mascara and a soft brown eyeliner—black is too hard for my coloring. Today top lashes are not enough—you have to have top lashes, then bottom lashes. So he cut up my old pair and affixed them tediously lash by lash.

When he whipped off my apron, I was lit up like a Christmas tree. Then they combed out my hair—now it was a lush, rich auburn. Eddie and Jack and Ruby stood back and beamed as if they had just created a new woman and they liked what they had done.

I kept wondering, what's in this for Eddie? I paid nothing for the session, and if the agency did, it was the first time any agency had ever done anything like this for me. Finally I realized that what Eddie got out of it was a customer. The only thing I bought from him was his rouge, and he gave me a little bottle of the white liquid as a gift. As usual with the best cosmetics, they are private formulas, not even on the market. I kept going back to Ruby every month while he kept working on my hair. It came out a little too dark on black-and-white prints, and he wanted it a little softer. Eventually he got it just right.

It's no news anymore that lots of people in the advertising business are insecure. Lots of models ball around with lots of advertising people in order to get this job and that job. And since agency people and models seem to talk more than they ball, there often occurs that awful moment when an ad man is compelled to prove that he hired Miss Delicious for some reason *besides* her talents in the sack—or on the desk. When that moment comes, advertising people like to be able to say that Miss Delicious comes from one of the top stables in town. Coming from a top agency is supposed to mean that everything is on the up-and-up. Or was in the beginning. It doesn't, of course. But it's a way of changing the subject.

So nice men from nice advertising agencies who like you and want to use you are often afraid to book you if you don't wear a top agency brand. Often they will send you to a model agency so you can be registered there, and then and only then will they book you. They're too insecure to book you direct if you don't have a name brand on you. "We use all her girls," they'll tell you. "She's got great girls. I'll give her a call. You go see her, and I know she'll take you on."

So you go. This one happened to be an agency that booked girls only for TV. No print. But you have to have a portfolio of photographs to show anyway. No model can trot around like a TV executive with a little portable tape machine which you can set down on a desk and have it reel off cartridges of all the various commercials you've appeared in. This will happen soon. It's coming. But it hasn't happened yet.

It takes a very experienced photographer to be able to tell from a one-dimensional photograph how you'll look on film. But it's all a part of the ritual of mating the girl with the job. After you've sent in your portfolio, you sit in the reception room and wait until Madam decides to look you over.

And in you walk. Madam is a very beautiful woman. Very business-like. In her forties, certainly. Her dress is expensive but not very new. Very last year, as a matter of fact. But you're not supposed to be looking at her while she is looking at you. She is casting a cold eye on you, from the heel of your shoe to the roots of your hair. "Good morning," you hear yourself saying, and then you wonder if you have made a boo-boo because suddenly you don't know if it's eleven o'clock Tuesday or two o'clock Elevensday. There is a chair at the side of her desk, and she smiles at you like a dental assistant about to wrap one of those towels around you and begin to poke at your teeth. She permits. You sit down carefully.

"You have a very interesting portfolio," Madam says, as if she were looking at an X-ray picture of your insides and this were a diseased organ. "Thank you," you say as if she had given you a 100 cc blast of morphine just before the operation. There's something wrong, and you don't know what it is.

"That mop of red hair!" Madam is suddenly screeching. "*Look* at it! Certainly this is not the way you go out on interviews." She was talking about my hair as if it were dirty, sooty grime on a windowsill and I were the lazy maid who hadn't cleaned it up. I was so shocked I didn't know what to say. Ruby had done my color on Saturday. My hair had been washed last night and combed twelve times today, the last time in the hall outside her office.

"You'll just have to do something about that hair before I could do anything with you," she said, slamming my portfolio shut. The whole scene was eerie, completely irrational. A year ago this kind of outburst would have sent me weeping and panting back to my friends at the Make-Up Center. Now I was as indifferent as if I were a corpse on a marble slab and she were the undertaker's wife. "Thank you very much," I said, very icy. I just looked at her and tried to guess what her problem was.

At one time or another, every model in New York worth sixty dollars an hour had to cope with a man whom I'll call, in this book, Philip Barker. Mr. Barker is a well-known philanthropist with a loser's genius for turning interesting projects into business fiascoes. Now my time had come. It was one of those late-spring afternoon cocktail parties at El Morocco. You never know who is giving it or why, but you are always told about the important people who are going to be there. And the important people are probably promised that the top models in town will be there. So the upshot is that the place is crawling with guys and gals pretending to be one or the other.

This TV agent had invited me and threatened me with the direst of consequences if I didn't show. So I went, and I was introduced to what seemed like hundreds of people, but the only one who really rang any bells was Mr. Barker. He was sitting at a table of guys and girls, and he took the pains to stand up when I was introduced to him. He wasn't so tall that one could suspect him of showing off, so I had to put that down as some kind of consideration for my sex, my profession, or perhaps the cut of my dress.

After I'd milled around for almost two hours with a drink in my hand, this very nice man introduced himself to me and told me he was Mr. Barker's press agent and that Mr. Barker had liked me and he wanted to get us together sometime. So I gave him my number and my agency number and said I was charmed I'm sure.

Well, anyone who can read a newspaper knows a little bit about Philip Barker. He is known as a very rich man, and he has corporate tentacles everywhere.

A couple of weeks later I got a call telling me that Mr. Barker wanted to see me. With these intermediaries you can never tell. Probably Mr. Barker was told I wanted to see him. I usually try to ask as many questions as I can about these appointments so I have some kind of idea what they're looking for. Well, said the press agent, Mr. Barker was having a big opening at a new cultural venture of his between five and ten o'clock one evening next month. In order to make sure the crowd was photogenic and attractive, he wanted to sprinkle some lovelies among the uglies he had to invite. He wanted a few models around in their best bib and tucker. For just showing up we would be paid a hundred bucks for the night.

That sounded kosher to me. They did it every week at the Coliseum on Columbus Circle. If they could do it for boat shows and auto shows and tool and die shows, why not for Mr. Barker's new cultural venture? It was also understandable that Mr. Barker might want to interview the girls he was hiring to dress up the opening. Maybe he even wanted to brief us and see if we could pass the test as culture lovers.

When I arrived at Mr. Barker's swanky office over near Rockefeller Plaza, the nice press agent, Vince McKinley, was there. He explained that Mr. Barker was interviewing another lady and it would just be a minute. Meanwhile Vince looked at my portfolio. "Beautiful book you have," he said. Then a model made her exit. She looked at me and I looked at her. We didn't know each other, so it was a kind of standoff. Then Vince explained that Mr. Barker had a few important phone calls to make before he could look me over. Finally I was ushered into the inner sanctum. Vince carried my portfolio in and put it on Mr. Barker's desk.

The office was fabulously furnished. He had a hidden bar with a wet sink in it tucked away among the shelves of his library. The furniture was low and spacious and tastefully arranged. The walls were hung with paintings, and he had a skyline view. Vince introduced me, and Mr. Barker said, "Oh, yes, I remember meeting you at El Morocco." I wondered if he really did or if the pad on his desk had a little notation next to my name to remind him.

"What can I get you to drink?" he asked me when he saw me noticing his hideaway bar. At an ordinary interview you were lucky if you got cold coffee in a paper container. I allowed as how this was a special occasion and so I'd let him treat me to a Scotch.

"Make yourself comfortable," he said. So I sat down on the couch —smack in the middle. When he brought me the drink, he said, "Now why don't you sit over there?" indicating the end of the sofa next to the table with the lamp on it and the telephone. It wasn't that I was afraid of the light. I had spent plenty of time doing my face up right so I had nothing to fear from any man's kilowatts. It was just that the phone seemed to be ringing every five seconds. And in case he SHOULD deign to answer it, that was the place he might want to sit.

When he insisted, I sat next to the phone and he sat down beside me. I noticed I had a drink in my hand and both his hands were free. This I figured was unilateral disarmament right there. Step Number One. Then the phone rang again. As he leaned over to answer it, he put his left hand on my knee and then picked up the phone with his right hand and started to talk.

He kept talking and talking, and I kept squirming and squirming. When he hung up, I said, "Gee, Mr. Barker, wouldn't it be easier if we changed places? The cord is not that long." He was rich enough to have a cord from here to California, but he had the shortest one in town. It was all part of the choreography. He seemed quite familiar with the procedure.

"What's the matter—does that bother you?" he inquired.

"Not particularly," I said. "But I imagine it might be uncomfortable for you."

The phone rang again. When he leaned over to grab it, his left hand slid right up my leg under my dress. He had me pinned there. Anything I said the phone would pick up. Maybe he was daring me to scream. Maybe he liked to live dangerously because the voice on the phone was a woman and he was calling her honey and arguing with her about whether or not he would be home for dinner. I had read in the papers that he and Mrs. Barker were having trouble and headed for the Supreme Court.

Now I was angry. I disentangled myself and walked to his desk to pick up my portfolio. Now *he* was angry. He slammed down the phone, stood up, and confronted me. He had his hands in his pockets. He pulled out a five-dollar bill and said, "Here's five bucks for your cab fare home, dear."

"Thanks very much," I said. "I'm independently wealthy."

I walked out. The press agent wasn't there. Nobody was in the outer office. The day was over and playtime was here. I never expected to hear any more about marching around his new cultural venture on opening night. And I never envied the girls who did.

If you're a secretary or a typist, you get paid for being sick. Everybody is entitled to a couple of weeks' sick leave with pay every year, so they feel cheated if they don't get some kind of fashionable flu. It's a chance for everyone to show how much they love you and you loll in bed telephoning your friends to drop by with hot bouillon or cold fruit drinks—all this on company time and money. If you have to go to the hospital, it's that much more chic. You've got sickness insurance, which they call Health Insurance or Blue Cross or something. Get some groovy doctor to certify that you need a few days' confinement for tests or observation and you get your sick pay, plus your meals. Insurance can cover everything but your telephoning, and the maid service is free. You get yours and the doctor gets his, and the insurance company picks up the check. You feel cheated if you pay those premiums every month or they take them out of your salary automatically and you don't come down with something gruesome enough for you to be confined to some smart undercrowded medical pavilion.

But if a model gets sick, she's out of luck. I once had a cold sore on my lip, and it cost me almost two thousand dollars in bookings. I wasn't photographable for more than ten days. When Elizabeth Taylor has one, they shoot around her for a few days. Or failing that, they take long shots and do the close-ups later. If the worst comes to the worst, they shut down the picture for a few days. And there's insurance to take care of that. Lloyds of London picks up the tab. But if you're just some hard-working little Miss Model booked for a juicy commercial with possibilities for residuals, they may love you to death, you can be just what the story board calls for, the client may be sold on you, the art director may think you're irreplaceable, but when the chips are down in a glamour job, nobody waits for you. The meter is running, and time means money, and at $60,000 a day, this is a total loss—the kind of check nobody picks up—not the client, not the agency. Even if you've slept with everybody who's anybody on the account and think you have it sewed up for keeps and forever, you're out on your ear. The economics of the business demands that they get themselves another girl. So if you don't learn how to be healthy, don't bother about being a model.

Sunday night after the Thanksgiving weekend in Vermont, as I headed back to Manhattan in my Thunderbird, I could feel my temperature going up and my residuals going down—the drain. What they called the Hong Kong flu that season hit Middlebury just about the time I did, and by Sunday night I was in no shape to make the trip. But I had to be in New York for an early morning booking. The producer, Jay Columbus, was one of the sweetest guys in the business, and he had gone to bat to get me the principal part in a commercial for the new Funk & Wagnalls encyclopedia. It was too late to call in sick. There was no way of reaching anyone until Monday morning.

When I got to Albany, I was so pooped I drove to my sister's house hoping I could bunk there for the night and drive the rest of the way in the early morning. I had a habit of using her place as a way station to break the trip. But that night of all nights there wasn't a soul stirring at their house. Nobody, but nobody, home. I kept on driving. I navigated that turnpike all the way to New York. When I pulled up in front of my apartment, I could barely let go of the wheel—I was so tense. I was too tired to park the car. I unloaded and just asked Charlie, the doorman, to take care of the car.

I went upstairs, flopped in bed, and set the alarm. I went to sleep before counting my teeth one time around. I wasn't sure I would even be able to speak above a whisper in the morning. Luckily my wardrobe and tote bag had all been packed tidily before I left for Vermont. My hairpieces were all set, and all I had to do was pick them up and carry them. Ordinarily they were a breeze—but the next morning any ounce might be the one that broke my back.

Fortunately the studio where we were shooting was only two blocks from my apartment. When they passed around the coffee and muffins at 9 A.M., just the smell of food made me nauseous and dizzy. I was afraid to look at myself in the mirror because then I might not have the confidence to face the makeup man. I had such a fever it was like being under the color film lights with Barbra Streisand in July. I had to patch up my makeup every five minutes.

When everything was ready on the set, I walked on with the sleeves of my suit stuffed with Kleenex—just in case my nose ran. I was way past hiding my infirmity; the crew were marvelous. Before each take the director would ask, "Are you OK, Carolyn? Your nose all set?" I was trying to remember my direction while worrying that my nose would run or I might sneeze in the middle of shooting and blow an otherwise good take. In between takes the makeup man was right in there dusting my nose with powder. I kept going the entire day on hot soup and hot tea, and we finished the entire commercial by four in the afternoon—an hour ahead of deadline. At last I could collapse. I'll never forget how sweet that crew were to me, especially Jay, the producer, who came to me afterward and told me everybody knew how sick I was, and how grateful they were that I'd kept going.

I was in bed for two days afterward and lost two fat days of bookings. But I'd managed the Monday job, and it has been paying residuals ever since it broke in the New York market. Not only that—because I made that special effort, the producer became a good friend of mine. He has used me in several lucrative commercials since that time, and we have more scheduled for the future. The only capital a model has besides her looks is her professional reputation. The French have a word for it. They call it *l'esprit.* The English word "spirit" doesn't mean quite the same thing.

When crack photographers and great producers want to use you again and again, it means you've got it. No amount of bed hopping or crotch politics is any substitute. You've either got it or you haven't.

Whenever you're mad, keen, determined not to be late for a booking, there are absolutely never any taxis to be had. I stood on Park Avenue ready to get down on my knees in the litter and pray for a rickshaw. It had been another rush-rush day with no time for lunch, but I was prepared. My early morning grapefruit and melba toast felt like hours away, so I dipped into the emergency rations in my tote bag and hauled out a box of cookies. I think it's hideous to eat in the street, but there I was, munching chocolate cookies like crazy, with my tote bag and my portfolio parked on the sidewalk. Whenever I saw what looked like a taxi, I was out in the street flailing my arms and posing like a lady in distress, hoping some cabdriver would melt when he saw me. Even if he wanted to bend my ear for three blocks about his beautiful daughter who wanted to be a model, I wouldn't care. Just as long as he got me to the church on time. I had seven minutes to get to this important booking on Park Avenue South. Even if I gave up and ran for the subway, I was lost. It would be too late. Something told me to pray. It was then I saw him walking toward me. He was so beautiful he looked like an archangel. He had as much hair as I did, blond and bouncing and fresh as a commercial for Prell. His face was thinner than mine, with beautiful high cheekbones. He had a see-through yellow voile shirt on with the sleeves rolled up. His skinny chino pants were bleached to a bone color from a thousand washings, and on his bare brown feet he wore mahogany leather sandals. He was gliding toward me, smiling this beatific smile as if he were the love of *my* life and this were the most important moment in *his*. It was like a slow-motion Clairol commercial gone wrong. If he's a male model who once worked with you and you don't remember him, there's something wrong with your antenna, Carolyn.

It was goofy of me just to stand there and stare at him as if I'd never seen a gorgeous hunk of man before, so I took another bite of cookie and waved frantically at a cab across the street.

The next thing I knew he had grabbed the box of cookies right out of my hand and was staring at the fine print on the package.

"Help yourself," I said in the snootiest of tones. He was frowning as he walked toward the big trash basket on the corner. Then he pitched my cookies into this pile of garbage and debris as if they had been contaminated by atomic fallout. He dusted his hands off and smiled so guilelessly that I melted. Then he walked up to me, took a piece of chocolate cookie right out of my hand, and tossed it away.

"If you want to be radiant, you can't eat junk like that," he said, beaming. I'd heard of people being mugged and raped on the street. I'd heard of purse snatchers and body snatchers. I'd even heard of boys in the subway snatching wigs off girls' heads and running off and selling them, but a *cookie* snatcher—this was ridiculous.

"I'm hungry," I protested. "I haven't had lunch, and I have a booking at two. If I don't get to Park Avenue South and Twenty-fourth Street in five minutes flat—well, it's a *catastrophe* already."

He wasn't paying the slightest attention to me. People were walking past, rush-rush-rush, minding their own business, not paying the slightest attention, either. And now he was unzipping my tote bag and going through it like a customs inspector.

"Wait a minute, Charlie!" I hollered. "What do you think you're doing?" I was too flabbergasted to fight with him. Maybe he's deaf, I thought. He's got to be deaf. No matter what I say, he just smiles at me with that beatific smile. He's gorgeous and he knows he's gorgeous and that entitles him to do anything. Anything indeed.

There he was rummaging through my tote bag like the fuzz with a warrant. Fuzz! Maybe there's a city-wide raid on pot smokers, I thought. Maybe undercover cops with synchronized watches are pouncing on photographers' studios and models all over town.

I was so fascinated I stood there, bolted to the street, as he fished out a bottle of diet soda and a package of gum. All the rest of the precious props he ignored. He held up this bottle of soft drink as if it were one of the Dead Sea scrolls and began to read off the fine print. He had a spellbinding voice, all molasses and honey. Aha, I thought, he's an actor, and this is some sort of improvisation he's practicing. He's been sent out by some kooky drama teacher to create a scene in the street. Probably someone is zooming in on me right now from the roof across the street with a film camera. Maybe he has to do something weird like this to get into the Repertory Company at Lincoln Center. Or maybe it's a final exam for an apprenticeship in The Living Theater. "Carbonated water. Citric acid. Calcium cyclamate. Sodium citrate. Saccharine'—with an asterisk yet. 'Flavor derived from lemon and lime oils.' And what does the asterisk tell us? Put on your glasses, lady, and read the fine print. 'Contains one-tenth of one percent calcium cyclamate and one hundredth of one percent saccharine, non-nutritive artificial sweeteners, which should be used only by persons who must restrict their intake of ordinary sweets. No fat or protein, less than fifteen-hundredths of one percent available carbohydrates. One-sixth calorie per fluid ounce.' "

When he'd finished intoning the litany of chemical compounds in my bottle, he walked over to the trash basket and tossed it in. Then with great ceremony he tore up my package of chewing gum and dropped it in. Dusting off his hands, he smiled that wild, enchanting smile and talked to me as if I were five years old.

"If you have to face a camera every day, you can't go on eating junk like that."

"But I'm dying of hunger, and if I don't get to Twenty-fourth Street in three minutes flat, it's going to be a disaster."

"Here's a taxi for you now," he replied calmly. I looked around and, sure enough, he was right. The driver flung the door open. My gorgeous friend dashed back to the curb and picked up my tote bag and my portfolio and shoved them into the taxi behind me. After he'd carefully slammed the door, he reached through the open window and handed me something in a waxed paper envelope.

"If you want to be radiant, try this," he said. "I made it myself." Then, as the cab pulled away, he shouted, "Chew each mouthful fifty times."

I leaned out the window to take another look at him. I wanted to ask the cabdriver if he had seen what I had seen. The waxed paper envelope in my lap was real. The tall blond boy in the street was real. Everything he had done was so perfectly natural. It was the timing, the strange way it had happened, that made it seem like a dream.

I opened the waxed paper envelope. In it were two thick slices of bread. I had to believe he had made it himself. I had never smelled bread like that in New York. It smelled of Vermont and my grandmother, and it tasted like heaven on earth. The more I chewed the more delicious it tasted. He had to be one of the flower people. The whole-wheat flour people. The love people.

I was so busy chewing that we were at the studio before I knew it. I didn't have a minute to spare. I dashed for the elevator, I lunged for the dressing room to fix my hair.

"Hi, Carolyn," the stylist said as she poked her head in the door.

"I hope I didn't hold you up. I wanted to be early," I said. "But the strangest thing happened on the way to the studio..."

She wasn't listening. She was on her way out. Never mind. I didn't want to tell her anyway. I wasn't sure I wanted to tell anybody. If I said he looked like an archangel and he destroyed my cookies with mad, keen love because he wanted me to stay radiant, and he made his own bread, they might think I was on LSD.

"I had hell getting a cab," I said, half to myself. "Absolute hell."

THIS must be what they call a crash pad.

It looked as if the police had raided a wild party just as it reached its peak, and had carried everybody off, leaving the debris frozen in place.

It was a huge industrial loft on the West Side of Manhattan. I checked the address; the sign on the door was the name the agency had given me. It was supposed to be the studio of this new hot-shot photographer from California who wanted to do some test shots with me. I had seen some strange setups in my time, but this topped everything. It had a split-level bathroom with no door. A dirty old bathtub was sunk about six feet into the floor, and you would need a rope ladder to get into it. There were mattresses scattered about the place covered with ratty fur that seemed half alive. Here and there was an orange crate with a coffee can full of cigarette butts on it. There were cardboard boxes full of old clothes looking as though they had been left where someone had dropped them making a getaway.

Larry finally wandered in from another room which he used as a

204

darkroom. He was a very jumpy guy, dressed in washed-out chino pants and a magenta jersey. He didn't make the slightest apology for the madhouse decor. He showed me a cracked makeup mirror lying on the floor as if it were a completely outfitted dressing room. There wasn't a chair in sight—nary a table to put my things on. Well, I thought, he must be a mad genius to get away with this; I'll do it his way. I sat down on the fur-covered mattress, propped the mirror up against the wall, and began fixing my hair. He wanted to shoot me in about four outfits. He liked everything I showed him. Now all I had to do was change into a bikini with a diaphanous jeweled caftan over it. As soon as I stripped, workmen started walking in from four directions, carrying lumber, cement, pipes, and paint. Apparently the place was under reconstruction. Strange people kept breezing by me, carrying strange tools and props, not paying the slightest attention to me.

I wondered if they were really construction workers or if this was some mad character shot Larry was cooking up for one of the magazines. Photographers are always doing that. One man wore a welder's helmet. He plugged in his little electric tool, turned on the gas, and began attacking a tangle of pipes. Sparks were flying like fireworks.

Larry wandered around in a state of intense concentration, glassy-eyed, as if all this hubbub weren't really happening. "OK, baby," he smiled. "Let's attack." Before I finished wiping my feet to get on the seamless, he began shooting. He had the lights set up exactly the way he wanted them. He knew exactly what he wanted, and he knew when he had it. We shot about four outfits in less than an hour, and that was that. He turned off the lights and walked off the set. When I walked into the crash pad to change clothes, he was lying on one of the fur rugs, staring into space, completely out of it. I just pretended he wasn't there at all and finished dressing. "*Ciao* for now, baby," he said. "I'll buzz you in a couple of days when we have the contacts." Then he rolled over, closed his eyes, and was gone.

The welders and the carpenters and the plumbers were still doing their little ballet when I walked out. It was all pretty weird, but that's what everybody is buying nowadays so I didn't think anything of it.

In a couple of days Larry called me, all excited. Some of the contacts were great. He wanted me to see them. He invited me down that evening to look them over and pick out the prints I wanted for my book.

This time when I walked in, the crash pad was alive with people. It was like a permanent party that had been going on for days. Six people sat around on the fur-covered mattresses. The missing bathroom door was suspended from the ceiling on thin, thin wires. The floor was littered with wine bottles. Tin cans held stubs of burning candles. The whole floor had been turned into a multicolored psychedelic painting featuring one-word abstractions like: PEACE DEATH LOVE WAR LIFE—plus a few of the more familiar four-letter words.

I might as well have been invisible. Nobody paid the slightest attention to me. Suddenly a girl walked in wearing a floor-length red cape in dirty crushed velvet tied at the neck with gold thongs. Underneath she wore transparent white pajamas that looked as if they'd been made out of worn embroidered altar cloths. She was topless, and her straight, dirty hair hung over her bosoms. She looked so strange and so terrible that it took me a minute to remember that I knew her. We had worked on a job together just a few months ago.

"Hi, Johanna," I said.

She looked me up and down as if I were a disgusting sight. "*Ciao,*" she said. "You still peddling it?" I decided to ignore the dig. She looked like a medieval mental case who didn't know where she was. Six months ago she had been a raving beauty.

"I did some test shots with Larry. He asked me down to look at the contacts."

"Oh, yeah," she said. "What ever happened to Larry? He was a doll." I hated to remind her that he was her host. "You want a little swizzle of anything, help yourself."

People outside the tribe always assume that if you're a model you must know lots of other models. Actually most models are loners. We're all doing the same thing at the same time in different places. You work with someone once and then you may never see her again for months, for years, or ever.

"I haven't seen you around," I said to Johanna, perfectly aware that it was a stupid statement.

"Yeah," said Johanna. "I got crabs in my portfolio, so I went skipping off into new things. I been through that movie too many times. So I got this new agent, baby. He set me up with a real crazy cigarette commercial. I had to ball twelve guys and kick back thirty percent of my residuals to get it. But I screwed all those bastards and got even."

"Good for you." I said. "I'm glad."

"Yeah," said Johanna, "I got a gorgeous case of cancer. And this gorgeous cigarette company sends me a gorgeous check every month to keep quiet about it."

"*Ciao*," was all I could think of to say.

I got out of there fast.

Ever since I can remember, I wanted to blow myself to a European vacation. Whenever I had the money, I didn't have the time, or whenever I had the time, I didn't have the money. Last June—one of the slowest months in the business—I had both, so I made my reservation.

All I had to do was set the date and they wanted me to do two days of glamorous yachting on Long Island Sound—shooting a cigarette commercial for South America. So I rescheduled my trip. I caught the cold of the year on that glamorous yachting party; when I finally caught the plane for Rome, I had a fever of 102.

My first and favorite all-time roommate Clem and her handsome Italian husband met me at the airport, took me home, and nursed me until I was in shape to cope with the sights and sounds of Italy. Then I took off for London.

A few days in London helped me to understand and appreciate my British grandmother, but it was in Paris that I first understood my French papa. In Paris you could just smell it. There the man and woman thing has been refined into an art. It's so easy to be discovered in Paris. A woman just sits still in a sidewalk café, and the *men* make the rounds. They have such a civilized way of flirting that it's a pleasure to learn their way. They understand that the preliminaries are more than half the fun, so nobody is ever in a hurry.

I began to feel sorry for any girl whose daddy wasn't a great lover. That had to be Daddy's story. They didn't call him the Great Rinaldo for nothing. His name was René. Mom called him Rainy—and that was enough to dampen anyone down—but not Papa.

Having a father like mine makes every boy and girl thing that happens to you absolutely epochal. You find out someone cares, even if the boy doesn't. With four daughters on his hands, no wonder Papa tried to keep us under lock and key; no wonder he whipped out the big black strap when Mom told him she found me in the cellar with two older boys. I didn't know what it was all about. Since I never had any brothers, I thought boys and girls were identical in the front like they were in the back. These older boys were just about to show me the difference when Mom walked in on us. I didn't understand what it was all about. But Papa did. And he knew the boys did. When you've been a great lover, you suspect every other male of attempting what you would have done—or did do when you were a boy. Papa gave my boyfriends a hard time; when he watched them and suspected them and even chased one off into the woods, he was telling me he loved me in his own way. And he was telling me in his own way that love and everything about it was too important to play fast and loose with.

So excuse me, kids, but from the hate-Mama-hate-Papa section of the Love Generation, I'm a dropout. It's OK for Bob Dylan and other Pied Pipers of the Now Generation to distrust and hate everyone over thirty—their parents included—but don't make a religion out of it and don't expect me to join.

Sitting alone or with somebody at a sidewalk café in Paris is one of the greatest shows on earth. You don't realize the hideous poverty of a city like New York until you spend some time in Paris. In Manhattan when I was starting out as a model, I had to lope around like a criminal on the run, going from the public library to some dirty park, going from hotel lobby to hotel lobby, looking for a place to rest and relax between appointments. In Paris you can check in at a front table in a sidewalk café—any time of year—you can order a cup of coffee or a beer or a glass of wine, and you can sit there all afternoon holding court. You can write your novel, study your script, pose, flirt, brood, sulk, be sad, be happy, watch the passing parade or ignore it—and nobody bothers you every five minutes for fear they're going to lose a nickel unless they sell you another martini.

Sitting alone at a sidewalk café, you can also be auditioning for a job as a model in the most dignified and civilized way possible. I stopped at the Café de la Paix near the L'Opéra one day and the waiter gave me a front table. I was alone. I had my camera over my shoulder—the badge of the tourist. I noticed two young men noticing me. They smiled. I smiled back. One of them came over and introduced himself. He was a photographer. He was sure I was a model, and he wanted to know where I was from. When I said I was from New York, he introduced his friend who worked for RTF—the French TV network. The photographer wanted to book me for a job on the spot. I'd had only one commercial job to do in Paris, and that had taken only a day. "When would you like to shoot?" I asked him.

"Oh," he said, "right now, or as soon as possible."

There was no casting director who needed to see me? No art director who had final approval? I didn't have to be seen by the client?

He laughed at my description of the American way of modeling. His little car was around the corner. He drove me to the Plaza Athénée, and I picked up some clothes. Then we drove into the countryside near Versailles, and he began scouting for a spot. No location director had been out the day before. The French are supposed to be inefficient and bureaucratic, but from what I saw, Madison Avenue could give them lessons in wasting time and money. The two young men were probably as old as I was, but they seemed like college kids to me—so eager, so direct, and so simple.

Pierre-Domenique finally found a spot that suited him, and he asked me to pose in the pants suit I had on. I didn't even bother to unzip my clothes carrier. It took him about ten minutes to get the shot that made him happy, and that was it. When he'd finished, he put his hand in his pocket and handed me a thousand-franc note. That's a little over twenty dollars. He apologized and said he knew in the States I would probably get much more. Yes, I admitted, but I would have to get a voucher signed—then pay the agency ten percent, then twenty percent more might be held in a reserve fund until the agency received its check from the client. It might be three months before I would see my sixty dollars, but with the voucher system I'd get seventy percent of sixty dollars—forty-two dollars—in two weeks. In the meantime I might have spent at least twenty-two dollars in cab fares running around to be looked at by various people who had to give me an OK.

My friends wanted to take me to dinner and give me a real conducted tour. They took me to Versailles, and we walked around the fabulous gardens of the Palace. I was dying to take pictures of that, but to the French Versailles is like Central Park Lake—it's been used up as a backdrop for fashion photographs. Then they took me on a walking tour through Saint-Germain-des-Prés on the Left Bank, where all the boutiques and shops are—the capital of the student-led revolution that had erupted just a few weeks before. Then Pierre-Domenique's friend suggested that they take me to dinner at La Coupole. I had never heard of it, and when they said it could not be described, they were telling the gospel. On one level it is just a restaurant, one of the biggest restaurants I'd ever seen—the size of Grand Central, so huge you wonder how the food could possibly be as good and as cheap as it is. On the other hand, La Coupole is a Paris landmark. The decor is absolutely zero. It looks like every other restaurant on Boulevard Montparnasse—plain tables, electric fans dangling from the ceiling, plain tile floor like the one you have in your bathroom. It has been a hangout for artists and literati since the days when Matisse and Picasso were young. It comes back to life every few years, and now it has been discovered once again by the young people of Paris. It needs no decor because the customers bring that with them. It is always crowded and impossible to get a table right away, so there is a permanent floating floor show of customers wending their way among the tables, greeting friends, seeing and being seen—it's the most fantastic fashion show to be seen in Paris.

Pierre-Domenique said, "It's the biggest zoo in Europe. If you come here often enough, you meet everybody you know."

I didn't know a soul in Paris, but I realized he had spoken the gospel when I heard someone scream, "Schatzi!" I looked up, and it was Pollo shouting, "Where did you get zat red hair?" He looked taller in Paris than he had in California and even better-looking. He was with another tall, handsome Latin type who, I guessed, for some reason or other, had to be the French actor who was the love of his life.

We made room for them at our table, and his friend Tino turned out not to be French but Italian. And he wasn't Pollo's old lover at all—the one who gave him so much trouble. He wasn't his new lover. As a matter of fact, if I could trust my vibrations, he wasn't a boy lover at all. He was a girl lover of the old school, and he was crazy about red hair, too. He wasted no time at all giving me the full Roman treatment. He was a painter, and he'd started out working as an extra in American films in Italy in order to make money. He'd begun to act more and more and paint less and less. At the time *Ben-Hur* was being made at Cinecitta Studios, they picked him to be nailed to the cross in the role of Jesus. He was signed, put under contract, paid to stand by for weeks, and when his big moment came and they fitted his costume, the producer decided he had too much hair on his chest. They wanted to shave him, but that wasn't in the contract, so Tino refused. He got his money, but he never got crucified. That sounded like the business I was on vacation from. All we talked about was hair.

We had a jolly big dinner with wine and twelve kinds of hors d'oeuvres, entrée, and dessert. When it came time for someone to take me home, I had my choice of escorts. It had been a busy day, and tomorrow would be hectic, so in order to avoid any complications I decided to let Pollo take me home. After all, he was my oldest friend in Paris, and besides, I knew enough about him to know he was harmless. I wouldn't have that late night entanglement problem to contend with.

So we all said our good-byes, and off Pollo drove me in his Volkswagen convertible. It had been two years since I'd gotten into the dyepot and become a redhead—I'd begun to take it for granted. But Pollo was carrying on the way David had the first night he saw me. Pollo insisted he would never have recognized me at all *without* the hair.

"First I saw ze hair, schatzi," he kept saying. "It was only after I realized I knew the face underneaze it from somewhere. If you ever go back to zat mousy brown, I'll scratch your eyes out."

He carried on so about taking me dancing that I finally relented. We ended up at New Jimmy's where Regine presides over the discotequeing—in a red wig. Pollo was a terrific dancer, and we were having a ball doing the Bugaloo, whipping my long red mane around. When they played a slow number, we danced cheek to cheek and Pollo made love to my hair as if it were a Revlon commercial gone wrong. It was all a huge inside joke, I thought, until something happened that is not supposed to happen when you're dancing with harmless pansies.

"Pollo!" I shouted, drawing back in horror. "Are you all *right*? What's come *over* you?"

"The body does not lie," he smirked. "You're no faggot moll tonight, schatzi. Zat red hair of yours does somesing to me. Isn't zat marvelous? If zey throw me out of the faggots' union, so what?"

I'd thought I had trouble with men before. That night I had more trouble calming down one reformed pansy than I'd had from ninety-nine men who had never left the straight and narrow path. He insisted on proving to himself and to me that this was no temporary aberration. He was furious when I couldn't take him seriously. I had been in all sorts of situations with men in my life, but this was the switcherooney of all time. I'd had four men to choose from. I'd picked the harmless

211

type so I could get home early, and it was 5 A.M. before I finally wore him out and got to my room at the Plaza Athénée. Like a determined German, he wasn't giving up the struggle just because he'd lost the first round. So I relented, and we arranged that the big seduction scene would take place the following Friday. And I left Paris on Thursday. Forgive me, Pollo.

# CHAPTER 9

"Does a girl gotta?" That is the question.

The Gallup Poll had never grappled with this question. So fools rush in where pollsters fear to tread. I had answered this question for myself after a couple of years in the business. But my answer was a little iffy. It was yes and no. I often wondered how it looked from the other side of the casting couch. I had been modeling for almost three years before I knew any Mr. Bigs well enough to ask them point-blank. I began my poll at a private party when I ran into a producer of TV commercials who had been successful in the business for almost fifteen years. So I asked him, "Does a girl gotta?"

And he said, "Sometimes, yeah. Sometimes she does. But the trouble is most models think they have to every damn time, and that's where things get ridiculous."

It only takes a couple of squares to turn a dialogue into a round table. Before many minutes had passed, we had a round table going on sex in the modeling racket. And everybody spoke his piece.

My producer friend thinks most models are stupid and trying too hard to be weird, and God knows he had the facts to back it up with.

"Look," he began, "the other day we were shooting a commercial in the studio for a food company, and we had picked this gorgeous blonde. Some outfits have elaborate systems for casting, but I pick my own talent. I get approval from my clients, but they give me the freedom to pick people I like to work with."

"So if you wanted to, you could sleep with every girl you hire?" said a square.

"Right. But the real scoop is I usually can't be bothered. I love my wife and I haven't got time enough to make love to her. So here we are on the set. Miss Gorgeous arrives at ten in the morning ready for work. She brings along this guy—the most sickening, disgusting-looking guy I'd seen in months. He's wearing dirty striped bell-bottom pants tied

213

with a pajama string. He has on sandals so you can see his dirty feet. He's wearing a black Homburg hat from the Salvation Army. He has a dirty beard, and long hair tied in the back with a string, and no teeth. So she brings him on the set and introduces him to everybody. I wanted to vomit, but I let it go. An hour later we're ready for her and she's not ready yet. So I send my assistant director into the dressing room to tell her she's wanted on the set. He comes back a little shook. He knocks at the door. She says, 'Come in,' and when he walks in she's having liquid sex with this toothless creep on the floor of the dressing room."

"I don't believe it," said a square.

"You've got to have brass balls to do that," said another.

"Right," said the producer. "But what was she trying to tell me? Last week I worked on location with another girl in the Pocono Mountains. It was an elaborate commercial, and this attractive girl was an actress who had appeared in quite a few Broadway shows. We had a nine o'clock call, and when she doesn't appear I send my makeup man to the motel to get her. He finds her sacked out with some guy in bed. When I get to her room to try to hurry things along, I find her sitting there nude with the makeup man trying to fix her hair and this guy is lying there in his shorts posing like some Brooklyn pasha, acting as though we were interfering with his private life. This time she doesn't even bother to introduce this creep to me. When she saw my one eyebrow ascending, she said, 'Oh, this is Bill.' Now what was she trying to tell me?"

"Some girls have a thing about having sex in crazy places at surprising times. Maybe she was trying to tell you she's a free soul," I suggested.

"She had already proved that to me," said the producer. "I don't have to be hit on the head. I can take a hint. I don't need her to give me a three-act play on my client's time."

"Yeah, taking care of two clients at one time is a little brassy," said another square.

"Models don't have to convince me they're weird. I get it all the time. Last week I worked with a girl on location upstate. By the time we got back to the city it was almost eleven o'clock. I didn't want to leave her standing on the corner waiting for a taxi, so I asked if I could drive her home. My sound man walked her to the door. While I'm waiting in the car, she invites him in. She invited me in, too, but I was in a sweat to get home. Next morning the sound man tells me about the

214

weird setup he walks into. This girl has a roommate—a Negro girl. The Negro girl is furious with her for bringing a guy home. He gets the picture—they're both lesbians. He wants to get out of there, but he hasn't got a chance. The white girl insists he ball her because she wants to get even with her black roommate. After he's finished and trying to get out of there, he finally has to ball the black roommate to prove he's not an enemy of Black Power. The next day he's no good to me for anything. So please don't ask me whether a model has to ball the guys in this business. They *think* they have to. Or they want to. Or maybe they think they want to. They've heard somewhere this is the way it swings, so they go along with the herd and that's it.

"You wouldn't believe the propositions I get," the producer went on. "Last week I cast a girl for a job, and when I asked her to bring her wardrobe in the day before shooting so I could check it with the client, she gets suddenly very la-di-da and says it's her maid's day off, so she asked me to stop by her penthouse for a drink. She's living in a penthouse on East Seventy-ninth Street. I don't drink. I went over just for the look. She started climbing all over me like in a BB movie. What do I need this for? What does she need this for? She already had the job. I hired her because she was right for it. She had the looks and the talent. If she hadn't bothered me with this cheap sex stuff, I would have hired her again. I like to work with regulars—people I know and can depend on. There are enough surprises in this business coming from the weather, the clients, the whims of this one and that one. It's nice to have the talent under control. But the things girls do to get jobs in this business are unbelievable. They bring me in eviction notices, they bring me in their starving children to show how much they need a job. Another model I know is married and has five kids. She has a house in Westchester, and her husband is an artist with a big advertising agency. She invited me to a party after we had worked together a couple of times. My wife didn't want to go. It's a lucky thing. Another producer I know went, and it turned out to be a nude swimming party. If this is what her home life is like in Westchester, what does she do when she swings?"

Outrage and shock have become very commercial these days. Does that help account for the fact that weird sexual behavior has become fashionable?

"No, ten years ago I think it was worse. It's just more in the open now," the producer insisted. "Ten—fifteen—years ago when I started in this business, things were really rotten. A girl really had to sleep with guys to get a job in commercials. She had to start out sleeping with the guy who did the casting in the model agency or the casting agency or the advertising agency. And then when she got the commercial she was expected to kick back part of her fees to some guys along the way. This used to be routine. But now that's been cleaned up inside the business. That's why today most of the casting people in the ad agencies are women. I'd say ninety-five percent of them are female. Today if a girl is ready to sleep with a man to get a job, it doesn't mean anything. She's wasting her time—wearing out her delicate membranes for nothing. She's got to pass some lady who's going to be looking at sixty or seventy girls for one job before she even gets to see the producer. She has to be right for the job—she has to have the talent to read lines, act, move, do something the job requires or she'll never get the opportunity to sleep with anybody who can help her get a job. So that narrows it down considerably."

"All right. Say she has the talent and has the looks and she gets a crack at the job. What then?"

"She's sent over by the casting lady to the producer and the client. To get two or three girls, a client like Buick might interview a hundred. The girls walk in a room. There sits the director, the producer, the art director, the copywriter, the musical director, and the client. At least ten people. She meets them all. It's hello Miss Jones and good-bye Miss Jones, we'll let you know. Don't call us, we'll call you. What good does it do her if she's full of birth control pills and she's brought her coil and two diaphragms along? Sex is irrelevant."

"Then a girl doesn't gotta."

"That comes later."

"Aha! After she gets the job."

"Sex comes in from left field when you'd least expect it. Life is not like the movies. It's no one-two-three deal. After the girl has been selected, the client might turn to the producer and say, 'I'd like to go for the redhead, but *will she?*' The producer doesn't know. But he might want to find out. Or he might have eyes on her himself. He might take the initiative and call the girl and tell her he'd like to use her but first he'd like to talk it over. He suggests coming up or she asks him over."

216

"How often does this happen?" a square wanted to know.

"Sometimes. Not most of the time. Nobody has the time or the energy. Everybody has too many commercials—the clients do, that is. Some of them have to oversee as many as fifty a year. It happens sometimes—that's as close as you could get to a percentage."

"In the cases where it happens, what percentage of the models would say no?"

Not many, all of us had to admit. It depends on the girl, the amount of money involved. But if it's a big national commercial with a fifty-thousand-dollar pot of gold at the end of the rainbow, most girls would. Definitely.

"It happens. We know it happens," I explained. "And after it happens, almost always the girl and the guy grow to hate each other. The man feels cheated. The girl feels used. They end up avoiding each other.

"Top models, of course, don't have to. If a client wants them, he has to pay for them, and that's it. The girls most ready to hop into bed to cinch their job security are the green newcomers. That's what I feel. They do it because they're scared. They feel they can't take a chance. There are guys around who say ball with me and I'll get you this and get you that and see that you get this gig and that gig. This is amateur night, and these girls have to get burned before they smarten up. Then they learn to say promises, promises, but let's sign the deal first before we hop into bed. In many cases these men are fascinating guys, creative, amusing, good company, so the girl takes the pill and she gambles. If he's a real horror, that's something else again. But a girl has to think of her reputation. This business is a very small world. It's like a small town, really, and people talk more than anything. It soon gets around, and when a girl gets marked easy, she's in for trouble."

"True," said my producer friend.

"It may be the IN thing to do to ball everybody, but once you get talked about, you can be very OUT in a hurry."

"But how often does it happen?"

"It happens plenty. Nobody can tell you. But when a good job is hanging in the balance with lots of money and fringe benefits, like fancy de luxe travel to smart locations, I doubt if very many or any girls would say no."

"And here again is where it makes trouble," said the producer. "I've

217

had clients who picked a girl for a big commercial. When we get out on location, the client takes a shine to the girl. She plays up to him. But when bedtime arrives, she says no. The client doesn't like her anymore. He hates the sight of her. And he hates the commercial. As a producer I get the headaches from it all. The client can be very blunt about it. If he likes a girl, he can do a lot for her. A girl is better off being sought after by the client than a big producer. A producer has only so many spots. A client can have a whole campaign that might go on for a year or more."

"If a girl screws around with a client only—she's whoring on the very top level—what about her reputation here?" one square asked.

"It depends on the girl," I tried to explain. "If she's sharp, she does the right thing at the right time and she knows the client is a married man with a family and a reputation of his own—so she has to protect him as well as herself. But if she's green and careless, she's apt to be dumb about the way she did it, and two years later everybody says, 'There's Joan—everybody's had her. . . .'"

"OK," a square wanted to know, "when you talk about the client whom are you talking about? I don't expect you to name names. When you're working on a Buick commercial, she doesn't sleep with Mr. Buick, he's dead. Who *is* the client?"

"He's the vice-president in charge of advertising. The vice-president in charge of marketing. The marketing manager, sometimes the owners of companies. With many companies their TV advertising budget is their single largest item of expense, so it's never far from being the top guys."

"Location seems to be the spot where the action is—is this where it happens? How does it happen?" this avid square demanded.

"Location is *la dolce vita*—no doubt about it. The cost is all deductible. It can all be wrapped up in the advertising budget. Everybody is free from routine. Few telephones. No wives. No commuting trains to make. The climate is usually groovy. A model is thrown together with a lot of highly paid professional, creative, intelligent people—artists and technicians. Everybody has his job to do, but there's plenty of time after and in between. For four or five or six days everybody lives more or less together—at the same hotel. After work is funtime. The setting is right and the time is right and there's this normal pairing-off. This is when it happens. This is normal—natural. It's like convention time in any other business."

"If the client takes a shine to a model on location and she doesn't respond, isn't it too late for her to be fired? Will they sack her and get another girl?"

"Not usually. But it would have repercussions. The client just drops a subtle hint to the producer, 'Let's not use her anymore.' And let's face it—his whim is law in a business where money talks and lots of money really hollers."

"What happens if the client has eyes for Miss Gorgeous and she has eyes for a handsome propman?"

"That happens—don't think it doesn't. But usually the crew members need their money worse than the models. They know the client comes first, so before a member of the crew would make a move, he'd check with the producer and get a security clearance. Has anybody got anything going with this girl, he'd ask. If the producer says yes, he could be speaking for himself. He might be covering for the client. He might even be covering for the girl. But that's enough to settle it. The crew have the native girls to pick from."

Now for the first time the producer delivered himself of an unsolicited opinion. "You still hear a lot today about people in this business being hung up on drugs and marijuana. I have to say I've seen no evidence of it after fifteen years in the business. Lots of people take pep pills, sure—but people in this business, especially models, can't mess around with drugs. It shows. They get very old very fast. Most girls have no more than three good years. They age terribly. I see girls every day who are twenty-two or twenty-four and they look thirty already. The thirty-year-old ones look forty. Once they start on that stuff, they can just forget it."

"How about birth control pills? What do they do to girls?"

"Maybe that has something to do with it. I know measurements mean nothing anymore. You get a composite from some agency giving a model's measurements, and by the time she rides across town in a taxi she's put on five or ten pounds around her middle. Now every time they get a little fat it's fashionable to blame it on the pill."

"I know plenty of girls who take them, and it raises hob with their figures," I said. "Those hormones have to go somewhere. Then some girls get bloated and they take more pills to counteract that. I won't take them. My gynecologist said I would have bad side effects, so I stay away from them. After all, one day we may get a pill with no side effects, and in the meantime there are other devices."

"A few years ago big busts were all the rage, and a lot of girls were taking hormone shots. Then they found out it threw their whole figure out of wack." This was the producer talking again. "It's unbelievable what girls will do to get a glamour job today. Now big busts are out of fashion. The fashion is no boobs at all."

"Some men just aren't turned on by boobs," I said. "They're leg men or derriere men or feet men—even ear men. I know one guy who's crazy about my ears—"

"You're getting off easy," a square broke in.

"Maybe because he's up to his ears in boobs all day. He designs brassieres."

"Does this mean a hat designer might hate ears and be crazy for boobs?"

"I don't know. Some men are crazy about feet. There's an old saying that more than a handful is a big waste anyway."

"What about dentists? What do they yen for?"

"I don't know. They might be big crotch men, for all I know."

"Do models have any generalizations about men—photographers are this and clients are that—Italians are this, and clothes designers are the other. . ."

"No, there's too much individuality in every category to make generalizations. Most of the men in this business—the professionals— are attractive, successful married men with families. Every once in a while there are ones who turn hippie and try to be a little weird, but they're the exceptions."

"The professionals have the responsibility for getting work out worth millions of dollars," the producer said. "There's too much money hanging on every move on the chessboard for them to suddenly turn into sex maniacs. Whenever sex rears its ugly head, money talks louder and money always wins."

What a shame. If sex were rampant in the sea of communications media, this might be a more interesting book. But then it would have to be written by someone outside the business—someone who's never been through it. Someone who could write his fantasies—tell the public it's exactly like what they suspect.

"Leaving aside all questions of personal advancement and limiting it strictly to taste, what kind of men do models go for? Are they attracted to male models?" asked Square Number Three.

Every working model within earshot gave a negative moan.

"We hate male models," said one.

"Can't stand them," said another.

"They're more narcissistic than we are."

"I couldn't stand a roommate who was a model, let alone a lover."

"Male models are free-loaders—professional house guests. They diddle around with rich old girls."

"Some girls don't like the competition," I suggested.

"You mean some girls actually like uglies and oldies?" the square wanted to know.

"Uglies make you look better," I admitted. "I only know one married couple who are both models."

"Yeah," someone else chimed in. "And they have different agencies. They let their *agencies* do the competing."

"Well, then, what other men do models prefer? Photographers?"

"We've been overexposed to photographers, you might say. Familiarity breeds contempt. A lot of girls marry photographers. Some do it to get ahead. But it doesn't work out. It's a bad combo. I know this young model who married a successful photographer. Everything was groovy until the day she dropped in at his studio to surprise him—and DID. He was balling another model in the dressing room. The wife was only eighteen and she couldn't cope with being rejected. She thought, migod, if I can't hold a man in my prime, what am I going to do when I'm an old hag of twenty-three? She went berserk and made the rounds of every one of her husband's competitors and friends. She balled every one of them who had time for her, and she ended up way off the deep end—what used to be called perverted. You know, like the ugly little fat girls who trail around after rock 'n' roll bands and make plaster casts of their private parts—three-dimensional beefcake. You know, what's under the fig leaf in the museums. But *only* what's under the fig leaf—the rest of the body they don't bother with."

"You're putting me on. There *are* such creatures?"

"Of course, dear. It's a whole movement. Where have you been?"

"Models like successful, interesting, rich men—tycoons. Smooth tycoons. Conglomerators. Guys who are here today and in Hong Kong tomorrow and don't mind taking you along for the ride. They want the kind of guy every girls wants. They're usually normal in that respect, I think."

"Well, then, how about the life style of models today—what are the percentages and how do they live?"

"Well, I think the greatest number of models you'd find living with guys."

"Unmarried, of course."

"That goes without saying today. The next biggest group lives alone. The rest are married or living with dogs or lesbians or living with lesbian dogs or some combination."

"When a model lives with a guy, who pays the rent?"

"There are no rules. Sometimes he does and she uses that margin for her own financial security. Sometimes after she gets going they split the rent. Sometimes when a model is successful she pays the rent. There are plenty of models who support guys, back them, invest in their futures—"

"Well, a model is in the sex appeal business. She spends all day every day peddling her body to someone who's going to use it to peddle some product. To what extent does this rub off on her so she ends up with strange or warped notions of sexual behavior?"

"I think girls working in TV have more chance to be normal. Girls working in print—for them it's easier to go off the track and end up icily frigid or lezzies or just too madly in love with themselves. Just yesterday I went on an interview, and this producer asked me if I was from California. No, I said, I'm from Vermont. Why did you ask that? He said because you're smiling—you're not blippedy-blah and affected. Some girls are so busy playing the role of models. They think they have to act that way or somebody is going to forget. They end up forgetting how to act like human beings."

"Then some girls take the world's image of a model so seriously they overreact. They're aggressive sexually in order to try to get ahead because they think they have to be—they think it's expected of them. And they act blippedy-blah, as you phrase it, because they think that is going to advance their career also?"

"I think some of them start playing the part and forget who the hell they are. They start out with fake names, fake hair, and fake fingernails, and after a while Samantha Severe forgets she ever was

Sarah Kerplunk, the little campus queen from Sheboygan."

I knew we were getting near the nitty-gritty when a bystander felt free enough to ask the seventy-nine-dollar question. "What's all the shouting about?" he wanted to know. "Are models so great at balling, or are they just good to look at?"

There was a moment of silence and then it became a chorus.

"It's better to ball a lady uglier than you."

"Fat slobs work harder."

"Older women think each bang might be their last—they're the best bang of all."

"Models are too scared they'll crack a nail or muss their hair."

"Maybe they're great when they see something they want out of you, but as a steady thing they're a bust."

"They're not what they're cracked up to be."

Finally I felt I had to rush to the defense of the profession. "Some of all that may be true," I admitted. "I've heard guys beef that girls don't want to muss their hair, they don't want any man to see them without all their trappings on. Some girls sleep in their eyelashes, with full makeup on. They're scared to let any man see them the way God made them."

"But on the other hand doesn't a man want to forget this public image thing? Doesn't he want to think a girl is HIS—even just for the night? Doesn't he want to see her the way no one else sees her?"

"Sometimes yes, sometimes no. Sometimes he's buying illusions too. He wants this doll thing."

"Can a model call up her retoucher and have him come and do repairs at three o'clock in the morning? Does she have a makeup man and a hairdresser standing by to put her back together between orgasms?"

"They could use it," quoth the producer. "Some of them have horrible figures, horrible shapes. Without clothes they look ridiculous—they're just too skinny and lumpy and bony, and a man who's looking for fun would be better off with a twenty-dollar trick he finds in a Hilton lobby."

"I know some men have told me they could never marry a model. They're completely turned off by them—too self-centered and egotistical. I know I'm always getting accused of that. It's a horrible habit we all have. We have to be perfect all the time so we're constantly

223

checking ourselves in the mirror to make sure every seam is straight and every line is in place. We do it all day every day. And it's pretty hard to turn it off when you're with a man you care about. But it's something more than ego. It's an occupational disease. Nasty maybe and annoying, but there it is. A good man can cure you of this nasty habit. I know one man who told a model to go scrub her face. When she came back with body makeup on, he took her in and scrubbed her all over. He didn't want any of the gook on his leather pillows, and he didn't want any pink foundation on his fur rug. He was a guy in the business—an art director—and he wasn't buying her public image—he wanted her body. If that happened to me, I wouldn't be offended. I'd be thrilled to death the guy cared enough about me to make a big scene out of it."

"How about girls who are frigid and narcissistic or AC-DC?"

"Men find that out soon enough. They're turned off by it. There are very few who want to suffer. Sufferers sometimes like it. Some men think girls are lesbians because they haven't found the properly equipped man to really arouse them. Some men insist on climbing mountains because they're there. Others insist they can thaw out confirmed lesbians. Some men thrive on obstacles—they want to accomplish the impossible."

"Some men have plenty of time for that stuff. They don't have to work hard to make a living. If they do, they got no time for it," said our producer.

"A good model has to change to stay alive," someone said. "She has to move with the times. Self-improvement is a way of life to her. Does that include sex, too, Carolyn?"

"I don't know," I admitted. "I haven't made any charts lately. But I think in my attitude—as well as my actions—concerning sex I have become freer and not so uptight as I was at the beginning. But that's a part of growing up. That happens with experience. It happens with every girl."

"A model can't be like any other girl. She has to be different."

"How is she different?"

"Well, she learns to become a performer of a sort. A professional in the razzle-dazzle business of sex-appeal. Wouldn't that make her more accomplished in bed, more interesting, more creative, like a European courtesan?"

224

"Have you ever met a European courtesan?" I asked this square. "I met one in Paris. She had to be pointed out to me. From the outside I couldn't tell. She was hanging on to her mystery."

"I'm talking about reality, not appearances."

"Well, I suppose a model gets better at posing, presenting a picture, flaunting her body, draping her sheets around her. She learns how to do a striptease with a towel and all that sort of stuff. But today any girl can pick up those tricks at the movies. Bardot did it all years ago."

"But doesn't she learn to perform better just from being a performer in the sex appeal business?"

"You learn to act. You learn to swoon over a dish of spaghetti or a flowered towel or a male model whom you just can't stand. So you learn how to act in bed—to make a man think he's the greatest lover since Don Juan. How to make him think he's super when he's really a panting slob. But this is a female thing. All girls learn to do that. If she's smart, any girl can hoodwink a man in bed. That's the easiest place to do it because a man wants to be hoodwinked. He wants to believe he's great. He wants to believe he's got you in ecstasy when he's not doing a damn thing for you."

"Well, if models are so hot on the market—so much in demand— doesn't it mean men expect great things from them in bed? Isn't that a dangerous situation right there—when they expect more than you can deliver?"

"Anticipation is the greatest part of it, anyway. You can do it only so many ways. I think it's the mystique of the model men are after. They're buying a brand name. Look, there are thousands of good-look-ing girls in New York who are great in bed. I'm sure of it. And yet when these big-deal males give a party, they all want their places decorated with models. I always get invitations and they always ask me to bring along extra girls—as long as they're models. They want that stamp of approval. They want to be able to say they're going to have a dozen models or twenty models. Why? Because models have the reputation of being freewheeling in the sex department. They want that insurance that they're going to have a few wild ones on tap. It was that way when I started in this business, and it's still that way."

My producer friend began mopping his brow. "And the girls try to live up to this notion," he said. "They're expected to be kookie so they work at being kookie. Holly Golightly in *Breakfast at Tiffany's* was a kook who made it, and life imitates art. But the average professional man—if he's really interested in having an affair with a model—he wants one who is cool. He's married and he has his professional standing—he can't afford to be harassed at home or at the office by some kooky lady. We have to get the work out, and models are a part of that job. Kooks don't last."

I had to agree. "Just the other day I dropped into an ad agency to leave a new composite and I saw this art director with a picture of a girl I know. When I said I knew her, he said, 'Oh, God, she's a kook, that one. She's wild. In bed she's really something. A friend of mine had her on the desk in his studio once for four hours and he had sixteen orgasms.' When they start that, I just turn off my hearing aid. I know they're giving me fantasies—what they wished had happened. The guys I can appreciate are the guys who just give you an old-fashioned look and never say a word. There are other ways of communicating than loudmouthing around. But this is a business where you have to create some individuality for yourself or you're lost in the mass. Every girl tries to have a gimmick. Some the them fake a British accent. Others try to be blippedy-blah. Others play crazy or kooky."

"OK," said the square. "If everybody has a gimmick, what is yours? Do you mind telling us?"

"No, of course not," I said. "I try to be natural. The friendly barefoot girl from the mountains of Vermont."

"The red-headed farmer's daughter?"

"Sure. I'll settle for that. If that isn't sexy enough for them, it means they don't know anything about farm girls. Or sex, either."

Thank you very much, Miss Greta Gimmick.

Movie stars are now making anticigarette commercials for free, and soon you may have to have an authentic case of lung cancer to play an extra in one of them. TV cigarette commercials seem to be going out like the dinosaurs. But they're going out in style. The more the tobacco industry is on the spot, the more imaginative and creative they have to be to sell their wares without rousing the public's ire. With much bigger budgets per minute of film than *Gone With the Wind,* a cigarette commercial is still a stunning showcase for a model. So the competition to get those few choice remaining spots gets fiercer by the minute.

This particular final competition was being held in a bar on East 81st Street in Manhattan called The Right Place. The bar has a huge glass skylight, and many of the film people use it for auditions because the flood of natural light allows them to see the way our pores will look when we get on location. It screens the hothouse flowers from the hearty, healthy, outdoorsy types the tobacco industry wants identified with its controversial product. It was early morning, and an array of judges sat at a table opposite the bar behind an array of coffee and Danish. The tables were filled with girls waiting to be looked at. Traffic in and out was constant. The judges—producer, art director, director, assistant director—have the job of confronting a cattle call of sixty ladies and cutting them down to four. All the girls had been sent by agencies after preliminary weeding out at the agency from photographs. There was no signing in; no secretary with the clipboard to call your name and announce you. The honor system prevailed. And after one girl did her number, the AD called out, "Who's next?"

Then, "What have you got running?" the AD asks.

"I've got a detergent, a deodorant, and a decongestant," says the blonde.

"No cigarette? Very good, Miss Dee-Dee." This exchange is also on the honor system. They want to know what commercials you appear in are currently being shown on TV. They are leery of someone who is overexposed and overidentified with one kind of product or another. Cigarette companies like not-too-young virgins: FCC regulations demand that anyone in a TV commercial for cigarettes be twenty-five years old or more, and the tobacco people like someone TV viewers have never seen smoking a rival product in Salem springs or Marlboro country.

Then they ask to see the model's portfolio of pictures. It's never that important or crucial for TV, but it gives the judges something to do. It gives them a prop to fiddle with. So you bring it along, and the judges pore over it as if it mattered.

Then the AD says, "Would you mind getting up, please, and standing over there under the skylight for us? That's fine." So she takes a nice position.

"Would you turn sideways slowly, please?" they ask her. She turns.

"Turn around now and walk back this way. That's right. Now stand over here." The audience of her peers watches the ritual intently. They ignore the girl subject and watch the judges. If the judges seem to snap back quickly and reach for their coffee and their Danish, it means she is no competition. If the AD says, "Thank you very much. We appreciate your giving so much of your time," that means you've had it. If they like you, they will ask you to stick around in the far corner of the room where the semifinalists are waiting, having passed the initial hurdles. Those who don't get asked to stay trip out looking neither to right nor left.

You never know who has dressed right and who has dressed wrong. You can ask your agency to give you some clue to what they are looking for, but they never give you very much to go on. You have to guess whether to come riding the fashion thing or done up like plain little Miss Jones. You try to look pretty, but after you've been through a few of these you learn that you never know who your real competition is going to turn out to be. Sometimes they're looking for someone who's not too pretty, and the hour you've spent putting a fabulous face together may be what did you in. Finally it's your turn. The questions are the same. The choreography is the same. You wait for them to thank you and they don't. They ask if you'd mind hanging around a little longer. You go over and sit down in the charmed circle, and you tell yourself, "I've got a chance now."

Now everybody who got a thank-you-very-much has left. The cattle call of sixty girls is down to about fifteen. Now they ask to see all the blondes together. Four blondes stand there like slaves on the block. The men caucus and mumble and whisper among themselves. Then the AD says: "You're Joan, right?" She nods, and he says, "Thank you very much," and blah-blah-blah, and Joan trips out. Another one is dismissed. There are only two blondes left. Now they ask for all brunettes, and a whole drove stands up. They follow the style of the Miss America judges. If they call your name, it means you've had it. If you don't hear your name called, it means you've still got a chance.

Why do they always get to the redheads last? There are only three of us, and you know two are going to get the thank-you-very-much. If they have four girls, two may be blondes or brunettes. Two redheads, never.

"Do you have hairpieces?" they are asking. Of course we have hairpieces. I have more hair at home than the entire panel of men have. They know, so why do they ask? Every model has hair enough for an army. We have to. We can make long hair short and short hair long. It

228

gets tougher to take the thank-you-very-much when you've survived the competition up to now.

Now they are concentrating on the profiles. They ask us to stand close in profile with the light behind us. Why didn't they ask us to smoke? It used to be SOP to light up, turn, take a draft, inhale and exhale, and then wait for the applause. I have seen girls who had smoked for ten years, and yet when they were asked to give a performance of a lady lighting up, they would come apart. They just couldn't do it naturally.

Now something new has been added to the panel of judges. A VIP has just arrived and taken his place in the center of the huddle. This must be the client.

"You're Samantha, right? Thank you very much, Samantha," says the AD. Exit Samantha. And then in quick order exit another blonde and another brunette. Suddenly there are only four girls left standing, and Kenmore is one of the four. Congratulations, kid. You survived. You may yet get to be one of the last red-hot cigarette-smoking TV mamas.

Now the producer is coming toward me. "You're Carolyn, right?" I nod, of course, and I smile. What could happen now? If they've been quietly casting Negroes in another building, they would knock out one of the brunettes, wouldn't they? That would make it a balanced ticket: one blonde, one brunette, one Negro, and one redhead. Redheads are always last.

"I picked you the first time around, Carolyn," the producer is saying to me, "but now the client is very hesitant about you. He thinks you look too young."

"But I'm not. I have my driver's license here—I'll show it to you. I'm twenty-five, honest I am. I wouldn't try to get you into trouble. Not me."

"Of course not, baby. He's not hesitating over your actual age. What bothers him is you *look* too young. I'd marry you tomorrow. I tried to thrash it out with him, but after all, it's seventy thousand dollars, baby. We'll use you in something else."

The word went out when one of Eileen Ford's bookers left the agency, taking Jean Shrimpton and several other big models with her, and set up a rival agency. Everyone adores this kind of bacchanal;

everyone wonders and asks everyone else what the new agency is like. I wondered, too. But I've learned most dressing room scuttlebutt gets rancid from repetition. I lean toward the direct approach.

I decided to go see. First I called. I was surprised no secretary came between us. I was talking to the Boss Lady herself. I introduced myself and asked, "Are you taking on any girls?"

"Yes, we're always looking at girls."

"Fine. What day do you see them?"

"On Thursdays. Have you modeled before?"

"Yes. I've been around a while, as you will see from my portfolio. I'm with an agency at the moment, but I'm also looking around."

"How tall are you?"

"Five foot eight."

"What color hair?"

"Red."

"What do you weigh?"

"One eighteen."

"How old are you?"

"Twenty-six," I said. I could tell from the pregnant pause that I had made my first mistake right there. I might have been thirty-five and said I was twenty-two and she could have been thrilled to death.

But she said, "We usually don't look at girls over twenty-five—"

"Well, if you don't, you don't. Thank you very much—"

"But we'd like to have a look at you, anyway. Why don't you drop by?"

"Would any special time be more convenient?"

"Three o'clock would be all right."

"Fine. I'll be there."

Suddenly this chronological age thing had reared its unsurprising head. I caught myself looking at my portfolio with a jaundiced eye. Oddly enough, my old pictures taken when I was young all looked older than my new pictures taken since I was twenty-five. So I did a little discreet weeding out before I sailed over to the new agency. The office looked like it had opened the day before yesterday. It was spacious and neat but it hadn't been fancied up yet. There was no receptionist or secretary, no outer darkness and no inner sanctum. Just two rooms, with a booker in one and the Boss Lady at her desk in the other. Inevitably she was on the telephone. While I was waiting a sweet young thing slouched in with her hair flying. Her bell bottoms had been sweeping the streets and looked pretty grimy. Her makeup was early Bronx Renaissance hippie, and she looked untidy and unkempt, but one thing you had to give her. She was plenty young. Ten years younger than the twenty-six I had already admitted to.

"Oh, hello, Priscilla, how are you, darling? Maurice sent over the new prints, and you look divine!" Praise the Lord and pass the brown mascara, some things never change. Since she had interrupted her telephone call to salute Priscilla, I explained I was there as a result of our conversation on the phone. "Oh, yes, dear," she smiled. "May I see your book?"

I wonder how many times I had listened to that unnecessary sentence as I plopped my portfolio on her desk and unzipped it.

The sound of a zipper unpeeling in the office of a model agency is like the wail of a police siren in the New York streets. Automatically a crowd gathers around to gape, drawn irresistibly to its cellophane pages as if to blood on the sidewalk. The booker came in from the other office. She and the Boss Lady began discussing me as if I were an unconscious accident victim lying in the street.

"She has a marvelous face."

"The beach shot in the silver slip is really stunning. I wonder who did that."

"Beautiful wide-apart eyes."

"Makeup very good."

"Yes. A little too much darkness under there maybe, but lovely bone structure. She has a very IN look. Her hair is very now."

"She has a wonderful book, but she's twenty-six."

"Oh."

Finally the Lady turned to me as if I had regained consciousness and said, "You have a very fine book, dear." She knew I knew I was twenty-six, so she didn't have to explain that to me.

"Thank you," I replied.

Then she began name-dropping, telling me about Jean Shrimpton and Vicky Hilbert and all the people she had on her head sheet. As if I didn't know. Everyone knew Vicky had left Ford to go with her. They said she had immediately lost a bunch of big accounts she'd had, and one big commercial she had running was yanked right off the air. There were all kinds of jealous feedbacks about the whole thing.

231

I knew everything she was telling me and a little more besides. If you're thirty and making money, any agency is perfectly happy to handle you. If you're nineteen and a beginner, they'll have a try at shaping you and steering you and see what happens.

"Well," I said finally, "thank you for seeing me."

"Right now I doubt if we could do much for you, dear. In another six months or so, let's meet again."

It had to happen eventually. I had been waiting for someone to tell me I was too old. I had often looked into Dovima's fabulous dark eyes and wondered how she felt that first moment of that first day when she realized time was catching up or running out on her. The Boss Lady hadn't told me in so many words that I was too old. But the next time I got turned down for a cigarette commercial, maybe I'd quote her.

Since Joanna Shimkus and Ali McGraw went from modeling to movie leads in one short leap—and made a success of it—it has made things easier for all of us. Today in New York, model agencies get lots of calls from film people wanting to look at girls. Working in commercials is good experience in front of the camera, and lots of models are studying acting just so they'll be ready in case lightning strikes. So a call to test for a film is not nearly so unusual now as it was even when I began. I don't even get excited anymore about a film audition. I've learned to take it in stride. You show up just in case you might accidentally have something they think they are looking for.

I was in that kind of mood when I kept the appointment the agency made for me with a new production company in a big office on Third Avenue. Sometimes you have the name of the man who's supposed to look at you and sometimes you don't. This day I just had the time and the place. I hoped they knew who was supposed to see me.

When I walked into the office, the producer turned out to be someone I hadn't seen since my early days as a TV extra. He was still as tall as ever. He had taken on considerable bloat; his eyes were puffed into slits, and his hair had receded in the front a bit so he let it grow down his cheeks in huge Heathcliff sideburns. My old friend with the bubble bath commercial in Palm Springs, the man with the chiropractor's grip, the irresistible—he thought—F.G.

I knew better than to let on we'd met before. I showed him my book and wondered if my name might ring any bells. Certainly there must have been hundreds of girls he'd done the same thing to. But I wondered if my having walked out on him was rare enough to ring any bells. Which kind of girls do men remember—the ones they succeeded with or the ones who got away? Maybe they black out on the ones who didn't and remember the girls who did. F. G. looked at my pictures. He had never seen any of them except the early head shot by Phil Pegler.

Wouldn't you know that would be the one he was staring at! "Who shot that?" he asked me.

I told him.

"I thought that was a Pegler shot," he said.

Pegler is an institution in New York. Every model adores him because he's a whiz at lighting and he knows makeup to a T and if you do what he tells you to he can make you look gorgeous. Other photographers sometimes try to put him down, talking about his standard signature lighting, but they always got an argument from me. If they could do what he does, they would do it too. Today I wasn't going to argue about Pegler with F. G. If F. G. could spot Pegler's work so easily, why had he asked me first?

Now he had finished with my pictures and he was staring at me. "Seems to me I know you from somewhere," he began. "I just can't put my finger on it." His unconscious was showing, but I let that pass. I got very vague and said, "Oh, really."

"Did you work on the Coast at one time?"

"No," I lied. "Never. Did you?"

He started shooting me a whole stream of questions. He wanted to know whom I'd worked for, what commercials I'd done. I skirted around the edges of truth and never mentioned anything that could be pinned down. He finally got discouraged about playing Mr. District Attorney and began talking about the film. It wasn't one film they were doing. It never is. They're always doing several. They're going to be good films; they have to tell you what they're searching for is a girl who is new—who's unusual to look at and yet has a capacity for deep feelings and some mystery.

I tried to keep a straight face. He had mystery on his hands he wasn't looking for, but I listened to all the blah-blah-blah he had to spill as if I hadn't heard it every time I'd gone on a film interview. This first film was going to be shot in Canada, he told me, and he began questioning me about my acting ability.

"I've done quite a few things that called for acting," I told him. "I think I could do a decent job. When can I read for you?"

Well, it turned out the script wasn't QUITE finished. It never is. Besides it isn't lines that are that crucial. They're interested in emotional reactions. Lordy, I thought, if it's a horror film I could give a reaction right now.

"Come over here," he said, standing near the window. I rose and walked toward him warily, glad my appointment was not at the end of the day. He had a secretary outside. He had told her he didn't want to be disturbed by any phone calls during the interview, but if he tried any more of his chiropractic curves on me nobody could stop me from disturbing his little secretary with the heavy legs and the net stockings she never should wear and the hair pulled back and the mod watch so big I wondered how she could type with it on.

"You're nice and tall," he remarked. "Now I want you to stand over here and close your eyes. I'm going to put my hand out. I want you to lay your hand in mine."

I closed my eyes warily and I did what he asked. His palms were sweaty and clammy—he drank too much, and his kidneys were working overtime, I could tell that.

"Now I will mention a word—just one word—and I want to feel your reaction." I tried to take my mind off his kidneys and listen.

"Sex," he whispered.

Poor old F. G.; he hadn't changed a bit. I'd known he wasn't going to shout murder or cotton candy.

"I'm not getting any reading," he complained.

"It's a terribly beat-up word," I said. "Let's try something a little more surprising and see what happens."

"All right," he said. "Now I'm going to put your hand between my hands and we'll try again. Eyes still closed?"

"Yes," I said.

"All right," he said. "Now you're having an orgasm. I want to feel you having that orgasm."

Oh, brother, it was only eleven in the morning, and I haven't even had coffee yet, and I'm supposed to have an orgasm in some fat man's hand.

"Who am I having it with?" I asked, very coldly clinical.

"Does it have to be someone in particular?" he snapped angrily, as if

I'd broken some mood.

"Well," I said professionally, "the last time I went through one of these sessions, they wanted me to play a lesbian. Is this another one of those?"

"Forget lesbians. Forget the script. When I say you're having an orgasm, you have one if you have to have it alone."

"I'm sorry," I said. "I know masturbation is very big this year, but I'm afraid I'm not my type. Anyway I'll try." I knew I had gotten under his skin. I knew nothing would ever come of it, so I might just as well play with him the way he was trying to play with me.

"I'm a very good hand model," I boasted. "I've done a few commercials caressing soap and clutching diet pills. But it's very confining, doing a whole drama with your hands while you're hanging onto me."

"Well, let's try."

So I tried. I twitched and I clutched and I contracted and I released my fist, and then I began trying to move my hands like a belly dancer gone wrong, slower and slower and slower. I was afraid I might go to sleep standing there by the window. "Can I open my eyes now?" I asked.

"You know," he said, "you're a very talented girl."

"Thank you very much," I said.

"You have what we're looking for." I knew he didn't even know what he was looking for, and if I did have it, he would be the last one to know. His mind was somewhere else. Then he took his big clammy paws and grabbed me around the neck and started pulling me toward him. It was the same old F. G. procedure from three years ago. He was trying to pull me toward him—pretending to be casual as hell when every move was as calculated as a budget.

He was pulling me toward the sofa when his little secretary burst in with a telegram in her hand. Aha, I thought, she's wise to all this, and she's getting even for something he did to her.

"Oh, excuse me," she said in that certain suggestive way.

"I didn't want to be disturbed—I thought I told you that, Miss Chamberlain."

"You said you didn't want to take calls, but I didn't realize you meant—"

"Never mind," he said. "Give me the telegram."

235

He had worked for fifteen minutes setting up the mood. Now we were back where we started. "I know you from someplace," he kept muttering. "I wish I could put my finger on it."

I began babbling about having another appointment. That's always the best way out. He was cooled down now but with his kidneys he could start getting hot flashes any second. I told him I'd be anxious to read the script when it was ready and suggested he call me.

"Oh, yes," he said. "I'll definitely call you. It's going to come to me in a flash one day where I met you, and then I'll give you a buzz."

Oh, no, you won't, I thought. If you remember anything, you'll never bother. Seeing what you can get on an interview with girls was so old hat I hadn't expected it. I decided to call the agency and give them the tipoff. If they sent any other girls up there, they should bring their track shoes and their chains. F. G. was still F. G.

The bubble bath commercials had taken him as far as he could go. Now he needed a film script so he could cast for bigger fish. What he needed was a writer and a choreographer to work out a new casting act for him.

Everything in the modeling racket is definitely tentative. You can start out at the bottom, you survive a cattle call, get into the semifinals and into the finals. You may get the nod from the top man, and then you can get a veto from the man behind the man at the top. And sometimes when you start at the top you can be undone by someone in an echelon down below. One of the rare times I started at the top that happened to me.

The night Julie London opened at the Waldorf Empire Room I was invited to a private party in her suite after the show. She had done that famous "You've got a lot to like in a Marlboro" years ago, so one of the guests was a vice-president in charge of marketing for one of the cigarette cartels. I didn't know him from Adam, but there was something about me he liked, so he asked me to come see him. I brought my portfolio around; after it made the rounds at his office he invited me out for drinks. They were going into a new campaign for a new long, long cigarette and he wanted to use me. He explained that the campaign was going to start with a national ad saturation, and then if it worked in test market, the same girls would be used in the

TV commercial. He made an appointment for me to be interviewed at the studio of one of the big photographers who was very much in vogue and very temperamental and very hot at the moment. The photographer and the art director and some designers were going to select the high-fashion garments to be worn in the national ad.

The photographer was a real high-strung fag. When I walked into the studio, he was roaming around throwing peanuts at imaginary targets while the hard rock music was blasting away so loud he couldn't have heard if I had shouted in stereo. While I was shouting at him and he was pitching peanuts into the air, a strange woman in a pair of panty hose and no bra came out of the dressing room, screaming as if she had been attacked by a horde of mice.

"Federico darling," she shouted, "did you know your little dog has blood in his stool?"

"He didn't do it on the garment, did he?" said Federico, still pitching peanuts.

"No, darling. On the seamless."

Federico seemed slightly relieved at the news.

"You should talk to your doctor about it. It's frightfully bloody."

"It's TENSION," Federico explained. "We're all bleeding to death, but we hide it from one another."

"Yes, darling," said the woman, retiring to the rear of the studio.

Federico ignored me; he didn't so much as toss a peanut in my direction. Hating to interrupt his nutsy meditation, I looked for a secretary or a stylist or a coordinator or someone who might know what I was supposed to do. Then I saw a woman reel by, pushing a whole rack of designer garments. Well, I thought, this is more like it. Maybe SHE knows what's going on. I sat down and waited for her to notice me. She was a real tough cookie, with black eyeliner on, a suntanned skin that had seen too many seasons in Florida, and a low, husky voice. She continued to ignore me.

Then a model walked out of the inner sanctum wearing a gray chiffon dress and a blank look. "They don't like that either?" shouted the fashion coordinator. The model shook her head. Then the FC began railing at me.

"These tobacco auctioneers—what do they know about fashion? *Harper's* is showing this very same pants suit next month. It's one of our loveliest things. These men never know what they want. They can't even give you a HINT of what's in their tiny little minds. But they can sit there like lumps and veto all my selections."

"Are you here for the long cigarette thing?" the model asked me.

"I guess so," I said.

"I gotta get out of here," said the model.

"What's going on?" I asked her as the FC pushed her rack of garments into the dressing room, bitching and muttering.

"There are about eight men in the other room picking the clothes they want for the job. The FC brought in all these groovy things from all these name designers who'll supply the garments in return for a name credit, but they positively hate everything. I gotta get out of here. My boyfriend is calling me at four. He's flying in tonight, and I have to know what flight he's on."

"Well, can't he leave a message?"

"No, sweetie, you don't understand. I *live* with him, and he expects me to be HOME when he calls."

"Oh," I said. She climbed out of the gray chiffon she was wearing and traipsed into the dressing room to put it back on the rack.

"Look," she said to the stylist, "there's another girl here for the job. Why not have her put on something?"

I could hear the FC bitching and muttering, but finally she walked into the outer office and threw a dress at me. "Here," she said defiantly, "put this on." I looked at the dress. It was the gray chiffon the other model had just worn. It was a size five, which was too tight on me. It was cut so deep in front I had to take off my bra. It looked more like a period costume that a dress. It had a sash on it, and whatever way I wore it, it didn't work. If I'd had a parasol to twirl, I might have been able to get away with it. I asked the FC if she had any shoes to go with it. The shoes I was wearing looked ridiculous with that kind of garment.

"Accessorizing is somebody else's job, not mine," she exploded.

"Are there any shoes around here?" I asked the other model.

"I saw some, but I think the dog is playing with them in the other studio," said the model.

There were shouts of impatience from the jury room, so the stylist insisted I go in wearing that horrible gray dress. I felt like a fool. I wouldn't want anyone to see me in this outfit, not even my mother.

I walked in anyway. Eight men sat in a semicircle just outside a huge arc light which was turned on. The FC walked in behind me and started making a spiel about the dress, giving them its pedigree, yakking about how insinuatingly sexy it was. She had to be blind. The dress might look great on the drawing board, but it did nothing for me.

"OK, fine," one of the men said. "Now have her put something else on."

The FC walked into the dressing room, raving like a madwoman. "Have you ever?" she shrieked. "I simply cannot cope ... I simply won't be treated this way ... who are they to have the final say when it comes to fashion ... who are these men, anyway ... where do they get them from ... "

Just then a trucker arrived with another bag full of clothes on a rack and wheeled it into the dressing room. He arrived just as I unzipped the gray number and stepped out of it. I had already taken my bra off and hung it on my tote bag. Now it seemed to be missing. Maybe the bleeding dog had dragged it into the other room with the shoes. I stood there with my arms crossed in front of me, waiting for her to give me something else to put on. The other model waltzed in wearing the black and white pants suit. The trucker stood there waiting for someone to sign his receipt. The photographer walked into the corridor pitching peanuts at imaginary demons.

"Please," I said to the FC, "now that the other garments have arrived, can't you give me something else to try on?"

"Oh, you," she said spitefully. "I have nothing else for you to wear."

"What do you mean—you have a whole bag full of new things!"

"Nothing would fit you," she said. "You can't get into another thing. I can tell." The old battle-ax had to find someone to take out her frustration on, and I was the only available target.

"Have you seen my bra?" I asked her.

"I'm not a wardrobe woman," she said grandly, turning her back on me.

Now there seemed to be complete uproar inside. The photographer was screaming at the trucker, refusing to sign a receipt for the clothes. The blank-faced model rushed out, intent on her boyfriend's call. The FC was sulking in her corner, muttering curses on the agency men. All I wanted to do was find my bra and get out of there. Even that was too much to ask. I had to hunt in my tote bag for a spare.

The vice-president in charge of marketing met me in the corridor. "What's going on here?" he asked. "Why didn't you come in in another outfit?"

"I wish I knew," I laughed. "Why don't you ask that lady in charge of the clothes?"

Before he could open his mouth, she came out yapping. "I have nothing here that suits her," she said grandly, zipping up a bag of garments.

"Look," the Veep said to me, "we've been here for three hours looking at clothes and girls, and it's all been a waste of time. I'm washing my hands of this deal. This is not my bag. We're leaving anyway. Can I give you a lift home?"

When the hard-bitten lady stylist heard this, her face settled into a satisfied snarl. I knew what she was thinking. The client had jinxed her clothes, so she was glad to jinx the client's girl.

"Some people in this business don't have enough drama in their lives," said the Veep.

"Let's have dinner sometime," he said when he dropped me at my apartment. "We'll use you in something else."

Famous last words.

"Have you got your bikini on?"

I nodded.

"Maybe I better put mine on to save time." she said, rushing down the hallway toward the tiny dressing room. She pulled the door open on another girl who was in there changing. "Oh, excuse me," she said. I wondered what she was doing at a callback for a commercial on a slim cigarette. She looked more like a Westchester mother than a model. She was cute but definitely chunky. I sat in the reception room of this production house in the West Twenties waiting, waiting, waiting my turn. My agent had tried to get them to see me on the Friday before I left for Barbados. No dice. Here it is ten days later and they're still casting. I told him I came back with a little color and my bikini didn't quite match up with the bathing suits I'd been modeling in the Islands, and he said, "That's all right, that's great. They saw your composite and they asked for you by name."

Miss Chunky came out of the dressing room in a gold stretch suit, clutching her mink coat around her. She was just about to sit down when a tan beauty slinked out of the inner sanctum. She's wearing rose-colored granny glasses with metal frames, an Aunt Minnie sweater, knit bell bottoms, and this Zsa Zsa Zulu hairdo.

"Next," she shouts, but what she meant was, "Forget it, kids—I hit them and it's mine." Miss Chunky was ahead of me. It was her turn, and I felt for her. Her lips were shaking, her hands were shaking, she was trying so hard that she was a wreck already.

"Oh, I don't have any cigarettes," she discovered.

"Don't worry about it," I said. "Take these." I handed her a pack of Larks.

"Thank you. Thank you. I'll pay you for them. But I don't seem to have any matches, either."

All I had was a lighter, and that would be one prop too many for her to handle.

"Here you are, honey," said Zsa Zsa Zulu, tossing her some St. Regis matches.

"Do you think I should light the cigarette now and walk in with it, or will they tell me what to do when I get in there?" Miss Chunky asked us.

"Don't worry, sugar," said ZZZ. "They'll tell you what to do."

Now Miss Chunky was trying to pull her stretch suit down, and it wouldn't stretch anymore. "I know they won't like me because I'm too fat."

"Don't run yourself into a hole, girl," said ZZZ. "Maybe they're looking for one real hippy chick to make their *cigarette* look slim."

Before she could make her entrance, another black beauty came out swinging a huge beaded satchel bag.

"Would you take your clothes off, please?" said one black beauty to the other. Then they fell out laughing as they headed for the dressing room. Little Miss Chunky walked in. Silence. Quiet. Suspense. Then she walked out the door, even more flustered than when she'd gone in.

"See? I told you so. I'm too fat. They made me so nervous I couldn't even smoke," she said, handing me back my cigarettes. "And that happens to be one thing I do very well. Oh," she said, "I'm supposed to tell you you're next."

"Thanks," I said. "Better luck next time."

When I walked in, I wondered what the tension was all about. There was no grand jury, just an emancipated secretary no older than I am.

She sits behind a desk with her glasses on, trying to look very important. She doesn't have the final casting say-so. She's just weeding out girls. They tell her what to look for, and she looks for it. And she makes her little list. If there happens to be something about you that turns her off—if you happen to remind her of a girl who stole her boyfriend two years ago—she can leave your name off a list.

"Would you take your clothes off, please?" she asked me.

I unzipped my pants and slipped off my sweater.

"Would you please walk toward me at a sixty-degree angle?" You feel ridiculous parading around in a bikini in front of a girl your own age who's probably just been sprung from the typing pool.

"OK. Fine," she says. "You can put your clothes back on." She didn't even mention my suntan. Maybe she was looking for moles and warts.

"Now would you smoke for me, please?"

I gave her a Mata Hari ignition, a Bette Davis inhalation, and then I blew two kinds of smoke rings.

My athletic smoking must have gotten to her because she couldn't help cracking a smile. "I'm sorry," she said. "I have to ask you to do these things. That's my job."

"I understand," I said. "Is this a new cigarette?"

"Yes," she said.

"Has it been test marketed?"

She said it had. They were slotting this commercial for national exposure. It makes a difference. Doing a commercial for test market ties you up. It means you can't even audition for another cigarette until the test market period is over. I did a Lifebuoy deodorant soap commercial for test market one time and found myself tied up for months for both deodorants AND soap.

She looked at my portfolio. "Will you be available within the next three or four weeks?"

"I expect so."

"The director and crew are out of the country shooting on location now. I'm sort of filling in. There will be callbacks next week. Your agency will notify you when. Thank you very much, Miss Kenmore."

They were in Brazil, but she was not allowed to say so. I decided I wouldn't hold my breath over it. Maybe they're looking for two girls six feet two, one black and one white. No room for redheads.

Revolution is much more commercial now than it was when Karl Marx and Lenin were doing their thing. Look at Karen. In the fifties she would have been deported. In the late sixties she was considered one of the NOW people. During the revolution in Paris in the spring of 1968, she was getting invited out to dinner every night as a big inside authority on what was going to happen because she had once gone to dinner at La Coupole in Montparnasse with Daniel Cohn-Bendit, the little German boy who was leading the student revolution. Now she was very close to the leaders of the riots at Columbia University. One of her boyfriends had been locked up for setting fire to the Dean's office. Instead of keeping quiet about it, Karen was running around hitting on Establishment people all over Madison Avenue, asking them for contributions to the student revolt. Karen was such an all-American vision that she made me look like a Slav. She had whooshy blond hair, twenty-three shades all mixed together, as natural as Malibu Beach. She had the long legs and the tan and the flag-blue eyes. She was Miss Liberty all over. When I first met her at a cattle call and she came on with this heavy German sauerkraut accent like Erich Von Stroheim, I thought she was putting me on. You'd be surprised at how many all-American girls come from Stockholm and Düsseldorf. She was always agitating and trying to make trouble, and it was a hoot to hear her quote Mao Tse-tung. Karen was in a constant state of excitement over the imminent collapse of Western capitalist civilization, and she had the wildest fantasies about using her face and body to lure the American consumer to his doom.

When you show up for a cattle call, you usually have no idea of what product they want you for. The agency people and the client, the stylist and the propmen—all of them case you, steely-eyed and noncommittal because they know something you don't know. A girl is strictly flying blind. She never knows what face they're looking for. If you're done up with three sets of false eyelashes and a very exotic kissy mouth, they're looking for plain Janes. If you're *au naturel,* they're looking for tiger ladies.

Karen was always trying to close the communications gap by playing Mata Hari. While some propman wasn't looking, Karen would wander casually over into the corner of the salon where the girls were being sorted out. While she seemed to be casually adjusting her bikini, she was actually reading some top-secret agency memo on a propman's clipboard. She would parade around like a dumb blonde without a thought in her head, then she would come back and give the lowdown to any of us girls she happened to like.

"Zere out of zere minds," Karen reported. "It's another hair dye for men. Zey call zis one Sudden Summer. Are you ready for zat? Zey are going to shoot zis commercial on ze West Coast, so why are zey seeing girls in New York? Somesing is rotten in Clifton, New Jersey."

"Maybe if they get someone they want to go with, they'll fly her out," I suggested. "It has happened."

"If any of zese girls gets a callback on zis gig, I want to know about it," Karen vowed. "I sink ze fix is already in. Zey already have ze girl zey want, and so zey have to have a cattle call to make it look kosher."

There was no use arguing with her. Once she got an idea in her hard German noggin, there was no getting it out.

"Somebody wants to see sirty girls in bikinis, zat's all. Why bikinis, for God's sake?"

"They don't want to fly you to the Bahamas and then find out you've got an appendicitis scar," I explained.

"Zat's what zey say. But zey already have everybody's photo already. Practically nude."

"True, true," I admitted.

"Zen why zese silly bikinis? Well, I don't care—ze sooner all zese old American men start dyeing zere hair and painting zere faces, ze sooner it will be over. New York will collapse like Rome. Don't you sink so?"

"Did the men in Rome wear makeup? I never heard that."

"Migod," said Karen, "American children never get to study any *history.* How would you like it if your husband spent forty-five minutes in ze bathroom every morning putting his face on?"

I had to laugh. I hadn't thought about it. "It would be hell, I imagine," I admitted. "I couldn't stand having another model for a roommate. One bathroom is not enough."

"Zere you are," said Karen. "It will cause a revolution. Probably ze plumbing people are behind it somewhere. All ze bathrooms will have to be done over to make room for two to make up—ozerwise zey will divorce. Now zey have false eyelashes for men, you know."

I hadn't seen them, and I was sure Karen was stretching things, finding signs of decadence that hadn't been invented yet.

"Oh, yes, I've seen zem. Zey have Rhett Butler black and James Bond thick. Oh, yes," said Karen. "And anti-bag rinse for under ze eyes. And pancake they call Bronzer."

That I had seen. That was Man-Tan brought up-to-date.

"Have you seen ze transistor weight belts men wear under zere girdles? One night at Salvation I was dancing with zis very fat man, and he turned on his tummy transistor and tried to rub bellies wiz me. It was dizguzting. Wiz heart transplants and hair transplants, zey can't save zemselves. Wiz all zere money and all zere makeup, zey don't fool anybody. Zey are all dead at fifty years old, and ze young people will take over."

"Some of the young people are wearing more makeup than their mothers. Have you seen any hippies lately? They look like they put on eye makeup with a canoe paddle."

"Zose are not the real revolution, darling," Karen maintained. "Ze real ones can't be bothered. In China, in Cuba, you don't find all zis nonzenze. Imagine, you come home from an exziting confrontation wiz ze police—you come home after a manifestation in ze revolutionary struggle, and you have had maybe some nice vodkas or some nice pot, your man wants to whisk you off to bed, and you have to say, 'Just a minute, darling,' and you have to go in ze basroom and spend half an hour taking all zis damn gook off your face, and by zat time your poor man is asleep. Zat is the love story of New York women. Zat is why so many lesbians and so many women living with poodles and goldfishes."

No one hates makeup more than a model. Nobody looks forward more to the day without warpaint. But warpaint is work paint, and nobody works in front of a camera without makeup these days except Katharine Hepburn and look at her.

"Wait a minute, Karen. You're forgetting something," I protested. "You can't have it both ways. If men start wearing eyeliner and false lashes and Bronzer and ruddy translucent powder, when you come home from a party and he wants to whisk you off to bed, he can be taking off his while you're taking off yours. That will keep him awake until you're ready, and vice versa. If you both go to bed with vanishing cream on, it might be very groovy."

"Carolyn," said Karen, "you must be joking."

There was something vaguely familiar about the studio the agency sent me to. I had the feeling I had been there before. The photographer seemed vaguely familiar, too. "Don't I know you?" Stewart asked me. "Didn't you test up here once before?"

"I think I did," I said. "I know I did. With a guy called Larry something-or-other, I believe."

"Oh, my God, of course. My partner. My ex-partner."

"What happened to the crash pad? Where are the wine bottles?"

"Yeah, you tested here all right."

"He was the mad genius from California. I had the feeling the pictures were great, but he kept promising me prints for three months, and then he disappeared."

"Yeah. Shall we try it again some night?"

"I'd love to."

"You say that or do you mean it?"

"I mean it."

"I'm warning you I'm a nut on clothes. I won't shoot anything unless I really dig it. So don't show up here with all your clothes smashed into a bag."

"What do you mean—smashed into a bag? Excuse me, I'm a pro, and I have some respect for my clothes. I don't throw them around."

"Yeah. Well, maybe you don't, but I've been burned by models who say they've done testing, but when they show up it's just a big bore to them and they show up with a bundle of rags."

"Don't worry about me."

"OK, let's make it Wednesday around eight."

Wednesday afternoon Stewart telephoned to warn me he was depressed. He wasn't in the mood for testing. As soon as I volunteered to call it off, he insisted on going ahead. "Naw," he said. "Let's shoot anyway." I spent a good two hours packing all my trumpery. Four of my newest outfits—all my hairpieces, extra shoes, extras of everything. I began to feel that refurbished crash pad studio was a jinx. Nothing would ever happen for me there. But Stewart was loaded with talent. Of that I was sure. The work he displayed in the studio was the equal of anybody's. His printing was perfection itself. He might get something out of me no one else had managed. It was the risk and the uncertainty that intrigued me. It was a game like no other I knew. It was that man-and-woman thing—the duel thing—the challenge thing.

From where we started on my arrival we had nowhere to go but up. He reminded me again of his depression. "I feel God-awful. I don't expect anything to happen. You're not really what I'm looking for, but you're here, aren't you?"

I wasn't going to argue about that. "You're not the kind of girl I feel I want, but then I don't know what I want. I've kicked around a few ideas, but nothing has come up yet . . . nothing solid . . . it's this goddam depression—what do you do when you get depressed?

"I usually do my laundry or clean the house." I was carrying thirteen tons of clothes. I might as well unpack them and get the bad news. Maybe if he could let out some of his *angoisse* on the clothes, we could move on. "Shall I try on a few things?"

"All right."

I started with a brown crepe pants suit.

"That doesn't excite me very much, " he said. I told myself he could say what he wanted to about my outfits, but I wasn't letting him ruin them for me. A great talent, yes. But one can't dress all the time to inflame anguished photographers.

I put on a little blue number. "I don't like it," he flipped.

I tried on the black hiphuggers with the blouse and embroidered vest. "Nah, that stuff is like an army uniform by now," he brooded.

"Look, Stewart," I interposed, "we're just not scoring, so let's forget about it. You've already told me I'm not what you're looking for, so let's not take it out on the wardrobe."

As soon as I suggested calling a halt, he wanted to go full speed ahead again. "No, no, no," he said. "We'll go with this outfit."

"You just said you didn't like it."

"I don't. It's a uniform and I hate uniforms. We'll just shoot the black vest barely open with no bra. Maybe we'll go with the coat. I like your fur coat."

That was quite a concession, coming from him.

"Now go fix your hair. Put on all the hair you've got."

I went in and put on about three pieces.

"No, no. That's not enough. Put more on."

I put on everything I had.

"That's better. Now tease hell out of it."

I teased hell out of it until I looked like one of the bridesmaids at Frankenstein's wedding. "It's OK now," he said. "Let's try the coat." I put on the coat, and he put on the electric fan. I thought he had lost his mind. After asking me to tease my hair into extinction, now he had the fan on, too. Now he wanted the fuzzy-wuzzy collar of my coat up around my ears. I gave him everything he asked for. He's good, I know he's good, I thought. He's moody and he's depressed, but everyone can be happy as a lark for a whole afternoon and the pictures can turn out to be absolute crap. So it's up to me to go all the way and give him everything he thinks he wants. If he changes his mind every two seconds, I'll have to change with him.

"What's the matter with your mouth? I can't stand a turkey-ass mouth. Open it up!"

Now we were tussling. I hate open-mouth pictures. I don't mind the lips just parted, but I have the idea I don't look great with a great gaping gaggle of a mouth.

"Quit tensing up in the mouth. Why are you so nervous?"

"I'm not nervous. You made me angry. Now that I've gotten over it I can relax."

"You call that relaxed? Come on." He had managed to make me feel I had never been in front of a camera before in my entire life. But you never know what they're seeing in that damn lens. You may think you know, but you never do. Maybe he was getting something different. Maybe he was torturing me for my own good. He was really so creative you could almost smell something happening. I was trying my damnedest to just let go and leave it to him. He did a couple of rolls, and then he said, "OK, lemme see you in the vest," I put on the embroidered vest without any bra. When I came back, he had the fan blowing up a storm. When I walked into the wind, the vest flapped around until I might as well have been topless.

"Can we pull it together with just a thread?"

"I can try." I tried locking the two flaps together with a thin black thread. Now when he turned the fan on we had tension. The fan was blowing it open and the thread was holding it together.

"I know we're going to have trouble. One of your troubles is you've been doing too damn much catalog crap. You girls work all day to get these constipated catalog poses, and you're too damn stiff for anything else." I had been doing catalog work all week. This was a standard gibe, and I let it pass. I tried to be as fluid as possible.

"Oops, there goes that mouth again. You're fighting me." He had me

248

so mouth-conscious that my throat was dry all the way down to my lungs. When he stopped tossing nasty cracks at me, I felt we were getting somewhere. When he was depressed, he would call you up long distance to tell you. When he was happy, he wasn't even aware of it himself. Near the end of the second roll, I felt he was happy. I knew I was happy. The whole evening could have been a standoff. Instead we had muddled through, and perhaps when we saw the contacts it would all seem worthwhile. Anyway, now it was over.

I was in the makeup room changing into my street clothes when he appeared in the doorway. He looked like a different man. "I never even offered you any coffee when you came in. Would you like some?"

"Sure," I said.

When I joined him in what was apparently going to be his living quarters, I was amazed at what he'd done to the place. The split level bathroom had been turned into a darkroom. The orange crates and the dirty fur rugs were gone. The place was severe, immaculate and clean.

I couldn't help asking, "What ever happened to Larry?"

"Larry was a doll of a guy, but he turned this place into a zoo. Then he couldn't stand it himself anymore, so he fled back to California. I just got a hotel bill from somewhere in Pango Pango, so I imagine he's still running and still running up bills.

"You know, he went absolutely gaga on grass. I guess. He didn't know what he was doing. We've been cleaning up this place for a month, and every day we find a new stash of grass somewhere. It's hidden in shoe bags and hatboxes and books and in the darkroom. Every can in the kitchen turns out to be full of grass. I went to make some tea for a client one day, and the stuff tasted kind of strange, so I called the guy upstairs. He tasted it. He said, 'That's awful good stuff, but it's not exactly tea.' This guy is a connoisseur. He used to get a lot of free highs from Larry. Who didn't? This place was a damn community center for AA dropouts and groupies. I barely used the studio four times in six months. I couldn't work here. Larry had a continuous bash going on here. Girls would arrive from the West Coast carting everything they owned in tomato soup boxes. When they got high, they'd just go to sleep on the floor. People being sick all over the place. Everybody loved everybody, and then—whoosh—you turn around and one day everybody is gone. I'm still paying the bills. I guess that's what squares are for—to pick up the pieces and pay the piper."

He gave me a grand tour and outlined the plans he had for turning the place into an apartment and a studio. When we finished our coffee, he kissed me and said, "You're a very unusual girl."

Then he went out to the street with me and put me into a cab. Three days later he called me, and I got my prints. They were my best head shots to date!

I might not have the face that launched a thousand ships. But what kept me working and getting better all the time was meeting people I could learn from—guys who liked me because I was me.

*I'm on a diet constantly . . . I live on a diet . . . the first beautiful, delicious thing I eat and, boom, I'm fat. . . .*

It wasn't the usual kind of script. There were no technical details on it, just this monologue. The casting girl at the advertising agency handed it to me the moment I walked in the door, even before she asked me to sign in. I was trying to read it over quickly.

"I like your coat," she said. "What kind of fur is it?"

"Oh, thank you," I said. "China leopard fighting with Russian raccoon—"

*If you like going to the refrigerator and stealing a big hunk of chocolate cake with strawberry ice cream . . .*

"Miss Kenmore, you may go in now."

"I haven't even had time to read this over. My appointment was for eleven-forty-five. I came early so I'd have time to look at the script."

*. . . if you still want to have your rich, delicious desserts, try Yuban. It's rich and delicious. It costs a little bit more, but it's worth it.*

I schlepped my portfolio into the inner office where the jury was waiting. I stood there with the script in my hand, waiting to be told what to do.

"Sorry, sweetie," this little assistant said. "They shouldn't have sent you in. The client has decided to break for lunch."

"But my appointment was for eleven-forty-five, and it's barely that now."

"Sorry, sweetie, you'll be first call when we regroup at two o'clock."

I went back into the reception room. I took the script with me, and I studied it. I had lunch and rushed back at two. Now there were ten girls waiting. The man who'd promised me I'd be number one after lunch was nowhere to be found. Half an hour later the client and his entourage arrived late and apologetic and fat. *I'm on a diet constantly . . . I live on a diet . . . the first beautiful, delicious thing I eat and, boom, I'm fat. . . .*

It reads like a character part, anyway. It's not for the girl-next-door type at all. It's more for the noisy-yenta-from-upstairs type. Thank you very much. All a girl's got is her time. When it's costing them nothing, they don't mind using it up. It was three o'clock before I got out of there.

# CHAPTER 10

"Gil wanted to book you for two o'clock," my agent told me, but I had a TV show to do at that time, so they shuffled it off until four. It should run no later than five-thirty. He'd have a fit if he knew I was there from three to seven. I got there at three because I had bottom lashes to put on and those damn false nails. Besides, I had to unwind. Gordon, this nice male model, was sitting there. Gil uses him a lot. It was man-talk time, and they wanted to give me coffee.... I love to tune in on your stories, boys, but I have to get out of these duds. I hauled out my robe first thing and took everything else off....

Strippers have nothing on models. We spend most of our days dressing and undressing while the music is blasting away. The instant you walk into a studio, you head for the dressing room to take off your bra. While we're working on our makeup, we're topless. Some flat-chested girls tie a scarf around their chests. I usually wear a half slip and yank it up under my arms. There is a very basic reason for the first step. A brassiere leaves strap marks on your shoulders that show up on the photograph. Wearing nothing on the shoulders while we're making up gives the skin a chance to bounce back into Lady Godiva smoothness. If we're doing bathing suits, we have to take off all our undergarments and get into a robe pronto. Elastic on panties and other undergarments can leave ridges. Even belts and chains can mark your skin if you've been wearing them an hour or so, so off they come.

His floors were so clean, the whole studio was so clean. Guys who have mice in the dressing room usually turn out to be beasties. "Can I get you anything?" Gil said, ducking his head in the door. "The hairdresser will be here at three-thirty, and the client is due at four. Go ahead, take your time, if you need anything just whistle...." I had TVmakeup on, so I had all that to redo. I was brushing my hair, and Gil knocked. "Are you decent?" Sure.

"Oh, my God," said Gil. "I forgot. Lemme see your feet."

"Don't worry—I did my toenails last night at home on my own time."

"Good kid, you're a pro."

"If I wasn't a pro, I wouldn't be here."

A model has an awful lot more to do to keep herself together than an average woman. Vanity doesn't come near explaining what it's all about. Every morning I have to get myself ready to meet my maker because I never know who it's going to be. One body is all you've got. It's your violin and your saxophone. You may be booked for slacks, but at the last minute they throw you in a bathing suit, and if there's hair on your legs, that means no more bookings at that studio. Every morning you have to be ready for those surprise close-ups under your arms, and you gotta be prepared to let them zoom in your gray crevices and the roots of your hair. Your back teeth better match your front ones, and a hangnail cannot be explained away—if you had time for a sleep, you had time for a manicure. And you better have spare false nails with you, because you never know when they are going to ask you to hold something in your pretty little hand, and this is not TV, baby, where the hand shots are doubled and they can get some lady from Jersey who never takes off her greasy gloves even to answer the telephone. . . .

Gil went out of his way to prove he was all business and no hanky-panky. "Look," he said, "if I was trying to make any time, I'd take you out for a couple of martinis." What time is it? Three-thirty already. No, the hairdresser was early, too. He had another booking after me, and he wanted to get out early. He took all my hairpieces and went to the table and started rolling them and setting them. While he's combing my hair, he's bending my ear about the big trauma he had had on his last job that afternoon. He was doing the hair for a TV commercial that had a child model in the cast; a tiny bitch baby brat shepherded by a seamless stage mama. He is doing the long blond locks of Little Miss BBB when she goes suddenly ape, screams at her mother like Barbra Streisand in labor, and picks up his forty-dollar French curling iron and smashes it against the wall. Mummy turned white and said she was so sorry but Little Miss BBB had had such a beastly day.

So I have to listen to all this explanation. So the hairdresser has no curling iron and he will have to borrow my electric rollers. No wonder we carry around thirty pounds of luggage, schlepping forever, and yet nothing is unnecessary—everything has its own use in its own time.

Aha, the client is early, too. He's here already, and a woman stylist or someone from the ad agency. Well, it will be nice having another woman around for this gig. If I need help with this Cleopatra rig, a girl will be more help than a boy.

Gil came back again to introduce me to the client. I'm still in my robe and my hair isn't finished yet, but I have those damn false fingernails on. From now on in, I'm helpless as an arthritic—I don't even dare shake hands with the man. I can't curtsy either, because I can't hold my robe together for fear my fingernails will fall off.

Gil likes my eye makeup. Maybe it was all a waste of time and they plan to hang chandelier earrings over my eye sockets. Now the girl from the agency arrives with the precious see-through metal doodads for my breasts....Two sets, big and small, and she gets them on me, and they seem to work. Not bad. Not bad at all. The dressing room is suddenly crowded. Then the hairdresser arrives with all my hairpieces furled and curled, and there's no room for him to work with me in front of the mirror. He has consulted with the photographer and the client, and everyone wants me very hairy, so he begins piling it on by the pound. He piles one piece on the side to get real drippy curls over one shoulder, another up high, and then a long, long fall. He's putting the pins in from every angle. "How much more time do you need with the hair?" Gil wants to know. "We have to begin to drape her. We're all set out there with the screen." The hairdresser is getting nervous about his other job.... He wants ten or fifteen more minutes.

Finally I move out onto the set in nothing but my metal doodads and my robe. Behind the screen there are all these men waiting to festoon me with jewels. The picture everyone will see may be in beautiful taste, but what are we going to have to go through to get there? They have a rack with thousands of earrings on it, but at the last minute they have to take a pin and make it into an earring.

I could feel the wind between my knees. Under the lights it was warm and all I had to keep me warm was Con Edison and its kilowatts. . . ."You're not cut out for this," the hairdresser said to me. "You're too womanly. Some girls would just walk out there as if they were testing for a Swedish movie and say, 'OK, boys, drape.' "

Wouldn't it be easy without all these people? But they were nice to me because they could see I was slightly shy. "Just consider your skin a costume—Josephine Baker once said that," the hairdresser suggested. "A little modesty might make the picture more interesting."

Some man was putting a coiled bronze snake around my ankle, and the metal was cutting me. . . .I hope they don't move it around, or I'm going to have marks that will show in the shot. . . .I'm an easy bruiser, fellows. Another man was shoving three rings onto each hand. Then they were hanging chains on me and jewels and more jewels. When they started putting a snake ring on my toe, I said, "Hey, fellows, how am I going to walk from here to the seamless? Wouldn't it be a great idea if you got me in place on the seamless and then draped me?"

"Marvelous. Great idea. Why didn't we think of that?"

Because everyone was too nervous. The job was too important. The photographer has invested in the hairdresser and all the extras because he's trying to bag the client as a steady account. The hairdresser is under pressure because he wants to please the photographer and give him what he wants so he can get more work. Funny, four days ago I was too sunburned to pose in a bra for J. C. Penney, and today I'm OK wearing less than that. I brought along two whole bottles of body makeup, and nobody even suggested I uncork them.

I had dashed in between a test for Pepsi and a second fitting for my TV gig as a nun—contemporary apparel for the active sisterhood—because the white blouse had to be dyed beige for TV and the black skirt had to be redone in blue. I was just back from Grenada, and it was my first time at that studio. It was the end of the day and everybody in the place was ready to take off when they threw me this bra. "Here," said the stylist. "We're glad you got here. We want to see this garment on you. Would you put it on?" It's a small world. I recognized the bra. It was designed by a top bra designer I sometimes see a lot of. I had a whole drawerful at home he had given me; they were samples, and I'm a sample size. "Move, will you?" said the photographer when he got me on the seamless. "This is for J. C. Penney." Well, I know Penney's is changing its image, but it's not ready for anything utterly dramatic just yet, so I gave them the standard kind of poses, the kind of thing you do for a catalog. "You got it," said the photographer. "How are you in panties?"

"Fine," I said, "I've been wearing them for years."

"Well, maybe if you just pull that suede skirt down a little. Just loosen it and slip it down so we can see the hipline. . .the hipline is great. . . .Fine, you know what to do. No creases. But wait a minute—where'd you get that color? That bronze is not good. Where'd you get that color?"

"Well, I just got back from a week of shooting in Barbados and Grenada."

"I'm sorry, Red, but the client is very fussy. For a national ad a little color like that would be fine, but this is a color shot and that bronze might give us hell. That's a damn shame, Red. Well, I'll use you in something else."

They always say that, but wouldn't you know, in a couple days he called my agent and said he had me in mind for the jewelry thing, and you know what grabbed him, what made him remember me, what made him ask for me when this Lady Godiva thing came along? He told me later that when I slipped down my suede skirt just above the hipline where many girls have creases—Carolyn had no creases. So I was too tawny for J. C. Penney. Some people can slip on a bra and come up covered with precious stones.

"It's not exactly a nude," my agent told me when he called me about the booking. "All you'll have on is jewelry, but they'll arrange something for the breast and also downstairs."

When he gave me the photographer's name, I said, "Hey, that's the same Gil who couldn't use me for J. C. Penney, and he said he'd use me on something else, and he meant it."

Next day I went to see him, and he told me about this new jewelry account he was getting. "It can turn into lotsa work for you." He showed me the layout and told me about the budget. "I'm paying for a hairdresser because I want everything perfect and in good taste. You'll be making more out of the job than I am. But you gotta go through the art director—he has the final say."

Gil had hell finding the art director's address because he'd thrown the slip away and the secretary didn't have it in her book. But Gil finally reached him and said, "I got the girl here I wanna use. Her name is Carolyn Kenmore, and I want you to take a look at her."

The ad agency turned out to be right around the corner from my apartment, so I ducked in to see the A. D. between go-sees. He said, "You look perfect," right off the bat. He asked me what I had done and all that blah-blah-blah, and I told him blah-blah-blah, and he looked at my book. But the man who has the final say never turns out QUITE to have the final say. There is always some unseen someone who has something to say about it. There couldn't be too many in the chain of command because the agency didn't seem to be that big. "Can I take your book in to show someone?"

"Of course," I said, and I stood there on one foot and then the other, wondering if this would evaporate mysteriously, too, but no, he was back in a flash, and he said, "We think you'll be fine. You know what it's all about, don't you? It's not really a nude—you'll be pretty well covered with precious stones."

And here I am covered with precious stones.

Dripping as I was with precious stones, I had to toddle over to the seamless where someone wiped my feet, and then the moment came when I had to let go of the robe and pretend that five guys who were there weren't there. I had seen the sketch of the layout, and I tried to give them something close to that. The lady stylist adjusted my see-through bronze top and the bronze medallion I had covering my whatsis, but I could feel the wind on my bare bottom and nothing warming me but Con Edison. I was shifting from side to side and terrified one of the pins from one of those jewels was going to vaccinate me. The hairdresser was fiddling with my hair. Now they were taping wires down my back to hold other dangling jewels in place....Now the assistant was fiddling with the lights, trying to light up the jewelry so it glittered. The chains were hurting my neck, and that snake bracelet on my ankle was cutting into me. They were working with two cameras. Gil had his assistant with the tripod he had had set and sighted, and he was moving in and around with a hand-held camera. The lighting wouldn't allow any fast action—the jewels would all come out a smear—so every time I found a pose I had to hold it and freeze and then coast and then freeze and then find another one and then freeze. Every time I changed position it changed the focus on the jewelry. I psyched myself into thinking I was a piece of driftwood so the chains and the biting snake bracelet couldn't hurt me anymore. They loved the side view featuring the ears. I tried to loosen up, but when I did, the tape peeled and the wires bent. I worked hard trying to hold the pose, but it wasn't right and I knew it wasn't right. Come on, Carolyn, you can't duck nudity, it's all a part of modeling, your skin IS your costume, move that arm, hold that, bring your hip out, that's enough, spread those fingers, that's it, bridge that hand, that's enough, eyes this way, turn, no, back, the other way was better, one second more. I've never done nudes, and please, God, if it's good and done in good taste I'll have one for my book. OK, let's take a break. Take five.

All the men melted away and began lighting cigarettes. They could take a break, but what could I do? I was afraid to move. I wondered what they would say if they knew that two hours ago I was a nun on television. I could barely light a cigarette for fear I'd ruin my ersatz claws. I couldn't hold up a crew of ten people to fix my nails.

The hairdresser came to my rescue. They had decided they wanted to change my hair. They had wanted me hairy, and now they didn't quite like it. He led me to the mirror and began taking pins out. One by one, he began removing the hairpieces, undoing all the work he had done. Now we were down to the hair I slept in, piled tight and high to show the large drop earrings. Two puffs more of the cigarette and I was back on the seamless. OK, said Gil, now we were going to try a few standing up with me swinging a whole raft of belts and chains on my arms. We tried it and I held it and we tried another and I held that. Wait a minute, there was another huddle and the client wanted me to sit down. So we took a few more sitting and then a few in a kind of squat. "OK," Gil said, "now we're sailing. Do anything you want to do." The chains were cutting my arms, the snake was cutting my leg, but I didn't care—I was gonna give it to him and he was going to get it. That's right, hold it. Now we're moving. Turn this way. Look sophisticated. Look evil. Look bored. This is it. We got it. Just two more frames. I fell into a low squat, and I started working those crystal beads. It was hurting, but I didn't want it to be over. I didn't want it to be over until I was exhausted, until I knew I had given Gil everything he wanted. So he could get the account, so the hairdresser could get his account. It all depends on me. They all depend on me, so you give after it hurts. It's a little bit like skiing. Those first two runs you're not quite with it. You know what you want to do, but your body is not delivering the message. And on the third run your body knows and you know, and you're warm, and you can look like Stein Erickson. You go that whole damn hour, even though the photographer may guess and the client may think that you got the best you're ever going to get in the first five minutes. Because it's in that last fifteen minutes that it often happens if it's going to happen. "Beautiful," Gil said. "Beautiful, Red. I'm sure we got it."

And now you wilt, and the chains and the snakes really hurt, and when the agency lady helps you take the tape off and the wires off and the chains off, you've got marks all over you. Thank God this wasn't a two o'clock booking. Thank God it's after six and nothing can happen after this.

I slouched into the dressing room like a zeppelin fresh out of gas. The place was a mess, makeup all over that I had to collect. Hairpieces strewn around, and pins. The hairdresser had flagged off to do his other job. I started picking up the mess. My wigs and falls went into their boxes. I chucked my robe into my tote bag and slipped into my lingerie. Dressing without any music seemed sort of crazy. Wait a minute, where is everybody? Nobody signed my voucher! I took my pad of vouchers out of my tote bag. My voucher had to be signed by the photographer or the client or somebody, and where had they all disappeared to?

"Oh," said the elevator man as I left, "they told me they're waiting for you in the bar downstairs." I got downstairs, and suddenly I was freezing. After an hour and a half naked under those hot, hot lights, now I'm in the cold street, and it's seven o'clock, and it's dark already, so I rush into the air-conditioned bar to get warm and get my voucher signed so I won't have to make another round of go-sees to get my money.

## A Model's Day

*Monday*

| | |
|---|---|
| 9 | Sheldon Secunda Studios—112 Fourth Ave. |
| 9:30 | Mayo Studios—9 East 19 St.—see Darwin Davidson |
| 10 | John Rawlings—421 East 54 St. |
| 10:30 | Horn-Griner—415 East 54 St. |
| 11 | Pierre Drummond—1181 Broadway |
| 11:30 | Home—call agency and service |
| 12 | Hanover Studios—225 West 34 St.—take hairpieces, panty hose (nude), strapless bra |
| 12:30 | |
| 1 | |

259

**AGENCY COPY**

## ZIP Agency

MODELS

| | | DATE |
| --- | --- | --- |
| A S | MODEL | OF |
| | | JOB |

| A G E N T | | CLIENT STUDIO |
| --- | --- | --- |
| F O R | R HOUR <br> A <br> T DAY <br> E | DEPT. OR ACCOUNT |
| T I M E | FROM _____ <br> TO _____ | CHECK FOR FITTING ☐ |

**TOTAL**

SUBJECT TO SERVICE CHARGE

THE ABOVE WORK HAS BEEN DONE AND THE
BILLING INFORMATION IS CORRECT

CLIENT'S
SIGNATURE _____

SEND
INVOICE **TO** _____

ADDRESS _____ STATE _____

CITY _____ STATE _____

NUMBERED COPIES OF THIS INVOICE WILL BE MAILED TO YOU,
HOWEVER, IF YOU WISH TO USE THIS INVOICE FOR PAYMENT
PLEASE NOTE THE MODEL'S NAME AND DATE OF JOB ON YOUR
REMITTANCE.

**MODEL RELEASE:** IN CONSIDERATION OF THE MODEL FEES
STATED HEREIN I HEREBY GIVE MY PERMISSION TO THE
ABOVE ADVERTISER AND/OR PUBLISHER TO PRODUCE MY
PHOTOGRAPH FOR PURPOSES OF ADVERTISING AND/OR TRADE.

MODEL'S
SIGNATURE _____

260

| | |
|---|---|
| 1:30 | |
| 2 | |
| 2:30 | Ross & Weiss Studio—35 East 32 St.—take hairpieces, |
| 3 | lightcolored shoes, jewelry |
| 3:30 | |
| 4 | |
| 4:30 | |
| 5 | Dermatologist |
| 5:30 | Call agency |
| 6 | Home—call service |
| 7 | Test Reg von Cuÿlenburg—take pants suit, long flowing dress, bathing suit, 2 dresses (minis) |

*Tuesday*

| | |
|---|---|
| 10 | Bank |
| 10:30 | Warsaw Studio—40 East 34 St.—take hairpieces, wigs, body stocking |
| 11 | |
| 11:30 | |
| 12 | Agency |
| 12:30 | |
| 1 | Pagano Studio—206 East 65 St. |
| 1:30 | Grey Advertising—777 Third Ave.—see Claudia Walden |
| 2 | |
| 2:30 | O'Rourke Studio—1181 Bro dway—see Barry or Gene—take |
| 3 | hairpieces and wigs, shoes, 2 medium-tone dresses, acces- |
| 3:30 | sories |
| 4 | |
| 4:30 | |
| 5 | Shelton Towers Health Club—gym class and steam bath or sauna |
| 5:30 | Call agency |
| 6 | Call Syd Craiker re: testing |
| 8:30 | Birthday party at Bill Eagan's—175 West 72 St. |

261

*Wednesday*

| | |
|---|---|
| 9:30 | Post office—mail package to Mom |
| 10 | Good Earth Health Food Store—saw Rik van Glintenkamp (call next week) |
| 10:30 | |
| 11 | Voice Lesson—Florence Kyte—150 West 57 St. |
| 11:30 | |
| 12 | |
| 12:30 | Make-Up Center—150 West 55 St.—pick up eyelashes and foundation |
| 1:30 | Call agency |
| 1:30 | Al Karp Studio—118 East 28 St.—hair, jewelry, and shoes |
| 2 | |
| 2:30 | |
| 3 | Mel Sokolsky Studio—322 East 39 St. |
| 3:30 | Vogue Wright Studios—225 Park Ave. So. |
| 4 | Len Steckler Studio—33 West 67 St. |
| 4:30 | |
| 5 | Frank Lerner Studio—421 East 54 St. |
| 5:30 | Pick up dry cleaning—39th and Lex.—Call agency |
| 6 | Make personal phone calls, friends, etc.—rest,wash hair, do nails |

*Thursday*

| | |
|---|---|
| 9 | Dr. Most—111 West 57 St.—dentist |
| 9:30 | |
| 10 | Call Reg regarding prints. Stop at William Morris Agency —1350 Sixth Ave. See Lloyd Kolmer |
| 10:30 | Telefects Productions—268 West 47 St.—see Jay Columbus |
| 11 | Stop at United Beauty Supply—47th (5th/6th)—hair spray, conditioner, etc. |
| 11:30 | Drugstore—Executive Drug (39th/Madison)—prescription, toothpaste, hand cream |
| 12 | Home—call agency |

| | |
|---|---|
| 12:30 | Lunch |
| 1 | Central Park location—meet at Marty Block Studio—23 East 17 St.—take hairpieces, wigs, shoes, jewelry |
| 1:30 | |
| 2 | |
| 2:30 | |
| 3 | |
| 3:30 | |
| 4 | |
| 4:30 | |
| 5 | Shelton Towers Health Club |
| 5:30 | Call agency and service |
| 6 | |
| 6:30 | Home—call Mom |
| 7:30 | Dinner date—David |

When I was rudely awakened from my slumber by the tinkle of my private bedside phone, I looked at the clock. Nine-fifteen. Nobody, but nobody, calls me on Saturday morning. I had finished the week off dancing my brains out at Nepentha until three in the morning. Saturday is sacred. My very own.

"Carolyn? I'm sorry to bother you, but. . ."

"Yes, Ed. . ."

"I have to ask you a terrific favor . . . you were sleeping?"

"Yes, Ed."

"I'm out at La Guardia Airport. We've got thirty salesmen who flew in from all over the country to see the first live demo on the Magic Merge, and the model didn't show. . ."

"She didn't show!"

"You gotta help me out. You gotta save me."

"Ed, I'm unconscious. It would take me a half hour to get myself together and at least another half hour to get out there."

"I'll come pick you up."

"Oh, please, Ed, can't you get somebody else? Did you try?"

"I've called every girl we ever used and can't find a soul. I know you don't do this stuff anymore, but this is a crisis, sweetie. We got so much riding on this. We can only hold the salesmen here for a couple of hours, and. . ."

263

"OK, Ed. I'll try."

"I'll be in front of your apartment in twenty minutes." Crash. Bang. Up I got. I wouldn't do it for anyone but Ed, I told myself. I got my face on, eyes and all, in twenty minutes—a new record. Ed was downstairs when I arrived. I had forgotten to ask him what I would need in the way of clothes, so I had ten tons of blouses and scarves. The Magic Merge was a new kind of girdle—a garterless panty girdle that holds the fanny in and the stockings up. Ed had been working on the garment and the campaign for weeks. My trouble was I had only panty hose—I had kicked stockings. I never bought them anymore. To model the MM I would need some sheer hose in the right size and the right shade. I thought we ought to stop at a store on the way. Ed said there wasn't time. We could take my panty hose and cut them off. Cut them off?

"Don't worry," he said. "I made them agree to pay you your full rate. I'll see you come out ahead on this one."

We parked at this hotel near La Guardia Airport. The salesmen were having a lavish brunch in a private dining room. The sales manager almost collapsed with relief when he saw me. He would have been happy with Apple Annie if she was a 34 B and wore a small or medium girdle. They would have put a sack over her head and sent her out to show the garment. But to get a photographer's model—that took connections. Where did ya get the lanky redhead, everyone wanted to know.

There was no time to lose. Ed threw me the garment, and I picked out a beige blouse to wear up top, tied in the front. I wiggled into the Magic Merge while Ed was performing emergency surgery on my panty hose. He handed them back to me—three pieces instead of one. I pulled the stockings up, tucked them under the MM, and I was ready.

If it hadn't been for my training on Seventh Avenue, I couldn't have done it. At ten o'clock in the morning, with no music, immediately after bacon and eggs, I trotted out into the center of the private dining room, moving from table to table in my MM. It all came back to me in a minute. You have to be fluid. A lot of photographer's models cannot show a garment live. Posing for a photographer is static; showing is fluid. You never really stop. You come out with one foot exactly in front of the other, you take a nice position with the hip angled a little bit, you put your hand on your hip for just an instant, and then you

264

move it away and you turn, trying never to touch the garment very long, holding your arms out of the way so they can see every detail of it.

The only music I had to dance to was chin music—the sales manager gave his carefully written spiel while I moved. They had a big blowup of a bulging rear end with a dotted line slicing off the excess flesh. This launched a competitive slap at panty hose.

"It may be a swell little panty when it comes to holding up stockings without garters. But as for control, forget it. . . .

"Peter Pan has something to get the no-garter customer back into the girdle department. . . Magic Merge. Inspired by Oleg Cassini exclusively for Peter Pan, the first garterless panty girdle that succeeds on every count. No tourniquet bind. No phony band. No hookups. No hang-ups. And plenty of control. Like you'd expect to find in the girdle department. Magic Merge. The panty girdle that's going to make hosiery come to it instead of the other way around. We mean that literally."

At this point I slipped the stockings out and showed there was nothing holding them up except the lightly ribbed bottom of the MM.

I smiled and I kept moving and showed them how it worked. It took only about ten minutes to save the day. The crisis was over, and now I had some friends at Peter Pan.

It was nice to be reminded where I got my start. Any time things got dry on the seamless, I could make a comeback on the runway.

Now I was completely awake and feeling like dancing, so Ed took me to lunch. I thought of all the money I'd saved by not being able to do my shopping, and I had him drop me off at the health club for my regular weekend ritual: exercises to keep me out of the girdle department.

"I hate you," the blonde said to me. "I hate your skinny ass."

"What did *I* do?" I asked her.

"Look at you," she said, eyeing my svelte midriff and pinching the roll of flab that spilled over her half-slip. We had been working together in tandem for hours on an all-day booking. Between us we must have modeled thirty different brassieres. My shots were a breeze. Each one took about ten minutes. Hers were a drag. She had to have special lighting. She had to hold her breath until her face was out of shape trying to suck in her gut. She was almost in tears from the strain. The photographer was kind and patient, but she knew it was her last bra booking *there* for a while.

"You don't take birth control pills, do you?" she asked me.

"I wouldn't touch them," I said. We were in the dressing room together, getting glued up ready to go home.

"I guess they really are no good for you, but what do you *do*?"

"I'd rather be pregnant than sick," I said.

"Maybe your lover isn't as demanding as mine."

"Maybe not."

"Do you work out, too?"

"Three times a week."

"That's what I should do."

"You can work out until you're blue in the face, but you'll still be bloated as long as you take those pills. And as long as you don't watch what you eat."

"I'd give anything to lose about ten pounds."

"I just lost ten pounds evenly all over—especially in the upper thighs where I needed to lose."

"For God's sake, tell me what you did. I'm desperate."

"You won't believe it. I eat more than I ever ate, and I don't put on a pound."

"What is your diet? Tell me—I wanna copy it down."

"It's not a diet. I wasn't trying to lose weight."

"What were you trying to do?"

"I was having hell when I had my periods. Nausea and cramps and agony for hours."

"So what? Doesn't *every*body? Isn't that why they call it the curse? It's better than not having it."

"It's not normal. Nobody can tell me it's normal. I went to a gynecologist. He gave me pills."

"Did they do any good?"

"Pills are not the answer to anything. I know enough to know that," I said.

"Well, what is the answer?"

"I don't know. All I can do is tell you what worked for me."

"I'm earie, dearie."

"I met this kookie dentist," I said. "I didn't know he was a dentist

266

when I met him on the street. He was young and terribly good-looking. The LAST thing you'd expect him to be was a dentist—an actor, maybe, or a dancer, but a dentist never—*jamais de la vie*. He stopped me in the street, went through my tote bag like a customs inspector, and threw away some cookies I had in there and some diet soda. He said I'd never be radiant until I quit eating junk. And he gave me some delicious bread to eat. He made it himself."

"Wait a minute. Is he blond, with lots of hair and sandals?"

"Yeah. Why?"

"I know another girl who ran into him. He was doing his thing in a drugstore. He sat down next to her and read her off a list of poisonous chemicals he said were in commercial ice cream. She got sick and couldn't finish her lunch."

"It sounds like the same stud," I observed.

"Maybe he goes around hitting models. It's a new kind of come-on—you gotta admit that. How did you find out he was a dentist, for God's sake?"

"I ran into him again. He was working as a janitor in this building where a lot of photographers have their studios, on Twenty-third Street."

"Working as a janitor?" she gasped.

"That's nothing. Now he washes dishes in a tiny Japanese restaurant in the East Village."

"Anything is better than being a dentist. I don't blame him."

"The things these kids are into today—it's amazing. He took one look at me and guessed what was wrong. He told me I would always have trouble with my periods because I was full of toxicity, because I ate junk. He said he could tell. He walked down the street with me, carrying my portfolio. His name is Bernie. He told me to quit drinking coffee and stop eating sugar and candy and soft drinks and meat—he said there was no way a girl could look like a lady eating a steak."

"Oh, yeah, it's that Oriental thing," she said. "John Lennon and Yoko and lots of other people are into that. The ten-days-of-natural-brown-rice thing."

"That's it. He told me not to do ten days of rice because I might have a bad reaction. He told me to convert gradually and start eating more than fifty percent whole grains—rice and buckwheat and millet and whole-grain bread, some green vegetables and a little fish."

"You did it?"

"He gave me a book to read, and it made so much sense I tried it."

"For how long?" she asked.

"I enjoyed the food so much I just kept eating that way. And I just began losing gradually. The next time I had my period, I couldn't believe it. No cramps. No nausea. Nothing. I owed him twenty dollars. He bet me twenty dollars. It was so silly—he looked like the type that doesn't have twenty dollars to his name. When I went back to the building to look for him, he had split."

"Vanished."

"Disappeared. Then one night I went downtown for dinner in this tiny Japanese restaurant in the East Village, and there he was washing dishes."

She stared. "I don't believe it."

"I was so excited. I told him what happened. He just smiled and picked up a guitar and began playing these wild Indian chords."

"What a scene!"

"One of the other kids down there told me he was a dentist but he got sick of it. He said if people ate properly, they wouldn't need dentists."

"So that's what he does. You know something? I think that's beautiful."

"It *is* beautiful," I admitted.

"There is nothing more beautiful than discovering your own thing and just doing it. He got to you and now you're into it, and you got to me and now I'm going to get into it, and if I get into it and get rid of this bloat around the middle, then I won't hate your skinny ass anymore."

"Peace, sister," I said. And we walked together all the way home.

Backstage was a real zoo—a sugarless bubble gum tester, a man who manufactured castor oil, a chap from California who picked up tables with his teeth every night on Broadway in the musical *Zorba*, eight female impersonators from the Princeton Triangle *Follies* and, "Here's Carolyn Kenmore to show you the latest fashion in nuns' wear."

That was my cue to waltz out in a fitted black coat, black jacket and skirt—dyed blue for black-and-white cameras—and my white blouse dyed beige and a tiny slice of red hair showing beneath my mini-veil, false eyelashes, and a huge cross around my neck. Then I walked up and down in front with the TV cameras on me while Arlene Francis and the other *What's my Line?* panelists looked me over and ad-libbed.

I wasn't the mystery guest—that was actor Hal Holbrook—but I got the full security treatment. A lady with a clipboard made sure there was no one else on the elevator before they let me come down; then she instructed another member of the crew to shepherd me through a secret basement passage across to the other side of the studio and sequester me behind some flats. I had to cool it there while the panelists worked over Jim Fitzpatrick to see if they could guess that he designed and manufactured contemporary fashions for the active sisterhood. This would take a fast 180 seconds on the TV screen, but it had already taken twelve hours of my life. The agency phone calls, the appointment, the interview with the manufacturer, the inspection of my portfolio by the production staff, the visit to the downtown showroom for preliminary fitting before the garments were specially dyed for TV, then another fitting after they were dyed. Final approval might have to come from the FCC and the Vatican, for all I knew. Then lunch with the client. Getting up at 6 A.M. to get dressed and made up in order to hurry to the studio at 8 A.M. to wait while everybody had coffee and staff members rushed around with contracts and wrote down your Social Security number and your telephone number and your agency telephone number and your grandmother's maiden name, and then waiting for hours while the wives of the other zoo mates told me about their pretty little daughters who wanted to be models, and should we encourage that or shouldn't we, and how did you get your start, and telling the story of my life, suddenly everyone on the set is screaming. "Where's the model, where's the model?" I had to rush behind a screen and change in thirty seconds. It wasn't just a run-through showing me where to pose and where to stand and how to move from there to there—it was a *dress* rehearsal. Somebody wanted to see the outfit on camera. On your mark: Here's Carolyn Kenmore blah-blah-blah, walk in, show coat, unbutton coat, take coat over arm, then walk in front of panel while the MC describes the skirt and blouse, blah-blah-blah. Thank you very much. That's it. Now once more for camera angles. That's it. Please be back at one o'clock for a one-forty-five taping, they told me after I had been there for more than three hours. So I rushed home from the CBS studios in the Ed Sullivan Theater to my apartment to get the hairpieces I would need for my next booking after the TV thing. The last two blocks in the cab took twenty minutes, and the leisurely lunch I had in mind went out the window.

So I had a frazzled lunch with the client, and he wanted to know if I would be available to do another catalog for him and sometime in April to model for the firm at a convention somewhere out of New York, and then rush-rush-rush back to the studio to check my makeup and jump into my costume, and back through the passageway. Well, anyway, here I am, and the panel has just unmasked after failing to guess the Mystery Guest, and now Jim Fitzpatrick is signing in. Are you self-employed? Is there a product involved in what you do? Some assistant is checking that I am in place. A stagehand drinks his coffee and looks at me. I was wondering what a real nun would do in a spot like that, and I remembered the story of the two nuns in Sardi's restaurant tossing back a few. One nun was definitely loaded, and when she raised her voice to make some campy vulgar remark, one of the Italian Catholic waiters was so shocked he rushed over to their table and asked them please to lower their voices—the other customers would get a bad impression. And this loud nun straightened her veil and lifted her martini and said, "Up yours, buster, we're from *The Sound of Music*."

That story reminded me of Middlebury, for some reason, and that reminded me to ask when this taped show would be shown. I had to know so Mom wouldn't miss it. Maybe this joker staring at me might know. I was just about to ask him when I noticed my stocking. A nun with a run! Oh, no! The poor Catholic Church is in enough trouble already without me disgracing them. "I have a run," I whispered. "What do I do? Is there time for me to change?"

"Oh, I noticed that quite a while ago," said this girl with the clipboard. A great little efficiency expert you are, darling, I wanted to say. Thank Heaven I had schlepped my tote bag with me. I dove in and found a spare pair of panty hose. There was no time to care who was watching. I whipped up my straight little nun's skirt, and I kicked off my shoes, and I stripped off one pair of panty hose and climbed into the other. All right, Mr. Poker-Face Stage Hand, if you've seen everything, including the flying elephants, you can quit staring at me. "And here's Carolyn Kenmore to show you the latest fashion in nun's wear." The floor manager was there to give me a shove, and on I went. Thirty seconds seemed like an eternity on camera, and nobody kicked the habit quicker than I did. In thirty more seconds I'd jumped into my shirt and

pants, taken off the cross and put on my tons of chains, and out the door
I flew, red hair unpinned and flying.

"Now that's what I call a swinging nun," shouted panelist Soupy
Sales as he spied me waving frantically from the Broadway curb, trying
to snag a cab to get me to my next booking. . . .

After you've schlepped around in the cold since 9:30 A.M. there's
nothing groovier than a nice warm bath at the end of the day—even if
your bathroom has standing room only for three clients, an art
director, a photographer and his assistant, another assistant in charge
of blowing bubbles, an interior decorator, two carpenters, a prop man,
a stylist to squeeze water on my shoulders, and a hairdresser to make
sure those curls at the back of my neck dangle just provocatively so.

Bubble bath bookings are usually scheduled at the end of the
day—around five o'clock—so the set designer and the decorator have
all day to set up. The client was a manufacturer of coordinated
bathroom rugs and shower curtains—they weren't selling bubbles so
there was some question as to whether I would be paid paid straight
rate—$60 an hour—or $250 for baring my body. I called the agency in
the morning. The answer: straight rate. So just to make sure, I packed a
strapless nude bra and a teeny-weeny-nude bikini. Bubbles usually
make the whole thing academic, but it's the principle of the thing.

When I walked in, I took a look at the set and it was gorgeous—wildly
Spanish in black and gold, and very good for a redhead. I slipped my
bra off to give the strap marks time to go away. In five minutes nature
would take its course and erase all the telltale signs. The photographer
gave me a big hug when he stuck his head in to say hello. There is no
end-of-the-day nonsense ever in his bailiwick. Like all the good ones,
he doesn't have time for hanky-panky. "I don't even know the names
of girls after they leave here," he told me. "Nobody has to sleep with
me to get a gig. Just don't give me a hard time and run into overtime.
I'm not going to let any girl put me in that position."

I showed him my nude bra. "It's straight rate, so I'm wearing this," I
told him.

"OK," he says. "If we run into any trouble with the bubbles, you can
sort of slip the bra off in the water."

"If the bra slips, your client has to slip me bare body rate. 'Oh, they can't fool me, I'm sticking to the union,'" I said. That's the name of an old IWW song that the kids have rediscovered.

"You win," the photographer said. "It's unfair to ask anything else."

So we were all in the hands of the man with the bubble gun. When I walked on the set in my robe, the clients were all charming and smiling. And the water was absolutely perfect when I dipped my toe in it.

"Not too hot?" the assistant asked.

"Perfect," I said. He took his little portable mixmaster and gave the water another churn. The bubbles were huge and white and thick. It felt so good I wanted it to last. I pulled the bubbles up around my bosom, and they peeped at me through the lens. No trouble. No trouble at all. I pulled my knees up, and the bubbles bounced without breaking. Once I was in there I couldn't touch my hair anymore. So the stylist hovered around, watching that my curls didn't get too damp and stringy. She took a paper towel to make sure my shoulders were moist and glistening.

Serenity and meditation came so easily. I gave them the gamut of beauty-in-the-bath poses—arm up, eyes down—hand on knees, scrubbing gently—one arm out holding a magazine. Wait until my sister sees my rugs and my shower curtains—she'll tear the town apart getting the same kind.

It was all over in a few minutes and time to change the shower curtains. The decorator whipped one pair off and another pair on. Up near the ceiling somewhere the carpenter was pounding something together. The lighting was being changed slightly. The assistant excused himself, and once again he stirred up the bubbles with his little mixmaster, and once again the stylist checked my curls and dampened down my shoulders, and then I was all alone again, feeling like the most beautiful thing afloat. When we finished, everybody treated me like a star—the assistant put little towels on the floor; they handed me a huge clean towel to cuddle in and a fresh pair of scuffs to wear as I scooted back to the dressing room. Everyone was so sweet and took care of me so beautifully that it was a pleasure—even if it was only straight rate. When I got home, I was so relaxed I fell asleep on the sofa in my fur coat with the telephone in my lap. This is what I used to dream modeling would be like....

When you're hustling and struggling as a beginner, you go through twenty go-sees to get one booking. You run gobs of gauntlets to get one little job. You know you've made it when you begin to get bookings out of the blue from people you've never seen in your *vie*. I used to play the "Why Me?" game whenever I didn't get a job. I still play it now when I get one. If you can learn from hard knocks, you can also learn from soft touches. So when a booking happens out of the blue from a photographer or a client I've never met before or even heard of, I always try to find the answer to the question: What does he see in her? "Her" being that girl whose eyes I put on every morning.

Late Monday afternoon the agency called me and said they had an all-day location booking for me on Wednesday with a new photographer, new agency, and a client I'd never heard of. The location was an hour and a half out of New York. The photographer would pick me up at seven-thirty in the morning and drive me there.

"Where is the location?" I asked, since it was early April with its unpredictable weather.

"New Haven." New Haven, Connecticut! This would be round-tripping in spades. I'd spent almost a year commuting from New Haven to New York. Now that I lived in New York, they needed me in New Haven. It figured. It was a big company up there, the photographer told me when I talked to him. I would be working with computers and a sewing machine, so I would need at least four different outfits complete with disguises to make me look like four different ladies—glamorous—single swinger—straight secretary—and young housewife. I went into my wardrobe file and got two of everything and checked everything over: shoes and belts and scarves and earrings and hair that was compatible—two sets of accessories for each dress that could turn eight outfits into sixteen. The night before, I gave myself a manicure and set my hair and fixed a hem here and a zipper there. Before flopping into bed, I set my alarm. As insurance I asked Charlie, the doorman, to buzz me at 6 A.M.

The first thing I did when I was roused in the morning was turn on WABC. At that hour I need music. Very loud music—plus the weather report and the news. There was no telling what new city disaster might affect our getaway to Connecticut. Next came breakfast. With an all-day booking ahead of me, I need something with go power and staying power in my stomach: Rice cream with raisins—enough to hold me for the day. Next comes the shower. Everything goes carefully into my cloth-covered clothing bag; then the tote bag catches the shoes and accessories, stockings, extras, money, thermos, miso spread sandwiches—miso is a vegetable protein energy builder obtainable at macrobiotic food stores. Makeup is all set in a special double-zippered purse-size kit specially designed at the Make-Up Center. If we're shooting up the river, it can hang on a tree. I put in extra eyelashes—thin ones in case they want a natural look for the housewife. When everything is in place, I do my makeup while drinking my bancha tea—bancha tea is another macrobiotic speciality. I'm all ready at seven-twenty-five. At seven-thirty the doorman calls to say the car is here.

I was shocked that the photographer was on time, and he was shocked that I was ready. "I expected I'd have to wait an hour for you," he said.

"What kind of prima donnas have you been working with?" I laughed.

His car was full of lights and equipment, and he had a huge roll of seamless tied along one side so the doors couldn't be opened. Photographers have to be *semper paratus* too. It turned out I knew the route out of New York better than he did, so I was calling all the turns. He was thrilled to hear I knew enough about New Haven to serve as navigator. Three men from the ad agency were also going along on our junket, but they took the train. The photographer was young and cool—very easygoing and charming. He had braced himself for a boring trip with a blank-faced miss who would ride through two states looking at her own face in the mirror. He was so obviously leery of models that it gave me an opening to inquire discreetly why he had picked me out of the gorgeous things flying around these days.

It turns out he had been burned—and badly—by girls he had hired through some of the big agencies—Wagner and Wilhelmina and Ford. So this time—since he was doing his first work for a new client—he tried a new tack. He looked in the Madison Avenue Handbook intending to scout some new agencies. He'd stopped in my agency to look for new faces. Mine was one of many pictures they showed him. He liked the glamour pose they trotted out. While he was studying it, he noticed another shot of me they have on the agency bulletin board—hair pulled back, riding a golf cart, demonstrating a portable telephone.

"That's what I needed—someone versatile who could look like two or three different people. So I took your picture and two others over to the advertising agency. The agency picked you."

When we arrived at the corporate headquarters in New Haven, they rushed us up to the office of the president. The executive bathroom was mine for the day; they had coffee waiting. Receptionists and secretaries rushed around to make me comfortable—helping me with my impedimenta, hanging up my clothes on the president's rack.

The ambience was very familiar to me. Suddenly I realized I was back in New England. New Haven is less than two hours from New York, but it's another country. Everything was prim and functional— nothing was unnecessarily fancy. The girls in the office looked the way I used to look—a little bit heavy, with their conservative little dresses just a tiny bit above the knee, their pearls, and their hair pulled back. And they looked at me—in my swingy bell-bottomed crepe pants suit, my gaggle of chains, my false eyelashes, my outrageous sunglasses, my makeup, my kissy mouth, my trailing scarf, and my long auburn mane—to them, I was that mysterious glamorous thing from another planet—a New York model.

After I checked over my makeup in the executive suite, the jury assembled: the president, three ad men, assorted other executives, and the photographer. My clothes hung there on the rack. Presumably they knew what they wanted. I had no idea.

"Well, gentlemen," I said, "what do you want me to wear?"

Five men looked at me, and then they looked at my eight dresses. Four of the men waited for the fifth man to speak.

"Golly," said the president, "I think you look great just as you are." It took my breath away. It was a great compliment, of course, but when I looked at that rack of dresses and thought of the hours I'd spent getting them together, sponging them, ironing them, checking every hem and every seam, all I could think of was, "Isn't that just like a man?" If I had spent three days packing and brought twenty-four dresses, they would have wanted me nude. Of course, the ad agency men couldn't go on the whim of the president. What had the three of them come up on the train for if not to be available for advice?

So the seminar started, and after the jury had been polled three times, the concensus was that the first picture should be a little more conservative. They wanted the sleeveless navy blue linen with red-

and-white trim. Since I knew the president wanted to be a little bit swingy, I jazzed it up with a chain belt, and then we were ready to go.

After traveling two hours on location, when I got to the room where we were shooting I saw the photographer set up his lights over yards of the white seamless he had brought from New York. The whole thing could have been done in his New York studio in an hour. But it was a new account for the agency and a new account for the photographer, and corporation presidents—like Mohammed—don't always go to the mountain. Sometimes they want the mountain brought to them. We didn't finish until three-thirty, and instead of photographing me in four outfits with four faces, we never got past the first one. The job was too important. Everything had to be perfect. By this time I felt the shot had to be scheduled for the back cover of *Life* magazine, judging by the tender, loving care being lavished on it. When I asked, they told me it was to appear in the annual corporation report. Although my face had turned up in many strange places, I was a virgin as far as corporation reports were concerned. They promised to send me a copy for my book.

While the photographer was packing up, I climbed back into my New York uniform and called my sister Jean. She works for another big corporation in New Haven just a few blocks away. She came over, and we had a chance for a quiet chat. I introduced her to the girls in the office—the secretaries and the receptionist and all of them who had been so nice to me. I felt very cozy and comfortable with them. I know what it's like to be a bit overweight and looking for a husband. I know what it's like to work over a typewriter from nine to five. I've sold popcorn and jerked sodas and spilled food on people when I was trying to learn to be a good waitress during college days. I felt like just another working girl among a bunch of working girls. But when they asked me where I lived, I couldn't lie. I had to say Park Avenue.

I explained how convenient it is, how close to where I usually work. But there was this thing that hung between us. They still looked at me as if I came from another planet. My eyelashes and wigs, my makeup tricks and my swingy outfit are simply tools of a trade—but the girls were so goggle-eyed and awed and impressed by the mystique of the Park Avenue model that I couldn't get through to them.

It took me back a few years—when I was little Miss New England arriving in New York for the first time, giddy and green, gawking at the

276

starved-looking, hard-looking hothouse models in New York as if THEY were mysterious creatures from another world.

That was only three years ago. In three years I had become one of them. And where are they now?

Three years ago when I got twenty-five dollars a day, it seemed like a small fortune.

Now I get three hundred dollars a day, and it pays the rent.

For a model—like an athlete, a dancer, a thoroughbred horse, or a President—the years are numbered. From the moment you begin, you face that question: What are you going to do when it's all over? Even if you get to the top, there's only one way you can go and that's down. You have to know in your bones—you have to have a sense of timing to know when to move sideways into something else. The number of good years you have depends on how early you start. I was a very late starter. For some girls who start in their teens it's all over by the time they're as old as I was when I began.

Other girls start even later than I did. Ali McGraw was a stylist for a photographer for years until one day *Glamour* magazine published her picture in a spread on glamorous behind-the-scenes jobs. She went from there to the top as a model, and she went from there to play a young Jewish girl from Westchester in the film *Goodbye, Columbus*—when she was pushing thirty. She's passing for a teen-ager and doing it beautifully. Some kids in their teens look old enough to be her mother.

All of us get used up at a different pace. If you learn to be ready for anything and learn how to do every kind of modeling in the book—if you don't limit yourself to one phase of the business but exploit them all—and if you guard your health like a tiger, you can stretch out the years. You have to take care of yourself. Booze and drugs and trash-eating take the heaviest toll of all. The body does not lie. If you've got creases around your middle and bags under your eyes, it doesn't matter if you're twenty-two or thirty-two—you've had it. But the years are numbered for everyone—every time you have a birthday so does everybody else in this world—including the people who always want to know: What are you going to do when it's all over.

Some girls—like Wilhelmina, Eileen Ford, and Dorian Leigh—start their own model agencies, often getting the benefit of other girls—as bookers, for example.

Some girls like Dovima, who at first accept the booker's role, soon realize that they shouldn't waste their talents, and then they wing out with *their* own agencies. With her personality and warmth she gets a four-star rating from me.

Some girls like Ingrid at the Make-Up Center become teachers or experts in one phase of the business and coach newcomers.

Some girls like Sunny take permanent jobs with big companies with which they became identified during their career. Sunny now does all the casting for girls who grace the Clairol packages.

Some girls like China Machado go into the editorial side of magazines like *Vogue* and *Harper's Bazaar,* or into TV production.

Some girls just get lazy and tired and can't be bothered with testing and more testing. They wake up one morning and their portfolio is a year out of date, and they just take their money and flee.

Some girls marry photographers.

Some girls go the booze route and end up in AA.

Some girls go the drug route like Johanna and just disappear.

Some girls like my friend Bonnie, who did so many housewifey commercials that she ended up overexposed, leave New York and head for the West Coast to try to make it as an actress in TV serials.

Some girls, like my friend Judy, become photographers' reps. Judy is a very good one. She picked herself an upcoming photographer and doubled his business in one year.

Some girls, like Julia, marry happily outside of the business, have a child or two, keep working part time. When we were doing a big fashion show one night at the Plaza, we ran an hour and a half overtime. Julia's husband and kiddies were waiting for her downstairs. She told me she had lost her portfolio two days before and she wasn't going to get another one together. She never worked again.

Some girls like Virginia get married to millionaries. Virginia invited David and me to a little party at her summer house in Connecticut last year to meet her new husband. It turned out to be a thirty-room house with umteen servants, and there were politicians and film stars and writers and tents on the back lawn where cooks specially broiled steaks for two hundred people.

Some girls are forced to go back to what they were doing before they became models. It's one thing to work as a secretary or a receptionist to keep you going and pay the bills waiting for the breaks. But when the breaks aren't breaking any longer, a nine-to-five job can be the roughest thing of all to take.

But the girls I admire most—and the girls who've blazed the trail I'd like to follow someday when it's over—all over—are Betty Furness and Bess Myerson Grant.

It's very tough to be taken seriously if you're a good-looking woman. But Betty Furness and Bess Myerson have done a lot in recent months to make it easier. Neither of them were exactly models. Betty was an actress who ended up one of the most famous salesladies on TV. Bess Myerson came to television via the Miss America route and proved that beauty and brains are not incompatible. Betty did a beautiful job when she was appointed National Adviser on Consumer Affairs to President Johnson. Now Bess has the same job by appointment of Mayor Lindsay in New York, and I admire tremendously the job she has been doing.

I'm sure one of the things that appealed to me about modeling was the fact that it was such a challenge. From the outside it looks like a real breeze. Once you've got your foot in the door, if you're a rugged individualist from Vermont like me, you hang on and you smarten up and you learn the hard way how to survive. It's satisfying and it's fun to know that you can get into the seamless jungle and survive and make it without selling yourself long or short, body or soul.

Today modeling is much more chic as a profession than it was when I began, and it looked pretty glamorous then. Every girl wants to be a model, to look like one; it's a symbol of being something or somebody at a time when that is more important and more difficult than ever. But you have to make it as a model before you dare to say that it's a pretty empty game. When you take off your makeup and scrub yourself silly and face yourself in the mirror, you have to admit that all you've been doing, actually, when you strip away the tinsel and the hurly-burly, is rent out the face and the body your Daddy and Mommy gave you to somebody who wants to sell somebody's something to somebody else. We're all just pawns in a game—the money game.

We're out there teaching people that happiness is just around the corner, at your neighborhood druggist, at your nearest automobile dealer. We're out there trying to turn desires into needs.

And the time is coming when all the salesmen and salesladies on TV have to grow up.

If sugared soft drinks are bad for kids—and we know they are—then models who know better than to feed them to their own kids shouldn't peddle them to others—leave that to the former astronauts and TV millionaires.

If cigarettes are bad, we shouldn't be selling them. We shouldn't wait for Congress or the industry or the public to take the lead. Through our unions and individually, we should have something to say about it. If we don't drink coffee, we shouldn't swoon over it on TV. If aspirin and other pills are dangerous—and we know they are—we shouldn't take the residuals for selling them and duck responsibility by saying that if we don't do it someone else will, or sing the cop-out song, "Don't ask me. I only work here."

# CHAPTER 11

9 A.M. The ikons on the wall are early black-and-white photos of the founding fathers: Skippy Peanut Butter, Playtex, Vicks, Niagara, Mazola, Empress Rainbow Trout, The knee-high coffee table is thigh-high with showbiz trade magazines. There is a sofa, a skylight, and a swinging door to the studios. It is a reception area of a TV commercial production company. Third floor back. West Forties near Eighth Avenue. Enter Miss Mitzi McInstant—red hair in rollers under a Parisian scarf; navy shirt and bell bottoms, navy Gucci loafers, short gold raincoat. In one hand a green zippered garment bag. In the other, a makeup kit and a huge tote bag, zipper open, overflowing with plastic bags full of red, red hair.

Inside, out of sight, the producer talks with his associate.

"I need a check for two hundred twenty-eight-fifty, Jack. For the flowers. Another one for five hundred. Make it out to the New York Botanical Gardens. Mark it donation."

"To them it's a donation, but to us it's a location expense. I'll have to ask the accountant how to carry it. Who left last on Friday?"

"I don't know. Why?"

"Whoever it was left the lights on. Cigarette butts under my desk."

"Yeah? I gotta get a check for expenses. I'll give you the breakdown later."

Streaking through reception area, producer meets model.

"Hi, Carolyn."

"Hi, Jay."

Big kiss. Producer is tall, lanky, with a huge rubber-soled basketball-center stride. Short hair, tweed jacket, striped jersey, dark gray slacks, crinkly smiling eyes, baby face—warmly serene.

"Have I got a gorgeous Hawaiian flower garden for you! It's on its way to the Bronx in a truck. The flowers are so great we may not have to use you."

"Thanks a lot. Real flowers?"

"Nah. Artificial."

"We should have gone to Hawaii. That's what I want to do one day—take my mother on a trip to Hawaii."

"I had nightmares all weekend it would rain today. And you know where it's raining? Honolulu."

"No kidding."

"Have a good weekend?"

"All I did was work. I was in Westport Saturday on location. Lingerie in the bulrushes again. . . . Almost froze to death. It was so cold we couldn't do the bathing suits. We're lucky. It's supposed to be sixty today. Stripping in the Bronx won't be so bad."

"OK, dear. Make yourself comfortable. We'll be off in five minutes. Jack, call ABC for me, will you, and see if they left?"

"What's their number?"

"It's on the rack. They're over there getting loaded. . . . Oh, Cinderella, how about the slippers?"

"I found some new silver ones. I hunted all over."

"Good girl. We talked about going maybe barefoot, but the client wants slippers."

"They're plain with a little heel."

"Good girl."

| | |
|---|---|
| 9:05 | "Jay." |
| | "He's downstairs, Jack." |
| | "They had a flat tire—that's why they're late." |
| 9:06 | "Did they leave, Jack?" |
| | "They had a flat tire on one of the cars." |
| | "Flat *tire*?" |
| 9:11 | Producer on telephone: "I wanted to shoot a series of quick dissolves . . . not on the freckles . . . on the lemons. . . . Superimposed? Depends on the lighting. . . . A soft light is all right. I'm partial to black. I get very good results. I'm leaving now in two minutes. . . . I want him there at eight-thirty to work on the girl . . . she has no fingernails. . . . I had to send her out today to get fingernails. . . . OK. Speak to you later." |
| 9:42 | Safari assembles under Biltmore Theater marquee for *Hair*. |

Two station wagons full of cameras, lenses, reflectors, equipment. Director Bob Broekman, the cameraman, in beige safari jacket, black jersey, and boots. Two long-haired young male assistants. Young girl in magenta mini, black stockings, brown coat, hair up. Crisis Number 2: One of the station wagons is low on gasoline. The D/C bolts from under the wheel; an assistant drives off with it. Producer and model wait on sidewalk with their impedimenta.

10:05 Safari reassembles, ready to load.

"Jay, you got the towels?"

"Yeah. You know one time we did a thing where we had to simulate a factory with a conveyor turning out hundreds of cans of coffee. So the client gave us two thousand jars of coffee. You know he asked us to return every one of them?"

10:06 Safari heads toward West Side Highway, Bronx-bound. The producer drives one wagon, the D/C the other. Model, dress, tote bag, and red hair in the back seat of wagon Number 2, driven by D/C Bob.

BOB: Carolyn, did you ever take a course in writing?

CK: Yeah. I took a couple. Why?

BOB: I think I'll take one. I've just about had it with this.

CK: Oh, Bob, you know you'd be lost without all this aggravation.

BOB: I hear Jay made you a present of a hundred-dollar dress. You know, forty percent of that dress is from me.

CK: Yeah, Friday he came over and looked at all my things. He said he liked them, but he knew what he wanted. So we walked over to Lord & Taylor with this picture he cut out of a magazine. He had the idea he wanted pink, but they only had one thing in chiffon in aqua. I put it on, and it was a perfect fit. So he took it. I know you'll like it.

BOB: As long as you picked it out, it's OK. I don't trust his taste.

10:30 Entrance to New York Botanical Gardens. Full safari assembles. Two station wagons. Moving man loaded with artificial Hawaiian flowers and other props. Two more private cars. One for the set designer and the assistant director. The second is the hairdresser. Guards collect fifty cents for each vehicle. Producer leaps out to go to the office to confer about the permit and pay the five-hundred-dollar donation fee.

The safari wends its way into the park. The sun shines fitfully. Groups of schoolchildren are being sheperded through the grounds by their teachers.

BOB: We spent a whole day looking for locations, and this is the best we could find.

CK: We should have gone to Hawaii.

BOB: You heard about the guy visiting Honolulu who asked the natives how he should pronounce it: Hawaii or Havaii. The native said, "Havaii." The visitor said, "Thank you very much." The native said, "You're velcome."

10:40   Safari stops near location spot: a grassy knoll under a pine tree complete with rocks and rills. Its height gives the spot isolation. Producer and set designer direct the unloading and placement of huge grave-sized beds of artificial Hawaiian flowers mounted on wooden panels draped with green plastic grass; assorted ersatz palms, fronds, orchids, and other plants. One huge carton of real, live Hawaiian mistletoe. Mini Greek columns in white plastic, brass candelabra, vintage white tenement bathtub painted with gold scrolls; brass wire dressing table with mirror. benches, and dozens of Cannon towels in bold floral designs.

The camera is fixed and mounted on a tripod in place. The D/C pans and zooms to insure none of the props are wasted outside his range. The set is decorated in depth, with artificial orchids affixed to background trees blocks away.

Producer introduces model to hairdresser, then disappears. HD is young, good-looking Latin in chocolate mini-raincoat, gray turtleneck, Gucci loafers.

"Carolyn, this is Gabe Borgo."

"Hi, Gabe."

"Hi, Carolyn. This is Lever Brothers, right?"

"Right. Where are we gonna work?"

"Jay is getting us a room, he told me. You know, I saw your hands in some rushes at the studio. You got beautiful hands."

"What did you see—the diet pills or the decongestant?"

"Both, I think."

"I'm lucky. I got good nails."

"Tomorrow we're working with Heather McCrea for a Breck hair thing. Her nails are all chewed away. We had to send her to get nails. Hey, I like your ring, too."

"This? I got it in a little antique shop in the Village. I love emeralds, and this was perfect with the little diamond chips."

"You know, we were supposed to work together on that Balsam hair thing."

"Yeah, Jay wanted me for that. It was delayed four weeks, and I had an eight-day booking in Barbados for a film. What a foul-up! I flew down, and then they decided to do it in Grenada instead. So I flew to Grenada and the airline lost my suitcase. I couldn't work for three days. By the time they found my things and my eyelashes, the film was practically finished. Then it was carnival time and I couldn't get back. When I got back, I lost a bra booking because I was too red and Jay had to get another girl. Jay was upset about it. He said, 'I'll make it up to you.' Everybody says that, but he meant it. And here I am."

"Weren't you upset?"

"At first I was, then I saw the script. It had an awful lot of lines. I'm not sure I could have done it all that well. I'm not sure I was ready for that. The girl they used was mostly an actress, wasn't she?"

"I don't know. I wish it had been you. She had terrible hair. We should have finished at five. I had another appointment. But we weren't. I got my car towed away."

"Oh, boy! Where did you shoot it?"

"In a beauty salon on Seventy-second Street. Hey, I like your coat."

"I got it at Gimbel's. I saw the ad in *The New York Times,* and I rushed right down. This color is good for me. Hard to get."

"Yeah. A lot of girls get long ones and cut them down. Hey, I like your makeup. I just started doing makeup."

285

"Yeah, Jay told me. That's great. You keep an eye on me."

"You got blush on?"

"Just a little. I still have to put on bottom lashes one by one. That's the thing that takes lots of time."

"I just finished a course."

"You did? Who did you work on? Models?"

"Only male models. Well, they'd find kids walking around Forty-second Street, and they'd bring them in, and we'd make them up as monsters. . ."

"Monsters? I couldn't do that. I'm strictly limited to the beauty end."

"Monsters aren't that hard."

"Probably easier than putting on bottom lashes."

10:50    Producer arrives, escorting a portly gray-haired gentleman in his fifties, gray suit and hat. Manila envelope.

JAY:   Carolyn, this is Mr. Kelly. I want you to treat him nice. He's the client.

CK:   Hello, Mr. Kelly.

JAY:   (To AD as he schlepps by with a prop.) Hurry up there with that tree.

CK:   (To AD) Hi, Mike. He's so nice. He was the AD on the thing I did for Funk & Wagnalls when I was dying of the flu. He was so sweet and patient—whenever I needed a Kleenex, he was right there, under my nose.

JAY:   Kids, we've got a problem. The only room I can get for you to work in is the ladies' room.

CK:   Well, all you promised us was a room. You didn't say what kind.

JAY:   See, no temperament. You'll never get anywhere. With some girls that's the cue for a scene. Gabe, let your hair grow a little longer and you're in.

10:55    GABE:   Maybe I should take a look at your hair.

CK:   It's there in my tote bag. It's not all the same color, but I've got five bags.

GABE:   The color's not too different.

286

11:00     Sissy, the girl assistant, has been wandering around in search of her stopwatch and asking everyone for a copy of the script of the TV spot commercial on premiums to see if it really runs thirty seconds. Now she asks the producer; he takes one out of his pocket and gives it to her. She studies the script intently:

| *VIDEO* | *AUDIO* |
|---|---|
| OPEN WITH ECU OF FLOWERS ON TOWEL. START PAN UPWARD. | (DREAMY MUSIC UP AND UNDER) ANNCR: V.O: What could be lovelier than a colorful flower garden . . . |
| PULL BACK TO SHOW SEVERAL FLORAL TOWELS ON RACK. BATHROOM TILE BACKGROUND. | . . . right on the towel rack in your bathroom! |
| GLAMOROUS GIRL ENTERS AND TAKES ONE OF THE TOWELS FROM THE RACK. | Create one . . . with these gorgeous floral design bath towels by Cannon. |
| SHE HOLDS IT TO HER CHEEK, ADMIRES IT, AND REPLACES IT ON RACK. | So soft, fluffy . . . and lushly beautiful! |
| FREEZE ABOVE AND SUPER "FREE FOR BOX-TOPS." | Best of all, they're FREE for boxtops! |
| CUT TO TIGHT SHOT OF PRODUCT GROUPING. | Yes, free for boxtops and wrappers from RINSO, LIFEBUOY, IMPERIAL, AND STRIPE TOOTHPASTE. |

| | |
|---|---|
| WIPE TO GLAMOUR DIS-PLAY OF ALL CANNON PREMIUMS AND THE TABLE-WARE. SUPER (flASHING ON AND Off): "FREE FOR BOXTOPS". | You can also get other lovely linens . . . and stunning stainless tableware . . . too. |
| CUT TO CU OF RINSO PKGE, WITH FLORAL TOWEL IN THE BACKGROUND. | See details on the Rinso package. |

CLIENT          LEVER BROTHERS COMPANY

COUNTRY         HAWAII—PREMIUMS—FLORAL TOWEL INTRO
                3069TV—LB—PREM—E8

DATE            2—3—69

APPROVED BY

NATIONAL EXPORT ADVERTISING SERVICE, INC.

11:05     After perusing the script, Sissy starts unloading empty
          giant-size Rinso boxes and carting them over to the hill.
          Cigar-smoking Negro driver of moving van discovers glass
          top of dressing room has been broken in transit. "I had it
          wrapped in padding," he says. "But . . ." The moving van
          has a radio in the cab. He sits there listening to news
          bulletins from Prague.

11:07 Producer arrives with second client, a tall, thin man with glasses and a moustache. The producer says, "Carolyn, did you meet Mr. Hughes? He's another client."

CK: Hello, Mr. Hughes.

Model and hairdresser are in a huddle, mulling over five plastic bags of red hair.

CK: Can you get hair wholesale?

GABE: Yeah, I know a guy can get anything for me. It's not all Italian hair—that costs a fortune and besides, it flies around too much.

CK: I'd like to get a longer fall—longer than this one.

GABE: I think he could get you a good Slavic fall for half what it would cost you in the stores.

CK: Another thing I need is a good wig. I have a curly-curly one, but it's not that great for my face. I have a big forehead with an angle slant—that's why I wear bangs. I need something closer in here—styled so it hugs me more around the face.

GABE: Most stretch wigs wouldn't give you that. What you need is a regular wig, specially shaped for you.

CK: I had one like that once. I borrowed it from a woman I did hair work for.

GABE: Before the end of the day, give me your number and we'll shout about it.

CK: I'd also like some ringlets for evening.

GABE: There's a thing you can get for thirty dollars that you can use two ways.

CK: Next week I'll give you a buzz.

GABE: Lots of girls deal with Bob Blank.

CK: He's a thief. I know a girl who bought a twenty-two-inch fall from him. She paid $175, and it turned out to be all Hong Kong hair. When she tried to have it colored, it got limp and purple.

GABE: That's the trouble with Oriental hair—you can go darker, but no lighter. Your hair looks great. Very natural. A good color for you. Not too many girls can wear that color. Is that a two-process or one-process?

289

CK: One-process. I used to be a two-process redhead. Now I just have it touched up every four weeks.

GABE: Who does it for you?

CK: Ruby Gordon at the St. Moritz, in the Albert-Carter salon. He's fantastic. His nails are all black. He won't use rubber gloves—he goes by the feel. He really knows his chemicals. He's really an artist. When he's done you, he's like an artist who's finished a painting.

GABE: Funny, I almost bought that salon.

11:15    Producer comes down the hill. The set is ready. The D/C wants a run-through. Model and HD ascend the hill. The set designer, a woman in an orange dress, is running about, adjusting orchids on trees, sprinkling fake grass on bare spots in the turf. Cannon towels have been adroitly scattered across the landscape. What the D/C sees though his lens is a little corner of Oahu created on a knoll in the Bronx. The model is given her position. The camera pans left, zooming in on the towels. When it picks up the girl, she walks toward camera, takes a seat at the dressing table, and makes love to a wildly floral Cannon towel. Her walk is timed, shortened, timed again. The producer, the two clients, the D/C huddle. One assistant twists the zoom lens; two others hold reflectors that pick up sunlight and bounce it off the red-headed model. A Parks Department guard, in uniform and badge, surveys the landscape, standing beside a young man in sideburns and orange pants. Beside him is his harpoon and an empty bag. A manicurist for the Parks Department landscape, he is to keep the area policed of inanimate matter. The cop's job is to police the bystanders who have collected on the fringes to watch the show. The producer asks them, "Which way is the sun moving?" "West."

"Which way is West?"

They draw a line against the sky.

Three authentic Hawaiians walk up the knoll eating popsickles. A gray-haired Polynesian grandmother in aquamarine Capri pants and sweater and glasses. Her Polynesian daughter in a brown topcoat. A boy toddler who looks Japanese.

The model adjourns to an empty park bench where she chats with the two clients. Finally she rejoins the hairdresser. The girl assistant has scrounged containers of coffee, enough for all hands. "Thank you, no," says the model. She has a thermos of tea in her tote bag.

"Carolyn, don't you think we should start getting ready?"

"Yeah, I do. They spend all this time on the set, and then they're going to want us to be ready in five minutes."

"Why don't you speak to Jay and ask him? Better you than me. I have another appointment at five, but I don't want him to think I'm trying to rush him."

"OK, I'll speak to him."

Producer speaks to model.

"OK, Toots, let's get ready."

Producer escorts model and hairdresser past huge glass houses teeming with tropical plants. They are headed for the ladies' room, schlepping the dress, the tote bag, the hair, and the hairdressers' tools.

Model and hairdresser enter the huge glass house. The humidity is fetid, tropical. The ladies' room reeks of Urine Numbers 5, 6, and 7. The hundred-dollar Lord & Taylor dress is hung on the first of three toilet cabinets. The HD finds a steel chair on which the model puts her make-up kit. There is a high stand-up mirror on the wall. No windows. On the tile floor a crawling community of ants.

GABE: You go ahead, do your makeup first, then we'll get to the hair.

CK: Jay said keep it kind of simple.

GABE: Yeah, he told me. I'll just tie it up a little so it's not blowing around. We don't have to go too high—maybe something curling around one shoulder.

Out come the rollers, off comes the raincoat.

CK: There are no windows in here. I don't use any hair-setting lotion in my hair. I tried so many.

GABE: The best is Fermadol—in a glass vial.

CK: You brought a curling iron with you?

GABE:   Curling iron.

CK:   I chopped off a little last night.

The HD stands behind the model, who looks intently into the mirror. With his left hand he takes a fistful of red hair and holds it on top of her head. This is a rough sketch of where he's headed.

GABE:   Something on that order. I'll use one of your old falls under here just as a filler.

CK:   It's not too long?

GABE:   Not too long.

HD dives into plastic bags, selects a fall, combs it out, and reaches into his kit for a set of electric rollers which he plugs in.

GABE:   My lifesaver. Electric rollers.

CK:   Yeah, I have some. Mine are GE.

Model continues with makeup.

CK:   That's a cute little fall. I use it when I have to be Mrs. Jones from next door. The humidity in here makes everything icky. My makeup is glopping up on me. I have one little eruption on my face today. It never fails.

GABE:   It's like doing makeup in a steam bath. What kind of powder you using? Try this. You know Mark Trail—he makes it. I used it on the Frenchman on the Balsam job. He had a bald head, and I had to keep dusting him. He was in *Cactus Flower* with Lauren Bacall. Better use a little blue on the eyes. Looks pretty white out there on the edges. A little too much white under the brows.

12:30   HD puts hot electric rollers in the fall.

CK:   All I have left to do is bottom lashes and blush-on.

GABE:   OK, now we start.

Just as he starts to work, six little Negro girls come screaming into the ladies' room.

"There's a man in the ladies' room. I never saw that before."

"She's a model."

"Look, he's got a lot of tools and stuff."

"She's cute."

"She's got a boy doing her hair."

"You never saw that before? Where you been, girl?"

"She's a model, that girl."

"Get out of his way, girl—can't you see the man wants peace?"

Some of the youngsters form themselves into a silent choir and just stand there, forgetting why they came. One makes a rush call to the cabinet. Then their teacher comes in. Her need is so urgent she pretends the hairdresser and the model are not there. She enters the toilet where the hundred-dollar Lord & Taylor dress hangs, and does her thing. She starts to wash her hands. There are no towels. She dashes out, wringing her hands, and looks back in anger. Now the choir of Negro youngsters reenters, with reinforcements.

A dozen of them are screaming and chanting.

"There's a model in the ladies' room!"

"See, there! We told you."

"She's getting her hair done."

"Isn't she cute?"

"Juanita brought her camera."

"You got it loaded right, girl?"

"Mister, I wanna take a picture. Could you turn her head around, please? Thank you."

"She got it. She got it."

"There's some people out on the hill with cameras and things. Maybe they're making a movie."

"Is this for a movie?"

"Probably just TV."

"She nodded. He's doing her hair for TV."

"Look at all the wigs and things there on the floor."

"Let's go out and watch them take her picture."

12:35     The youngsters leave. The producer enters.

JAY: We're breaking for lunch. Gabe, you get her ready—everything except the dress. You don't have to look TOO good, Carolyn. This commercial they'll only show it for two years.

CK: What are you going to shoot? The towels or my face?

JAY: A combination of both.

JAY: Gabe, we're having top talent tomorrow. You'll have

a blonde tomorrow.

GABE: I like red hair.

JAY: Red hair for this job is perfect.

CK: I have my eyes open all the time, right?

JAY: Maybe not when you caress the towel. The Bronx Chamber of Commerce is going to cheer when you make your entrance. We're having heroes for lunch. For the Italians in the crew.

CK: Where'd you get them?

JAY: I sent Sissy out to get them. That's all she does. That's what I hire her for.

CK: What a way to make a living! It's almost as bad as mine.

JAY: She loves this business—everyone is attracted to this business. After all, it isn't just chasing sandwiches—it's part of show business. It's part of the excitement. Look at you—you were chosen over thirty-five girls.

CK: There have to be losers, too.

JAY: It's the sore losers I don't like. Girls who call me up and want to know why they didn't get the job.

CK: Girls actually do that?

JAY: One asked me why she didn't get the job. I told her to shave.

CK: She came in something sleeveless? What are they *thinking* of? I wore pants out here, and I'm wearing a full-length dress, but I shaved my legs this morning. With a Hawaiian thing going, you never know what somebody's going to dream up on the set.

JAY: One girl came in one day with her two-year-old kid. She trained the kid to sit in the producer's lap. She told me she needed the job bad because she had this daughter to support.

CK: Lord, the things people do to get a job! Some people don't look for as many jobs in a lifetime as a model does in one day.

JAY: For the Buick job they had six people who did nothing but look at girls for four days. They got it down to seventy-five girls. It's a hard job, being a model.

CK:   You know we know, but does anybody else?

GABE:   I just worked with Barbara. She asked me to say hello. She's a nice girl.

JAY:   She's cute. But that's not talent. I hate stupid people.

CK:   I think I know her. I did a job with her once.

JAY:   They all think they're going to make it. You have to work hard and hustle.

CK:   The voice of experience. There's no easy way, really.

JAY:   You gotta be lucky. Look at this girl in my movie, *Goodbye, Columbus.* She's a model, and she made a big hit. But will she ever get to make another? OK, kids, heroes for lunch.

The producer exits from the ladies' room just as a lady tries to enter. She does a long, silent double-take. She spies the HD and the model. Oblivious, she walks into the cabinet where the Lord & Taylor dress hangs, does her thing. She starts to wash her hands. There are no towels. She dries her hands on her plaid skirt and exits. The model and the HD barely notice her, so intent are they on the final stages of makeup. The model is putting on her lower lashes one by one.

12:45   The Producer reenters.

JAY:   This is too much in here. Gabe, if you'd feel better outside, work outside. Let her change and come out on the set where she won't wilt.

GABE:   I need the electrical connection for the rollers.

CK:   This glue won't stick on the lashes. It's maddening to have to put lashes on one by one. But that's the look now. If you see any lashes flying around out there, you'll know whose they are. I knew a girl once who put her lashes on upside down. Eventually that will be the fashion.

GABE:   That's so tedious.

CK:   I can't *wait* until they go out of style.

GABE:   Do you try to match your two eyes?

CK:   I just try to integrate what I've got with what I can stand to glop on.

12:50   GABE:   Is it a long dress?

CK:   Yeah, aqua chiffon. There—that's not too bad.

They're not gonna be that close.

GABE:   Looks good. I can do a little touching-up out there. We can even see better outside.

CK:   This light is terrible.

GABE:   That's a great makeup case. Where did you get it?

CK:   At the Make-Up Center. It's the first thing I ever found that you can drag anywhere.

12:55   GABE:   Shall we put the dress on?

CK:   Yeah.

Model goes to the sink to wash her hands. There are no towels.

GABE:   On the set we've got nothing but towels. We're giving away towels.

CK:   Isn't that something? Never mind. Here.

She finds a scrap of dry towel in the wastebasket. She enters the cabinet, kicks off her shoes, pants, shirt. Standing on the cold tile crawling with ants, she slips into bikini pants and bra. The HD removes from the green garment bag a wispy chiffon sleeveless gown, bare midriff held together with jewels. Simple, elegant, spotless. She steps into the dress and then rejoins him in front of the mirror. She slips into a pair of silver kid sandals.

GABE:   This dress is yours?

CK:   Jay bought it for me. He's so sweet. He could have asked me to schlepp all my dresses down to his office so he could look at them. Instead he came over to my apartment and looked at everything. He called me in the morning and said he would drop by for coffee. I was up, but I wasn't made up. And you know, I couldn't find my eyelashes. I ran around that apartment frantic. He was on his way, and I couldn't find my lashes. I had been reading in the living room the night before and I'd stripped them off and laid them down somewhere. I had to go through the trash. I was all over the carpet on my hands and knees. For the first time in my life I wished I'd bought a white rug.

GABE:   Where did you find them finally?

CK:   Under a magazine. Jay looked at all my dresses, and he said he liked them, but he had a picture of what he wanted, so we walked over to Lord & Taylor and he bought it for me. This was the only thing I tried on. What do you think of this bra?

GABE:  It sort of shoves you together.

CK:  I don't need this cleavage. Some clients hate boobs. I think I better take the bra off. What do you think?

GABE:  Let's try it without.  (Off comes the bra.) That's better.

HD has the red fall in his hand, complete with hot rollers, when the entire distaff side of the second grade of St. Anselm's Parochial School, Class 101, parades into the ladies' room. The model is up to her midriff in wide-eyed little girls in MacGregor plaid jumpers and white shirts. Most of them forget the intent of their mission and just stand there in a group, under the feet of the hairdresser and the model. With the flushing toilets as obligato, the youngsters turn into a cheering section:

"Boy, she's cute."

"What's she doing in here?"

"They're making a commercial."

"A commercial? For what?"

"A hair set, I think."

"In color maybe."

"Her hair is so pretty."

"She's got real hair and false hair together."

"Look at all that hair!"

"It's a very cute dress."

"It's cut out across the stomach."

1:05      Gabe removes the rollers from the fall and combs it out. Model takes a sip of tea from her thermos on the floor.

GABE:  You must be hungry.

CK:  I never eat on a job. I had my eating day yesterday. Last night I had millet with peppers and dill, and carob cookies and soya cookies and rice cakes. A friend came over and told me I never looked better than since I started eating grains like rice and millet and buckwheat. I lost where

I never lost weight before—in the upper thighs. I told him about this darling little Japanese restaurant on East Sixth Street in the Village. It's called the I-Chi. I went there again Saturday night for striped bass tempura.

GABE:  Know what I forgot today? Light bobby pins. It's lucky you're a redhead. If you were a blonde, we'd be in trouble. Every job I forget something.

1:10   The model is too tall for the hairdresser to work on her while standing in front of the high mirror.

GABE:  Can you scrunch down a little?

CK:  I'll try. Thank God for hairpieces.

GABE:  You're in very good shape.

CK:  I work out twice a week. I went to a class on Sunday and my legs are still sore. This woman really gave us a workout, and I did every bit of it.

GABE:  I used to work out, but I stopped about a year ago.

CK:  They really put me through the ringer Sunday.

GABE:  You take dancing classes, too?

CK:  Some girls take dancing, singing, yoga, and karate. I don't know where they get the time to do all that and work too. I take singing—I like that.

GABE:  I think you better sit down. I'll put your scarf on this chair.

CK:  Oh, my Paris scarf. The bottom of this dress is going to get dirty anyway out there in the dirty grass. The clean plastic grass is full of soot already.

GABE:  You think they'll want a flower in your hair?

CK:  Somebody will think of that.

GABE:  I think we need more height on top. Have you got a little switch?

CK:  Right there in the bag. I've got all shades. It's hell keeping your hairpieces in shape—so they don't fade and so they match. That's Yugoslav hair. Here, let me show you how you can part it in two, and we'll braid it.

1:20   Hairdresser has used three hairpieces. The last one he braids and twists across the model's head, above her bangs in a kind of halo. Producer enters and shouts.

JAY:   Lunch is ready, kids, whenever you're ready. Five minutes or so?

GABE:   That's all I'll be.

CK:   How about the bangs? Can you tease 'em up out of my eyes a bit? That's good. When Jay asked me if I'd need a hairdresser, I said please, please. I know location jobs, and I know my hair. Imagine me here in this tropical jungle all alone, up to my whatsis in little women just out of school, trying to get my hair together.

GABE:   It's a Hawaiian scene—we should have a little hair dangling on the side of your neck. Like that. I'm doing some things for *HairDo* magazine in a week or so. I'd like to give you a buzz.

CK:   You do the casting?

GABE:   Not all of it, but they usually leave us alone if we need an extra girl.

CK:   I used to do a lot of things for them, but I haven't done any in a while.

1:25    GABE:   You can stand up.

Model stands. Now she can see herself in the mirror.

CK:   I don't think it's high enough on top. The braid cuts off the height in back.

GABE:   You're right. I'll put a little wiglet on.

1:26    Model sits down again while HD adds another hairpiece.

1:30    GABE:   I'll give it just enough spray to keep the wind from ruining it. There. You're gorgeous. I'm not talking about the hair. The kids were right. It's your pretty face.

CK:   You're a darling. The face is not bad.

GABE:   A little cakiness under the eyes maybe, but we can take another look in the good light outside.

Model assembles all her gear in the tote bag, schlepps her clothes, hair, and wigs. With gold mini-raincoat over the chiffon dress, she parades with her hairdresser past the glass houses, past the visitors sunning themselves on the park benches, to the set, a quarter of a mile away.

CK:   These shoes are going to be a write-off. I can see that. That's why I have a closet full of shoes that don't fit me. I have to buy something in a terrific rush, and I have to take what I can get.

1:40    As model and hairdresser traipse up the hill to the location, they see something added. Sissy presides over a pile of hero sandwiches, potato salad, cans of beer, soda. The two clients are diving into a can of pickled Italian peppers.

Now the location is ringed with spectators. The cop is vigilantly keeping them out of camera range.

The model sits down at the fantasy dressing table, strewn with ersatz orchids and greenery under the cedar tree dappled with real Hawaiian greenery. The hairdresser gives her coiffure a final spray. The crew members stand by, catching the intermittent rays of sun in chrome arc reflectors. The D/C and his assistant have a low camera angle; they kneel or sit on the turf.

1:45    The assistant cameraman takes light readings of the model's face. Sissy has forsaken the hillside buffet and squats to the left of the cameraman, having become script girl. The model removes her gold mini-raincoat, leaving nothing between her skin and the wind except shreds of aqua chiffon.

"How many towels in the opening shot?"

"You got the stopwatch, Sissy?"

"Somebody gel that sun."

"Carolyn, you know the action?"

1:47    One client moves into camera range, takes a Cannon towel from the makeup bench and redoes the folds, then replaces it. The director huddles with the model, showing her how to caress the towel. The model is in place, the wind ruffling her skirt.

1:52    "Roll."

The camera pans from right to left, while the assistant twists the zoom lens.

"In Carolyn."

Young glamorous girl enters and takes towel from back of chair. She holds it to her cheek, admires it, and replaces it. The action takes twenty seconds.

Bystanders relax.

"We'll have to watch for this commercial."

300

"What are they selling, do you think?"

"There are Rinso boxes over there—maybe it's that."

Client walks into set and wipes the fantasy dressing table mirror. The client huddles with the cameraman and the producer.

1:54     "Roll. Take Two."

Camera pans, assistant zooms. "In Carolyn." Model enters with the wind blowing the lock of hair at her temple. She takes the towel, she holds it to her cheek, she reacts, she emotes, she is ravished with admiration, she still is romancing it as the director calls cut. Replacement of the towel has been dropped.

Client, director/cameraman, and producer huddle.

JAY:   More with the towel, Carolyn!

1:55     "Roll. Take Three."

"In Carolyn." The model moves into the wind. Now she lifts the towel to her face. Something close to ecstasy is what she's selling.

1:56     Take Four. "In Carolyn."

"Now the other side of the face. That's it."

Ecstasy has now become passion.

After the take the model smiles at two fat teen-age girls lounging on a park bench. The girls hide their heads. Perhaps the all-too-human smile destroyed the fantasy for them.

2:04     The hairdresser moves in for repairs.

GABE:   They like your hair. Everybody says it looks beautiful. Very natural. The client asked me if it's all yours.

CK:   What did you tell him?

GABE:   I told him it was all you. Your coloring is great with the Hawaiian flowers. It's even good with the towels.

Two middle-aged ladies appear in camera range, climbing the knoll. The one-man security force runs to meet them, gently chasing them away. They are so pooped from climbing the hill that they hardly know which way to turn. The cop guides them gently to the sidelines. They watch with fascination as the model stands there in the vivid windblown chiffon gown, and they clutch their heavy winter coats about them.

2:08    "Roll. In Carolyn."

Miss Mitzi McInstant, girl of the moment, done up to look like a blithe Hawaiian fantasy spirit. The fat youngsters on the sidelines dream of growing up to be her. The tired Bronx lady mountaineers dream of slimming, trimming back to be her. Mitzi McInstant promises us fantasy in return for boxtops. Her perfection leaps, leers, sulks, swishes toward us, enticing us, educating us, compelling us, selling us flowered towels—free for boxtops.

2:25    After a total of ten takes, the producer announces he is happy. They have what they want. They have all they need. The rest of the shooting will be devoted to tight shots of products and groups of products.

The crew members strike the setup and prepare a new one. The client searches for the model's gold mini-raincoat and gallantly delivers it to her.

"Thank you."

"Ten takes, six orgasms. That's a pretty good average."

2:26    Model stands under the tree in her raincoat. The client lights her cigarette. The producer brings her a can of beer. She thanks one and all and reaches into her tote bag for her thermos of hot tea and a slice of dark homemade bread.

CLIENT:   You eat that for your figure?

CK:   No, for my health. I know the boy who baked it.

GABE:   This is the easiest job I ever had.

CK:   These guys are great to work with. They know what they want. They get it and that's it. This is the easiest job I ever had. Imagine being finished at two-thirty. I hardly know what to do.

CLIENT:   They're very down-to-earth. Nobody's trying to be a genius.

GABE:   I'm driving back to Manhattan. Can I give you a lift?

CK:   That would be great.

2:30    Model and hairdresser start schlepping their luggage back toward the ladies' room. Suddenly the HD spies the giant moving van parked nearby. The Negro driver sits in the cab listening to the news reports from Prague: Soviet occupation troops are being beefed up from 70,000 to 100,000.

GABE: We're going to use the back of your truck to change, OK?

He hoists the model onto the rear apron of the truck.

She removes chiffon dress, slips into her blue bell bottoms, shirt, gold raincoat, and Gucci loafers.

GABE: You want me to take the pieces out of your hair?

CK: No, may as well ride home in style.

Having made her change, model ascends the knoll to extend farewell greetings to the crew, the client, and some of the bystanders. The producer is missing.

"Where's Jay?"

Model and hairdresser are about to leave when producer appears.

JAY: Don't forget your dress.

CK: Don't worry, I won't. Thanks, Jay, for everything. Do I have to sign anything for you or anything?

JAY: We'll do all that later. I'll give you a call. We'll shout.

CK: OK, dreamboat.

2:50     Hairdresser and model drive off.

3:30     Model arrives at midtown apartment.

6:30     Producer telephones.

JAY: It was great, Carolyn. The client loved you. They liked the dress.

CK: Everything went all right after I left?

JAY: Somebody hooked ten of the loose orchids, but that was the only crisis. We got off easy. We wrapped up by four-thirty, and I was back here by six.


WEDNESDAY, APRIL 16   6 P.M.

Producer telephones model:

"Well, Toots, you looked just great."

"Have you seen the rushes already?"

"Oh, sure. It came out great. The colors were fantastic. Your hair looked perfect. We're real happy—showing it to the clients on Friday. You're all right for a redhead. What did you think of Gabe?"

"He was terrific. So easy to work with."

"Yeah. I use him on every job. He knows what we want. He's a good boy, and he really liked working with you."

"He promised to get me some hair, and he called me already about it. He's coming over to get a color cut of mine."

"Sure. He's a good boy. He helps out lots of models."

## MONDAY, APRIL 21   6 P.M.

In the inner studios of the television production company. Producer and model are looking at the rushes of the Lever Brothers commercial as they are projected against the wall in a tiny room.

"The breeze is blowing my skirt. Look! The setting is unbelievable. It looks like a summer day. You'd never know I was freezing. It doesn't show. Would anybody believe this is the Bronx?"

"Your hair looks great. Look how the wind blows the curls over your shoulder. See?"

"The wind is blowing the flowers, too. They look fragile and real."

"Your makeup looks great."

"I did it myself, but Gabe helped me a lot."

"That towel will never be the same. You really showed it off beautifully. The client will love that."

"I don't often get a chance to see rushes of myself. You either see the final thing on TV or you see nothing. I really look good, if I do say so myself."

"Seventeen seconds of you and only thirteen seconds of the products. That's why we had to have the right girl."

"When will they run it, Jay?"

"It starts May first in Hawaii."

"So soon."

"I'm doing a Guiche thing, and they want a redhead, too. I'd like to use you, but they want short hair, and I wouldn't ask you to cut your long hair. Long hair is part of your image, and you hang on to it."

"I appreciate it, Jay, but there'll be other things."

"Sure. I'm gonna use you plenty."

Now they are in the tiny reception area. The ikons of the founding fathers are still on the wall. The knee-high coffee table is piled thigh-high with magazines. On top is a screaming headline of the New York *Sunday News,* April 20, 1969, reporting on another location job in New York:

## 6 TEENS SLAY FASHION FOTOG
## MODEL & CROWD SEE STABBING

I guess when wolf whistles follow you around town, when you're in a glamour business and have to look it, something's bound to explode now and then. Location jobs can be full of hazards—but fortunately most shootings are as harmless as orchids in the Bronx.

*It's not easy for a girl with tiger hair to hang onto her blistering temperament, while simultaneously transmitting waves of comfort, understanding, and durability.*
                                        —Vogue, op. cit.

You can't hide it if you're happy. The huge zippered leather portfolio you're continually schlepping, your heavy tote bag—sometimes you need them as ballast to keep your feet on the ground. Every girl has her eyes on at six-thirty in the evening as you're walking home through Times Square. It can't be the eyes or the pants or the banner you're flying. It's got to be what the sign over the marquee of the Biltmore Theater on West 47th Street says—*Hair.*

"Avco was down three quarters, and Lenny said we—Hey, looka that redhead!"

"Mike Nichols wanted me for a thing in *Catch,* but they were shooting on location and I couldn't leave the—hey, check *that* out!"

"Hey, Red, where's the fire?"

"Hey, Red, you know you've got one Roman toe and one Greek toe?"

"Hey, tiger, who you with?"

"Wilhelmina."

"You on her head sheet? What's your name?"

"Kendall."

"That red stuff will either kill you or cure you."

"Carry your bag, beautiful?"

"I won't be nobody's flunkey but yourn."

"Do you know what you do to me?"

"Are you as dangerous as you look?"

"Are you a model? I could tell. You don't even see birds out today, only crazy people."

"Hel-lo, bay-bee."

"Hey, Red! Hurt me. Beat me. Whip me, but don't ignore me, baby."

"Do you think you could handle something like that?"

You round the corner to Park Avenue, and you know you've run your last gauntlet for the day. Well, almost.

"Hi, Sam." Sam is one of the doormen at the building I call home.

"Oh, Miss Kenmore, you work too hard. You're always running back and forth. You should find yourself a nice rich millionaire. He'd keep you in style, and you could settle down and have a family."

"Sam, I told you you're my agent in that department. Keep your eyes open and I'll give you ten percent."

"Good evening, Miss Kleinmore."

"Hi, Charlie." Charlie is on the elevator. When Jack, the mailman, finds a picture of me in a magazine, he gives it to Charlie to check out if it's really me. He's been calling me Miss Kleinmore for three years. He's always formally introducing me to men in the building. I think he thinks I'm a nice Jewish girl who ought to be married. Here it comes again.

"Oh, Mr. Seitz, do you know Miss Kleinmore? She's the best tenant in the building. She makes us sandwiches and chocolate chip cookies and banana bread and poppy seed cake . . ."

"Good evening, Mr. Seitz."

"How do you do, Miss Kleinmore." Mr. Seitz bows and leaves.

"Charlie, I think you're overdoing it. You know all I make is the cookies. I bring the sandwiches and the banana cake from Vermont. I told you my mother makes the banana cake, and the poppy seed cake I get at the bakery. I hate wasting food, and whenever I have goodies left from having guests, I unload them on the boys."

"Yes, but Mr. Seitz is a very rich fella, and he has nobody to look after him at all."

"OK, Charlie, but you know I'm only paying one commission. Ten percent is all I'll go for."

Giovanni, our Latin cupid on the other elevator, always insists on locking the elevator while he carries my junk down the hall. So I stand in front of my door with the elevator signal buzzing like crazy, and while I'm fishing for my keys and Giovanni is scurrying back down the hall, I hear my phone ringing inside. The Super, Mr. Dezse, comes through the service elevator.

"Hello, Mr. Dezse. How are you?"

"Much better now I see you."

Now both my phones are ringing, and I don't know which one to answer first. I get the door open. I drop my bag and my book and lunge for my private phone.

"Hello."

"Carolina Moonshine?"

"*David,* where are you? What are you doing in town? When are you coming over? Hold the phone, will you, I've got tomorrow calling on the other line. . . ."

## A GLOSSARY OF TERMS
## USED IN THE WORLD OF MODELING

| | |
|---|---|
| AFTRA | American Federation of Television and Radio Artists. |
| BOOK | Big leather portfolio with cellophane display envelopes inside in which a model carries and displays her wares—her best and most recent photographs. |
| BOOKING | When a client, art director, agency, or photographer—or all in concert—agree to use a model, they notify her agency, agree on the rate, time, and availability. This commitment is called a booking. |
| BREAD | Money. |
| BUY OUT | When a model's services in a TV commercial get into fringe areas beyond that for which she is contracted, she signs a general release in return for a flat fee waiving claim to any future residuals. |
| BP | Short for beautiful people, the 1970 version of what was once the Four Hundred, later cafe society, later the jet set. |
| BX | Derived from Brand X, the stooge product which is inferior to the name brand. A BX cat is a man who's an also-ran. |
| CATTLE CALL | A mass audition or job interview when dozens of models are told to report for an interview at the same time. |
| COVERAGE | Covering up skin with hair, false or real. Usually male. |
| CALLBACK | After an interview for a prospective booking, it's always, "Don't call us, we'll call you." When they do, it's a callback. It means you've made the semifinals at least. |
| CLOSET MODEL | A girls who is sure she could have been a working model; one who worked briefly as a model and then settled for a job in the |

periphery of the model business when the going got rugged.

COMPOSITE
A printed brochure usually 8 x 11, of two to six pages displaying a model's recent photographs, test shots in a variety of backgrounds, to show her versatility, giving her vital statistics, measurements, specialties, sent or given to photographers, agencies, and casting directors as a reminder that she is alive and well-preserved.

CONTINGENCY FUND
or
RESERVE FUND
When an agency pays a model on a voucher immediately after she has completed a booking, after deducting their 10 percent commission, they can and sometimes do withhold or hold back another 20 percent until such time as they are paid by the client or photographer.

CONTACTS
A sheet of prints in which at least pictures are developed on an 8 x 11 sheet. The photographer looks at them with a magnifying glass to make the first rough edit of his work. This is where a model first sees herself as the photographer shot her.

DOM
Dirty old man.

DOLL
Dirty old lesbian lady.

DOLLY
Dirty old lesbian lady yenta.

EDITORIAL MODEL
A model who specializes in print work for the editorial section of magazines and newspapers, rather than in paid advertising. Most high-fashion models are called editorial models in the trade. Their rate is only $15 per hour, and they live off prestige and other fringe benefits from their publicity.

FAGGOT MOLL
A female who makes the social scene habitually escorted by one or more male homosexuals.

FITTING
If a model does not wear her own clothes for a booking and her wardrobe is supplied

| | |
|---|---|
| | elsewhere, she has to report for fittings. For this she is paid half her hourly rate. |
| FITTING MODEL | A live mannequin in the original French sense of the word as distinguished from a metal form covered with muslin. A model on whose body a designer works, draping fabric or testing other materials, seeing his work in motion in three dimensions on a living, moving body. |
| GRAVEYARD MARKET | Conservative customers, resistant to changes in products, packaging, fashion, change. |
| GIG | Employment of short duration. |
| GO-SEE | A rendezvous or appointment with someone who wants to look a model over with an eye toward booking her at some future time. |
| GROUPIE | Nonprofit uncalled-for call girl, a chick who hangs out with the rock bands. |
| HEAD SHEET | A brochure that is a composite of composites, usually $8^1/_2$ x 11, prepared by a model agency, showing head shots and full-figure shots and vital statistics and rates of their most wanted or hottest model properties. |
| INDUSTRIAL MODEL | A model who works live as a traffic-stopper or semisaleswoman at conventions, industrial shows, and trade shows. |
| LOCATION | A booking that takes a model out of the studio, in Manhattan or out-of-town. |
| PRINT | An 11-x-14-inch photo of yourself—test or for print. |
| PRINT WORK | Still pictures destined for publication in magazines, newspapers, brochures, or other linear media. |
| PORTFOLIO | See Book: a big leather portfolio with cellophane display envelopes in which a model carries and displays her wares—her best and most recent photographs—test shots as |

well as commercial and editorial shots.

**RAMP WORK** — Working in a fashion show or showroom on a ramp or runway.

**RATE** — A model's hourly fee—$40, $50, $60, etc.

**REP** — A photographer's representative is usually called a rep. He is agent for the photographer. He carries a portfolio of the photographer's best work around to the art directors and magazine editors, attempting to line up work for his client. Some former models end up as photographer's reps. For this they get 25 percent of everything they sell.

**RUG** — A hairpiece for male models.

**RESIDUALS** — When a model or actress appears in a TV commercial which is run repeatedly on TV, locally or nationally, she is paid what amounts to a continuing royalty in accord with certain scales set by the Screen Actors Guild.

**ROUNDS** — A very chic term for looking for jobs.

**SAG:** — Screen Actors Guild

**SEAMLESS** — A huge white carpet-size roll of heavy-duty white paper which is unrolled in a photographer's studio like giant heavy toilet tissue. The model stands on the paper, and it supplies a seamless, gently curved background with no distracting lines or angles.

**SPLIT** — To leave, depart, quit the scene. Originally Harlem.

**SPEC** — On spec, a model gambles her time, the photographer gambles his, on the chance that the resultant photos will pay off commercially for both of them.

**SHOWROOM MODEL** — A permanent model regularly employed by a company to be available from nine to five for showings to buyers who come into the company showroom.

311

STYLIST — Girl Friday or assistant to a photographer or client who worries about such details as accessories, wardrobe, jewelry, furniture, and props. Sometimes stylists get in on casting.
If a stylist works for a client, she is sometimes called an FC or fashion coordinator.

SCHLEPP — Originally a Yiddish verb, meaning to carry something not very chic, such as bags and bundles. Because of its expressive sound, it has passed from the garment district into general usage.

TEAR SHEET — A torn-out page from a magazine, carrying *your* photo.

TEST MARKET — An advertising and marketing campaign in any or all media limited to a single city for a specified time. The results are carefully surveyed, and if it works it becomes a regional or national campaign. If it doesn't work, the campaign is scrapped, and it's back to the drawing board.

THINK TANK — The last few minutes before a model starts her daily rounds in which she inventories everything she might possibly use and makes sure she has it in her tote bag.

TRAFFIC ENGINEER — A polite word for pimp, also called a TE. Someone who lines girls up for other males; viz: a TE in PA vines. A pimp passing as a press agent.

TUSH or TUSHY — Hind quarters, derriere, derived from the Yiddish *tuchas*.

TESTING — A noncommercial photography session in which the model and the photographer gamble on their time in the hope of producing pictures which showcase their talents more favorably than commercial shots which are ultimately produced and directed by others.

312

Pictures which happen in this context are called test shots. If later they are used commercially, the model receives her regular fee or an agreed flat rate in return for signing a release.

TRANSPLANT

An operation in which hair follicles are taken from the back of a man's neck or elsewhere and transplanted surgically to his head where he needs coverage.

VIB

Very Important Buyer.

VINES

Originally Harlem argot, now in general use for threads, clothing, wardrobe.

VOUCHER

A book of forms which a model carries in her gear. After she has completed a booking, it is filled in and signed. Getting paid on a voucher means the model agency pays the model immediately, deducting 10 percent commission. Sometimes agencies withhold another 20 percent until such time as they have received payment from the client or the photographer.

WEATHER PERMIT

A one-day insurance policy used in case of an outdoor booking or location work where the weather may interfere. If a client has a weather permit and it rains, making shooting impossible, he pays a model half her rate for the day and has an automatic option on her services for another day at full rate.

WWD

*Women's Wear Daily,* the retailing daily newspaper.

YENTA

A noun, originally Yiddish, meaning a loud-mouthed gossip of either sex. The word has passed into universal usage, meaning a loud and generally disagreeable lady. La Dona Yenta is such a female all done up, trying to make it as a lady.